GUIDANCE
An Examination

Edited by

RALPH L. MOSHER
Harvard University

RICHARD F. CARLE
Boston University

CHRIS D. KEHAS
The University of Chicago

GUIDANCE
An Examination

A revision and expansion of the 1962 Special Issue
of the *Harvard Educational Review.*

 HARCOURT, BRACE & WORLD, INC.
New York / Chicago / San Francisco / Atlanta

Library of Congress Catalog Card Number: 65-17350

Printed in the United States of America

"The Progressive Heritage of the Guidance Movement," by Lawrence A.
Cremin, first appeared in the Winter 1964 *Bulletin*, Harvard Graduate
School of Education Association.

"A Computer-Measurement System for Guidance," by William W.
Cooley, first appeared in the Fall 1964 Issue of the *Harvard Educational
Review*.

"Administrator, Advocate or Therapist? Alternatives for Professionali-
zation in School Counseling," by Dan C. Lortie, and "The School and
Self-Understanding," by Joseph Samler, first appeared in the Winter 1965
Issue of the *Harvard Educational Review*.

The remaining articles first appeared in the Fall 1962 Special Issue of
the *Harvard Educational Review*.

PREFACE

GUIDANCE—AN EXAMINATION is a revision and expansion of the 1962 Special Issue of the *Harvard Educational Review*. The book contains the articles that appeared in the original issue as well as four articles on Guidance that were especially commissioned for this volume.

The editors have aimed to subject the field of Guidance to critical and scholarly review, from within the field itself and from related disciplines, such as psychology, philosophy, and sociology. This symposium is not concerned with the common stereotypes of guidance (matching man with job; life adjustment; college placement; or clinical provision for the atypical); instead, it focuses on a search for theoretical models and substantiating evidence. It presents differing views by noted authorities upon issues that range from the counselor-counselee interaction to the professional development of the entire field of Guidance.

As an introduction, Lawrence A. Cremin analyzes the effect upon the Guidance movement of its progressive heritage. He argues for a drastic reformulation of some of the most fundamental assumptions of Guidance. Gordon W. Allport examines three psychological models of man and suggests that Guidance must recognize man's proactive, future-oriented growth as basic to effective professional practice. By contrast, Jack Michael and Lee Meyerson contend that the behavioristic model, rejected by Allport, provides the only sound basis for the development of a scientific and ultimately effective Guidance function. Subjective dynamics of the counselor and counselee interaction, dismissed by Michael and Meyerson, are seen by both Carl Rogers and Adrian van Kaam as crucial. Rogers hypothesizes that the effectiveness of counseling depends not upon the counselor's training or theoretical orientation, or upon the severity of the client's problem, but on the quality of the interpersonal relationship. He presents important empirical evidence in support of this position. Van Kaam examines the implications of the existential position of both counselor and client. By contrast, Raymond C. Hummel advances a model for counseling in terms of ego psychology and cognition.

Edward Joseph Shoben, Jr., provides a critical assessment of current Guidance assumptions and practices. His argument is for a transformed Guidance function which would sharpen the impact of the school and give it a greater cogency for the individual student. The importance of the social and cultural context for Guidance is further pursued by Dan C. Lortie and Dean K. Whitla. Lortie, analyzing the school as a social institution, examines alternative professional roles which Guidance practitioners might adopt. Whitla, assessing the college experience, stresses that Guidance personnel must be sensitive to the transaction between the student's feelings of competence and the qualities and values of the institution.

William W. Cooley proposes a provocative computer-based system of measurement to encompass a changing student and a changing world of work. Joseph Samler, seeing the implications of mental hygiene for Guidance, argues for increased pupil self-understanding through cognitive procedures. David V. Tiedeman and Frank L. Field present a theory for the development of purposeful action on the part of the individual, the counselor, and the Guidance profession. And C. Gilbert Wrenn, in a concluding article, notes the accelerating rate of cultural change. He suggests that the counselor's previous training and experience may often hinder rather than facilitate effective counseling.

The editors recognize that the discussion herein initiated is necessarily incomplete and believe that it merits extension, particularly in the area of philosophy. We consider this book, however, a substantial realization of our original intention.

RALPH L. MOSHER
RICHARD F. CARLE
CHRIS D. KEHAS

CONTENTS

GUIDANCE
An Examination

LAWRENCE A. CREMIN

The Progressive Heritage
of the Guidance Movement

IT IS NOW almost twenty years since the psychologist, Lawrence K. Frank, first published his intriguing little essay, "The Historian as Therapist."[1] In it, Frank pleaded for historians who would serve society much in the fashion of psychoanalysts, clearing away distorted versions of the past so that men would be freed to contend more effectively with the problems of the present.

Frank's proposals, of course, raise all sorts of difficulties for any historian who would take them seriously, notably in their subtle invitation to read the problems of the present into the story of the past. And yet, I would suspect my students and I had something of Frank's "therapeutic" goal in mind as we set out in the early 1950's to write a history of the progressive education movement. We wanted to do away with the cartoons and caricatures that had long dominated pedagogical discussion, and to substitute a clear and accurate account of what progressive education had really meant in the American tradition. Our goal, to be sure, was to discover the facts; but we also wanted to report those facts in such a way as to enable contemporary educators to respond more intelligently to the situations in which they found themselves.

[1] The essay is reprinted in Lawrence K. Frank, *Society as the Patient* (New Brunswick, N. J.: Rutgers University Press, 1948), pp. 298–307.

THE PROGRESSIVE EDUCATION MOVEMENT

I sketched some of our findings two years ago in a book called *The Transformation of the School,* and would like to use those findings as a basis for this paper. Perhaps I might summarize them in seven brief propositions:

First, what Americans refer to as *progressive education* began not in 1919 with the founding of the Progressive Education Association, but rather in the 1890's as the educational phase of the broader progressive movement in American life and thought.

Second, progressive education was not a single movement but rather a congeries of separate—frequently contradictory—movements, each seeking to contend in its own way with the central educational problem of the early twentieth century: how to adapt the popular school system to the needs of a democratic-industrial civilization.

Third, these movements enjoyed widespread support from businessmen, labor leaders, rural publicists, clergymen, academics, and social workers; they were not dreamed up and put across by a conspiracy of professional educators.

Fourth, these movements influenced all levels of education, public as well as private, rural as well as urban, southern as well as northern, western as well as eastern.

Fifth, John Dewey was the hero of the progressive education movement, not because he created it singlehandedly, but rather because he saw it whole; he was able to weave the *social reformism* of the urban settlement workers, the *individualism* of the Rousseauan pedagogues, and the *scientism* of the university psychologists into a reasonably consistent view of education. Seen in this light, the genius of *The School and Society,* the first great manifesto of the movement, and of *Democracy and Education,* its most comprehensive theoretical statement, resides less in their complete originality than in their synthetic character.

Sixth, the rise and fall of the movement was a political phenomenon comprehensible in political terms; progressive education collapsed as an organized movement in the 1950's partly because of internal dissension and partly because the political coalition supporting it in the schools dissolved.

Seventh, although the organized movement is dead, the ideas and ideals of the progressive era retain a distinctive relevance for our own time; but they need searching reappraisal and substantial restatement to render them intellectually tenable and politically viable.

THE LEGACY OF PROGRESSIVISM

Needless to say, the effects of the progressive revolution I have described here are everywhere with us: in the architecture of schools, in the arrangement of classrooms, in the programs of students, and in the attitudes of teachers. Nowhere are the effects more apparent, however, than in the work of the guidance counselor. Beyond any other individual in today's education system, he incarnates the aims and ideals of progressivism. He is the most characteristic child of the progressive movement, and as such is heir to all of its vigor and optimism, and all of its diversity and contradiction.

Consider, for a moment, the legacy of diversity and contradiction. The fact is that each of the principal facets of progressive education is reflected in a particular way in the early development of the guidance movement. The social reformism of the urban settlement workers, for example, is patently involved in the beginnings of vocational counseling during the first years of the present century. One need only recall that the work of Frank Parsons and Meyer Bloomfield emerged as part of the program of the Civic Service House, a Boston settlement. It was Parsons' idea that a Vocation Bureau attached to the settlement could be of substantial assistance to young people, especially those of limited means, in helping them arrive at wise, well-founded occupational choices. And he saw wise, well-founded occupational choices as the foundation of useful and happy lives.[2]

The key to Parsons' ultimate goal, of course, lay in his notion of the useful and happy life. Parsons, a significant figure in the history of American reform, believed not only that vocational counseling would lead to greater individual fulfillment, but that people suited to their jobs would tend to be active in the creation of a more efficient and humane industrial system. Intelligently practiced, the craft of vocational guidance would serve not only the youngsters who sought counsel, but the cause of social reform as well. Thus did the earliest, and to date the most stubbornly central, thread of the guidance movement connect with the broader progressive program.

In like manner, the effort to individualize education—which had always been the essence of the new pedagogy—was at the heart of what came to be known as "educational guidance." In 1908, the very year Parsons and Bloomfield opened the Vocation Bureau in Boston,

2 See Parsons' first and only report as Director of the Vocation Bureau, reprinted in John M. Brewer, *History of Vocational Guidance* (New York: Harper & Row, 1942), pp. 303–8; see also Frank Parsons, *Choosing a Vocation* (Boston: Houghton Mifflin, 1909).

a young teacher named Jesse B. Davis organized a program of vocational and moral guidance in the schools of Grand Rapids, Michigan. His effort included not only job counseling, but counseling with respect to courses and extra-curricular activities as well.[3] Six years later, Truman Lee Kelley wrote a Ph.D. dissertation at Teachers College, Columbia University, entitled *Educational Guidance*, in which he urged the need for general counseling programs that would aid youngsters in their choice of studies. The concept broadened steadily during the 1920's, especially under the influence of the child guidance clinics pioneered by the National Committee for Mental Hygiene. By 1932, Professor John Brewer of Harvard was advancing a conception of guidance that came close to being synonymous with the whole of education. Pupils, Brewer argued, should be guided in *all* of their life activities; the ultimate goal of guidance was unified, integrated, harmonious personalities.[4]

Finally, the effort to develop a science of education, also at the heart of the progressive movement, was reflected in the spirited interest in tests and measurements that grew up in the United States shortly after the turn of the century. By the time of World War I, a variety of intelligence and aptitude tests was already in fairly general use in the schools; and the wartime work of the Army Committee on Classification of Personnel (mainly in developing and administering the Army Alpha and Beta tests) really made testing a household notion throughout the country. Needless to say, the possibility of precise instruments for measuring and predicting achievement proved a boon to counselors, who were ever eager to make their work more scientific; and the tests rapidly became a standard counseling device. Thus the idea developed of the guidance worker as a trained professional, wise in administering and interpreting scientific instruments for the prediction of vocational and educational success.

DIVERSITY AND CONTRADICTION

Now, my effort here has not been to sketch a history of the guidance movement; that has been done elsewhere and well.[5] Rather, I have

---

[3] Davis describes his program in *Vocational and Moral Guidance* (Boston: Ginn, 1914).

[4] John M. Brewer, *Education as Guidance* (New York: Macmillan, 1932).

[5] The best history to my knowledge is the unpublished doctoral thesis of Ruth E. Barry and Beverly Wolf, at Teachers College, Columbia University, entitled "A History of the Guidance-Personnel Movement in Education" (1955).

attempted to document the close and inextricable tie between the guidance movement and the broader progressive movement of which it was part. Both movements have had a heritage of diversity, and both have had a heritage of contradiction. Just as various schools of progressives began to argue among themselves during the 1930's and 1940's over whether teachers ought to "build a new social order" or "develop the whole child" or "apply scientific techniques in the classroom," so did various schools of counselors argue the merits of vocational versus educational guidance, of systematic testing versus non-directive interviewing. One need only follow the long and tedious discussion over what kind of organization should represent guidance workers and what it should be called, to grasp the significance of these differences.

More important for our purposes, perhaps—and here I'm reminded of Lawrence Frank's plea—these differences and contradictions continue to affect the practice of guidance today; they are inherent in the very assumptions the counselor brings to his work. Permit me to illustrate with a few questions that might well come up in the day-by-day activities of any high-school counselor. How much social reformism, for example, of the sort implicit in Parsons' notion of vocational guidance, is the counselor going to permit himself in advising minority-group youngsters with respect to vocations from which they have traditionally been excluded? How much does the counselor's commitment to individual fulfillment in such cases ultimately conflict with his commitment to social reform? Or again, to what extent does the commitment to individual fulfillment in counseling lower-class children conflict with the knowledge that middle-class values are generally more appropriate to white-collar or professional occupations?[6] Or again, to what extent does the commitment to a notion of individuality lead the counselor to skepticism concerning scientific test data?[7] Universities, after all, are constantly taking chances on highly motivated youngsters who do poorly on every conceivable predictive measure. Or again, to what extent does a counselor support a personal sense of vocation where the market seems to call for different aptitudes (there's the old saw about Einstein doing poorly in school mathematics), or indeed, where there is little or no market for such a voca-

[6] Edgar Z. Friedenberg states the problem poignantly in "An Ideology of School Withdrawal," *Commentary*, XXXV (1963), 492–500.

[7] There is a considerable body of literature on this problem, varying in character all the way from John Hersey's mordant novel, *The Child Buyer* (New York: Knopf, 1960), to Robert L. Thorndike's scholarly treatise, *The Concept of Over- and Underachievement* (New York: Teachers College, Columbia University, 1963).

tion? How much does "realism" about the job market sometimes fly in the face of the deepest meanings of vocation?

One could go on with such questions, but perhaps my point has been made. My concern is not with the dozens of decisions a counselor has to make every day in the very nature of his work. It is rather with the contradictory values and loyalties he brings to his work as heir to a contradictory heritage. Ultimately, it is only as he becomes aware of these contradictions that he can really enter upon the difficult task of resolving them; and it is only as he resolves them that he can eventually overcome the confusions they inevitably generate.

REAPPRAISAL NEEDED

One other problem derives from the progressive heritage of the guidance movement: it concerns the need for a searching reappraisal of progressive doctrine to separate those notions that are still tenable from those that are not. In the extent to which progressivism has become the "conventional wisdom" of our time, it is increasingly prone to obsolescence. As John Kenneth Galbraith pointed out some years ago, the ultimate enemy of the conventional wisdom is not so much ideas as the march of events. The conventional wisdom accommodates itself not to the world it is meant to interpret, but rather to the public's view of that world. And since the public tends to prefer the comfortable and familiar, while the world moves on, the conventional wisdom is ever in danger of obsolescence.

The implications for guidance are profound. It is no news that the movement has entered a period of vigorous expansion, aided in large measure by the federal government's financial assistance and Dr. Conant's moral assistance. Yet at this very time, some of the most fundamental assumptions of the movement, insofar as they derive from the progressive tradition, stand in need of drastic reformulation. Put another way, contemporary guidance theory is shot through with terms and concepts handed down from the progressive era that are now anachronistic in their meanings. Let me cite three by way of example.

First, the concept of *education*. As I read the contemporary guidance literature—and I admit to oversimplifying here to make my point— I come away with the notion that the counselor is dealing with a changing individual who is growing up in a changing world that has a changing occupational structure. Yet in all of this, the agencies of education somehow remain constant. The point, of course, is that this is simply not true. The structure of education is changing more rapidly in our time than at any other in history; witness the rapid rise of public, social and recreational facilities, of quasi-public social service organizations, of teaching programs in business and industry, and most important, perhaps, of the mass media of communication, notably television.[8] All of these institutions educate, and as the counselor considers the range of educational possibilities open to his clients, he must bear them all in mind.[9] Few of these institutions existed during the formative period of progressivism, and hence the progressives thought almost exclusively in terms of an expanding *school*. To do so today is plainly anachronistic. An exciting case in point, by the way, is New York's Higher Horizon's program, in which counselors have turned to all of the city's educational resources—museums, parks, concert halls, theatres, libraries, zoos, and aquaria—in their effort to raise the intellectual sights of slum children.

A second progressive holdover I find in the guidance literature is a concept of *community* that almost always implies locality. Now, the community in turn-of-the-century America *was* the locality, and the early progressives—except for the more far-sighted among them—had every right to assume that most people would spend their adult lives in the communities into which they were born. Indeed, many progressives, especially rural publicists concerned with the flight of farm youngsters to the city, took this goal as not only probable but eminently desirable. Much of what we know about contemporary America indicates that this is no longer so. Consider a passage from a recent report of the United States Census Bureau:

> About 35.5 million, or 20.0 percent, of the 177.4 million persons 1 year old and over who were living in the United States in March 1961 had moved at least once since March 1960. Although this overall mobility rate has reflected to some slight extent some of the

[8] There is a good deal of literature on this subject, but it is scattered through journals in a dozen different fields. A useful synthesis is Margaret Mead, "Thinking Ahead: Why Is Education Obsolete?" *Harvard Business Review*, XXXVI (November-December, 1958), 23–30.

[9] The counselor must also bear in mind the continuing educational influence of these institutions. Note, for example, Harris Dienstfrey's incisive remarks on the vocational models offered youngsters by such television dramas as "The Defenders," "The Nurses," "Ben Casey," "Naked City," and others, in "Doctors, Lawyers and Other TV Heroes," *Commentary*, XXXV (1963) 519–24. Note also the magnificent Jules Feiffer cartoon in *The New Republic* for May 18, 1963, which says more about the educational impact of television than many a learned essay.

postwar changes in business conditions, it has remained relatively stable in the 14 successive surveys conducted since 1948. . . .

Of the 35.5 million persons 1 year old and over who were living in a different house in March 1961 from that in 1960, about 24.3 million, or 13.7 percent of the total population 1 year old and over, had moved within the same county; 5.5 million, or 3.1 percent had moved between counties in the same State; and 5.8 million, or 3.2 percent, had moved between States. In addition to these persons who moved within the United States, about 0.6 percent of the 1961 population had been living abroad in 1960. . . .[10]

Given these statistics, it is simply erroneous to assume that most graduates of a local high school are going to remain in the local community for the rest of their lives, and hence ought to be trained with reference to the occupational structure of that community. Today, the counselor must think in terms of a national—indeed, international— community if young men and women are to be prepared realistically for the world in which they will undoubtedly live.

A third anachronism from the progressive era that suffuses the literature of guidance is a particular notion of *vocation*. Based on the situation that prevailed in the first years of the present century, too many counselors have continued to assume that choice of occupation plays *the* determinative role in the development of adult character. Yet, as I read the sociology of occupations today, we seem to be moving into a period in which, paradoxically, occupation will probably play an ever more central role in the lives of those who enter the professions, but a less and less central role for those who enter the trades —witness the recent victory of the New York electricians' union in winning a five-hour basic workday.[11] If this be the case, the counselor will have to develop a much broader concept of vocational choice, one concerned with total life-style rather than merely with occupation. Here, I find myself much in agreement with the arguments of my colleague Edward Joseph Shoben, Jr. in his essay in this volume. Dr. Shoben proposes that the counselor assist the youngster not merely in choosing a vocation, but in the whole process of choosing the personal

---

[10] *Current Population Reports: Population Characteristics,* Series P-20, No. 118, August 9, 1962, p. 1. There are no accurate statistics on the mobility of the American population at the turn of the century; the earliest Census Bureau statistics refer to the period between 1935 and 1940.

[11] A useful summary of recent work on the sociology of occupations is Everett Cherrington Hughes, "The Study of Occupations" in Robert K. Merton, Leonard Broom, and Leonard S. Cottrell, Jr. (eds.), *Sociology Today* (New York: Basic Books, 1959), pp. 442–58.

models he takes for himself, or, if we use the Socratic terminology, in the process of learning to live the examined life. Incidentally, I might add that if the counselor is to play this role, he will have to prepare himself for it with a good deal more humanistic study than is currently present in most guidance curricula.

In connection with Dr. Shoben's proposal, I might also remark on one other educational change of extraordinary significance: the contemporary curriculum reform movement. The reader is no doubt aware of the excitement generated by recent curriculum revision in mathematics and the natural sciences; and no doubt there is equal awareness of the effort to extend this revision into the social sciences and humanities. This is not the place to debate the merits of the new reforms; suffice it to say they have produced some striking results that are patently here to stay. But they have also raised some thorny problems, one of which is a growing specialization, and consequent fragmentation, in the curriculum. Now, it may be that such specialization is unavoidable, given the nature and rapid expansion of knowledge in our time; I for one have not yet made up my mind on the matter. But I do know that as specialization moves down into the elementary and secondary schools, the role Dr. Shoben asks the counselor to play becomes all the more important. Ultimately, the counselor may end up as one of the few professionals primarily responsible for seeing the child's education whole.

THE PROBLEM OF OPTIMISM

My final comment is really in the nature of a postscript. Insofar as guidance is the child of the progressive movement, it is also heir to the characteristic vigor and optimism—some would say utopianism— of that movement. And this, too, has raised problems. After all, the counselor has dedicated his life to taking some of the waste, the accident, and the needless inefficiency out of the difficult business of becoming an adult. Yet however much he achieves his goal, he is ever doomed to a measure of failure. As Morris R. Cohen once remarked in a critique of John Dewey's perennial optimism: "So long as human beings lack omniscience they will lack omnipotence and will therefore have to face insuperable difficulties and evils."[12] The failure to recognize this, I would suspect, is the original sin of pride.

[12] Morris R. Cohen, *Studies in Philosophy and Science* (New York: Holt, Rinehart & Winston, 1949), p. 169.

Some years ago, Ruth Barry and Beverly Wolf observed the following about the literature they had read in connection with their history of the guidance movement:

> The guidance and personnel literature indicates that personnel workers are also unrealistic about their own work. Personnel work has had its successes and presumably its failures, but the literature would lead a reader to believe that no program or no aspect of a program had ever failed. Mathematically, the odds against 100 percent success in personnel work are infinite; yet, apparently no one ever fails in personnel work. Writers admit that a guidance program could be better, but never was it unsuccessful. . . . By refusing to recognize failure, personnel work creates a myth, an impossible ideal, a stereotype, which does not fool the public, but may mislead individual workers in the field. By reinforcing stereotypes, personnel work tacitly promises that it can be all things to all people and that each personnel worker can be everything to each individual student.[13]

I'm afraid I, too, come away with much the same impression. Somehow the guidance literature seems to promise that with more money, more personnel, and more effort, counselors could usher in some sort of utopia. I think counselors would do themselves and the public a great deal more good if they simply promised that they would try to make life a bit more planful, a bit more intelligent, and a bit more humane.

[13] Ruth E. Barry and Beverly Wolf, *op. cit.,* p. 441.

Psychological Models for Guidance

HOWEVER EXCELLENT his natural eyesight may be, a counselor always looks at his client through professional spectacles. It could not be otherwise. After all, he has invested time and money in his psychological training. Of what use is it unless it adds special prisms to his own unaided eyesight?

The lenses we wear are ground to the prescription of our textbooks and teachers. Even while we are undergraduates a certain image of the nature of man is fitted to our eyes. We grow accustomed to the image and when we become practitioners or teachers we may still take it for granted.

But every so often comes a time for optical re-examination. Perhaps the image we have is still the best fit we can get; perhaps it is not. We can tell only by examining alternative lenses. In particular I believe that three are worthy of special scrutiny:

1. *Man seen as a reactive being.* Under this rubric I would include outlooks known as naturalism, positivism, behaviorism, operationism, physicalism; these are also sometimes called—mistakenly, I think—"scientific psychology."

2. *Man seen as a reactive being in depth.* Here I include what is variously called psychoanalysis, psychodynamics, depth psychology.

3. *Man seen as a being-in-process-of-becoming.* This label covers recent trends known as holism, orthopsychology, personalistics, existential psychology.

These three images provide a focus not only for guidance practices, but for all other professional psychological activity whether it be teaching, research, counseling or therapy.

MAN: A REACTIVE BEING

One hundred years ago in his *Beiträge* Wilhelm Wundt mapped a program for the newly conceived science of psychology. His own view of the proper development of this science was broad and permissive, especially in the field of social psychology. But what has taken hold in the Anglo-American tradition is the experimental outlook of his *Physiologische Psychologie.* Fusing with Darwinism, Machian positivism, the quantitative outlook of Galton and his successors, as well as with techniques invented by Binet, Pavlov, Hull and others—this experimental outlook prevailed and has ground the lens that is fitted to the eyes of almost all undergraduate students of psychology. Many of us who continue in the profession feel no need for further correction in this image of man.

Seen through this lens man is no different in kind from any other living reactor; and therefore, like the paramecium or pigeon, may be studied biologically, behaviorally, mathematically. To be sure a few special concepts need to be devised to take care of the vast complexity of human behavior, but all these concepts—among them habit hierarchy, secondary reinforcement, input and output of information, and the like—are consistent with the postulates of physicalism and naturalism.

If we ask, "What does it mean to be a human being?" this school of thought replies, "Man is one more creature of nature; his behavior though complex is predictable in principle. His present state is determined by his past state. A man's consciousness is unreliable and must be distrusted, preferably disregarded altogether. We seek the general laws of nature, not personal uniqueness. We study man, not men; objective reality, not subjective."

In principle this broad positive tradition, which we all know so well, puts a desirable end to psychological naïveté. It cautions us not to believe every verbal report that comes to our ears; it warns us to be skeptical of our own naked eyesight; and from it we learn to check ourselves for observer reliability. It teaches us to use precise and repeatable methods. Because of its stress on reliable methods this favored tradition in psychology has become known as "scientific psychology." Its methods are indeed scientific; but its primary postulate—that man is simply a reactive organism—is no more scientific than any other postulate.

It is here that the counselor encounters his first difficulty. Trained in tests, statistics, and experimental design, he may think, quite mistakenly, that to employ these useful aids he must also view his client as a reactive being—an exclusive product of stimulus impact, homeostasis, drive-reduction and reinforcement learning. The term "scientific" has spread like a grease spot from method to theory. Just because most of our methods evolved through the positivistic tradition does not mean that the postulates of this tradition concerning the nature of man are the only acceptable postulates for scientific psychology.

A counselor whose theoretical spectacles disclose a merely reactive being, is likely to think of his client in terms of past conditioning and potential re-conditioning; in terms of reinforcements, in terms of environmental determinism. He will assume that his client's basic motives are drive-reduction or second-order conditionings which in some shadowy way are supposed to account for all his adult interests and vocational ambitions.

The vocabulary emanating from this type of postulate is replete with terms like *reaction, response, reinforcement, reflex, respondent, reintegration*—all sorts of *re*-compounds. The reference is backward. What *has* been is more important than what *will* be. Terms such as *proaction, progress, program, production, problem-solving,* or *propriate* are characteristically lacking. One would think that the client seated opposite would *protest*, for the language of response negates the subject's immediate certainty that his life lies in the future.

The positivistic view of man as a reactor has performed a good service, shaking us out of common sense naïveté, endowing us with useful methods, and correctly informing us that man is, in *some* aspects of his being, a simple respondent to simple pressures. Its postulates are, however, questionable. It sees reality as ordered but not as personal; it sees consciousness as a nuisance; it looks at man as reactive, not proactive.

It is probably true that no counselor fully follows this creed in his daily practice. Indeed he could not do so. It is too impoverished a view of real life. When a convinced positivist attempts to fit his image of man to concrete human situations, as B. F. Skinner has done in *Walden Two*, the result strikes many of us as threadbare, even pitiable.

Probably for this reason many behaviorists (starting even as far back as E. B. Holt in *The Freudian Wish and its Place in Ethics*) attempt to combine stimulus-response with psychoanalysis. Neal Miller and John Dollard in their *Personality and Psychotherapy* offer a good example. Man as a reactive being is combined with man as a reactive being in depth.

MAN: A REACTIVE BEING IN DEPTH

So influential is this image of man that we find it everywhere: dominant in literature, in social work, in guidance, in therapeutic practice, and in the market place. There is no need today to describe this image to any educated, or even semi-educated, American adult. Freudianism, like positivism, is our daily dish.

What I should like to do is to make clear that Freudianism (in spite of its less reliable methods) is a close kin of traditional positivism. The only change in the image of man lies in adding the depth dimension. To the long psychological vocabulary of *re*-compounds, depth psychology adds *repression, regression, resistance, abreaction, reaction formation*, and many others.

Like other simple naturalistic views of man, psychoanalysis puts its chief weight upon the press of pleasure and pain. This pressure produces in the organism a tendency to seek an equilibrium between the force of his drives and the circumstances of reality. The fact that Freud maximizes the role of sex and locates the whole constellation of reactive forces chiefly in the unconscious does not alter the essential similarity.

For Freud causation lies in the past history of the individual just as it does for the conditioned-response theorist. Both have a dismaying disregard for the person's phenomenology of the future, for his sense of personhood and sense of freedom. The ego is a reactive agent, having no energy of its own, but borrowing from the unsocialized Id.

Central to depth psychology, and important for guidance, is the doctrine of *recall* and *recovery* (two more *re*-compounds). Therapy, and presumably guidance, proceeds by disclosing to the client some buried motive, or a troublesome and repressed psychic trauma. The client's salvation, if indeed he has any, lies in this vital recall. A troublesome memory is brought to cognizable form. Presumably the result is helpful to the individual in solving his conflicts. The theory, however, does not allow for any interaction between the person and the recovered memory. Simple re-instatement is itself, as Freud says, the "pure gold" of psychoanalysis. What values a client should live by when once the re-instatement has taken place is not the "pure gold" of psychoanalysis. That all adult values are simply sublimated aim-inhibited wishes, is the central doctrine. Freud never allows for the individual's capacity to disregard his past or to reshape it freely. Indeed, since the structure of the Id never changes, the future can at best be a redirection, never a transformation, of one's purposes. What one becomes is essentially what one is, and what one was.

Among the valid portions of psychoanalysis of special use to all counselors, is the brilliant account given us by Freud and by his daughter Anna, of the defensive mechanisms of the ego. In dealing with our client we do well to follow the advice of psychoanalysis and watch for rationalizations, denials of reality through repression, and displacements of aggression. All these, and other, ego-defenses belong to the nature of man, and therefore must find a place in any theory of human personality.

But what perplexes me is why so many of the ego-processes described by psychoanalysis should be merely protective strategies. Are there no ego-processes that lead to a transformation of what is recovered? To a creative cognition? To a revised sense of personhood and a new phenomenology of the future? To Freud the person seems never to be truly proactive, seldom even active. Almost always he is seen as reactive to early fixations—perhaps to some castration threat that occurred years ago, or to some other unsocialized infant complex, especially to Oedipal fantasies. My difficulty with this image of man is summed up most tersely by the late satirist, Max Beerbohm, who said, "They were a tense and peculiar family—those Oedipuses."

There is, I am well aware, a large group of theories that derive from the psychodynamic tradition but at the same time deviate considerably from the orthodox view of reactivity-in-depth. All these theories, in my judgment, move in a desirable direction. Here I shall mention only some of the relevant authors: Adler, Jung, Hartmann, Horney, Erikson, Fromm. Still more deviant from Freud are Goldstein, Maslow, Rogers, and Robert White. These and other writers offer a type of theory that views man as a being in the process of becoming. Many of them ask the pivotal question differently from the reactivist schools of thought. And it makes a good deal of difference just how a question is asked.

A story is told about two priests. They were arguing whether it was proper to smoke and to pray at the same time. One said "Yes," the

other "No." To settle the matter they decided that both should write
to the Holy Father for his opinion. Sometime later they met and
compared notes. Each claimed that the Holy Father had supported
his view. They were perplexed. Finally one asked, "How did you
phrase your question?" The other replied: "I asked whether it was
proper to smoke while one is praying; and the Pope answered,
'Certainly not, praying is serious business and permits no distrac-
tions.' And how did you phrase your question?" "Well," said the
other, "I asked if it were proper to pray while smoking, and the
Pope answered, 'Certainly, prayer is always in order.' "

Instead of asking Aristotle's question, "What is the place of man in
Nature?" many authors today are asking St. Augustine's question,
"Who am I?" This question, rephrased in the 20th Century, has
opened the floodgates to a new theorizing of the broad type often
labeled *existentialist*.

MAN: BEING IN THE PROCESS OF BECOMING

Seelye Bixler, former president of Colby College, tells of a student
who recently remarked, "I can't tell you how much satisfaction I take
in my existential despair." In some student circles despair has always
been popular. To label it "existentialist" makes it doubly attractive,
in fact irresistible.

But overlooking the fashionable flavor of existentialism it is surely
necessary for the modern counselor to take seriously the present-day
anxieties of the younger generation. No longer can youth contemplate
its future under the protection of the great social stabilizers of the
past. No longer can one counsel within the framework of Victorian
decorum, theological certainties, or the Pax Britannica. It is obvious
to us all that some sort of shattering transformation is under way. The
comfortable stabilities of culture, caste, the gold standard, and military
supremacy are no longer ours.

Nor are the comfortable stabilities of traditional psychology adequate. Of what use is it to invoke an impersonal theory of learning, a
biological theory of motivation, and a late Victorian formula for the
unconscious, when youth's problems today are acutely conscious, in-
tensely personal, and propelling him like an unguided astronaut into
an unknown future? A counselor is not equipped for his job unless
he can share in some degree the apprehensions of modern youth, and
sense the swampy underpinning on which youth treads. Over his desk

the counselor might well tack the wisdom of the Spanish writer Unamuno, "Suffering is the life blood that runs through us all and binds us together." While not every youth who comes to the counselor is at that moment a sufferer, it is a safe assumption that he comes for guidance that will fortify him for the inevitable suffering that he will encounter in his course of life.

TENTATIVENESS AND COMMITMENT

From the existential point of view the ideal counselor will strive to develop two attitudes in his client. Taken separately they seem antithetical; but fused into a world-view they provide strength for the future. One attitude is *tentativeness* of outlook. Since certainties are no longer certain, let all dogmas be fearlessly examined, especially those cultural idols that engender a false sense of security: dogmas of race supremacy, of naïve scientism, of unilinear evolutionary progress. Let one face the worst in oneself and in the world around him, so that one may correctly estimate the hazards.

Taken by itself such tentativeness, such insightfulness, might well lead to ontological despair. Yet acceptance of the worst does not prevent us from making the best of the worst. Up to now psychologists have not dealt with the remarkable ability of human beings to blend a tentative outlook with firm commitment to chosen values. The poet Tennyson perceived the point.

> There lives more faith in honest doubt,
> Believe me, than in half the creeds.

A commitment is, as Pascal has said, a wager. One may lose it, but one may also win. Cardinal Newman warned us that our religion can never be a matter of certainty. It is at best a subjective condition of certitude which he defined as "probability supported by faith and love." Yet a mature religion, thus defined, can be infinitely sustaining and heroically motivating. Existentialism, whether theistic or atheistic, makes the same point. We have the freedom to commit ourselves to great causes with courage, even though we lack certainty. We can be at once and the same time half-sure and whole-hearted.

William James, probably America's greatest thinker, tried to teach us this lesson, but fifty years ago we were not ready for it. It is surely noteworthy that, writing as he did in a period of social stability, James saw clearly how ultimately uncertain are our foundations of value.

Wealth, he saw was a false god, leading us into a national disease that has recently been called "galloping consumption." The more we build up our material resources, the more we fear poverty. In religion, James knew, there was no certainty; yet, like Cardinal Newman, he recognized the constructive power of a mature religious commitment. Whatever ideal leads to long-range constructive consequences is psychologically sound. It is also pragmatically true. And who is to say that we have a test for truth more absolute than our own commitment in so far as it is validated by fruitful consequences?

Neither positivistic nor psychodynamic schools of thought allow for the fact that our psychological constitution permits both total tentativeness and total commitment. Such a paradox reminds us of the electron that is able to go in two opposite directions at the same time. Taken by itself tentativeness is disintegrative; commitment is integrative. Yet the blend seems to occur in personalities that we admire for their soundness and perspective. Presumably through teaching and guidance we may develop both attitudes in our youth.

Whenever the two attitudes coexist in a life we find important desirable by-products from the fusion. One is a deep sense of compassion for the lot of the human race in general and in each separate social encounter that marks our daily life. The other by-product is likewise graceful; it is the sense of humor. Humor requires the perspective of tentativeness, but also an underlying system of values that prevents laughter from souring into cynicism. As Meredith said, humor is a capacity to laugh at the things you love and still to love them.

RATIONALISM VS. IRRATIONALISM

The chief criticism made of existentialism is that it leads away from reason and exalts irrationalism. While this charge may apply to certain literary and theological trends in the existential movement I doubt that it jeopardizes the future of scientific psychology. The attitudes of tentativeness and commitment of which I speak are perfectly sound concepts—call them "intervening variables" if you wish. Indeed in so far as they reflect important states in human personality, and thus lead to improvement in understanding, prediction, and direction of human behavior, they are sounder scientific concepts than many of those we have been using.

And just what is rationalism? We venerate the ancient Greeks for their exaltation of human reason; and as psychologists we venerate Aristotle for asking the question, "What is man's place in nature?" But Greek rationalism was broader than the limited, method-centered, scientism into which it has degenerated. The Greeks themselves saw a place for tentativeness and commitment within the scope of reason. The case is beautifully stated in an ancient inscription found somewhere on the coast of Greece:

> A shipwrecked sailor buried on this coast
> Bids you set sail.
> Full many a bark, when we were lost,
> Weathered the gale.

The dead sailor urges us to make the wager, take the risk, although we cannot be sure of coming through to our destination.

IMPLICATIONS FOR THEORY

What does all this mean in terms of psychological theory, and in terms of guidance? First of all it means that in order to achieve a more realistic image of man and his potentialities, we need to revise our current theories of learning and growth, of motivation and personality structure. Elsewhere (in *Pattern and Growth in Personality,* 1961) I have discussed some of the needed changes in detail, and so shall say only a few words about each.

The trouble with our current theories of learning is not so much that they are wrong, but that they are partial. They fit best the learning of animals and young children. The concepts of conditioning, reinforcement, identification seem a bit hollow when the counselor tries to apply them to his work. They are not very helpful, for example, in explaining how a youth may learn both tentativeness of outlook and firmness of commitment. Supplementary theories in terms of organizational, biographical, and propriate learning are needed.

Except in the sense of physical maturation the concept of *growth* scarcely exists in psychology at all. Nor will it have its proper place until we have agreed upon normative standards for the maturity of personality. Up to now normative problems, except in the sense of statistical norms, are much neglected.

As for motivation and personality structure psychologists are in a state of turmoil and disagreement. That the past stages of a life do not fully explain the motivational "go" of the present, I for one am firmly convinced. Therefore we need a concept (*functional autonomy*, I think will do) to represent that portion of a life that is oriented toward the future and not toward the past. Also we need a theory of personal structure (of *personal dispositions*) to represent the important cleavages and foci of a given, concrete personality. Such a theory will, I am convinced, carry us much further than a conception of uniform variables to which every client is forcibly ordered, whether we call these variables factors, needs, dimensions, or common traits.

Most of all we need to surrender the models that would compress human personality into the routine homeostatic situation that we find in quasi-closed systems. Human personality is a wide-open system, responsive to tangible and intangible culture, on the look-out for new ideas, and capable of asking an altogether new type of question— asked by no other creature in nature, viz., "Who am I?"

There are, I am glad to say, many psychologists who feel as strongly as I that these various types of improvement need to be made before the counselor will have a fully fashioned science of psychology to undergird his practice.

IMPLICATIONS FOR GUIDANCE

Guidance is not a matter of gimmicks, nor of rules of thumb. A guide, like a philosopher and friend, is a person who loves wisdom and loves his fellow men. True, he has skills to mark him off from the professional philosopher or the untrained friend. To some extent the counselor's present-day skills are useful. Standard tests and measurements are helpful; so too achievement records and focused interviews. Most of our devices come from researches conducted under the positivistic outlook, or (in the case of projective techniques) under the psychodynamic. While many of them are serviceable I look forward to the invention of new instruments still better suited to the study of the central or propriate aspects of single personalities.

Most important, of course, are the spectacles the counselor wears. The image should no longer be borrowed from the tradition of simple naïve reactivism. Just as centimeters, grams, seconds are outmoded in modern physics so too are simple stimulus-response connections in modern psychology. In psychology, even more than in physics, we need theory capable of dealing with fluid becoming.

The plain fact is that man is more than a reactive being, more even than a reactive being in depth. If he were comfortably fixed at these levels we could with confidence apply a uniform stencil in studying his nature. But the life process is no less paradoxical than the processes of modern physics. How can one deal with space that is both finite and unbounded, with light that is both wave and particle, with electrons that pass from orbit to orbit without traversing the space between? Similarly, a human person is both structure and process, a being both biological and noetic, a being who changes his identity even while he retains it. Small wonder that at the end of his life, the famous physicist, P. W. Bridgman, said, "The structure of nature may eventually be such that our processes of thought do not correspond to it sufficiently to permit us to think about it at all."

We need not, I think, be quite so pessimistic. Our first duty is to affirm a new and wider rationalism; that is to say, to redouble our efforts to find a more adequate image of man to guide us in fashioning a more suitable science of personality.

And what about our personal attitudes as guidance specialists or teachers? Should we not cultivate the same twin virtues that we recommend to client and student: tentativeness and commitment? We can hold our own present image of man on trial, reviewing our own past psychological training in critical perspective. At the same time we can embrace courageously our task of interpreting the wisdom of the past in such a way as to make it most available to the youthful personality who is facing an uncertain, but not uninviting, future. Tentativeness and commitment are twin ideals for both counselor and client. To my mind they lie at the heart and center of guidance, of teaching, and of living.

JACK MICHAEL
LEE MEYERSON

A Behavioral Approach
to Counseling and Guidance

IT IS TEMPTING to begin an article of this kind with attention-compelling references to some of the seemingly spectacular results that have been achieved by investigators who have employed procedures derived from what has come to be known as the experimental analysis of behavior. It is fascinating to learn how pigeons were taught to guide a missile (7), how speech was restored in a catatonic patient who had been mute for many years (4), and how some long-standing undesirable behavior in mentally retarded and psychotic individuals was changed in a relatively short time (1). Not a great deal is accomplished, however, if the relevance of this work for the educator, the psychologist and the counselor is not perceived, and needless harm occurs if the results are dismissed as artificial, impractical experiments by laboratory scientists who "want to treat people like rats and pigeons."

A behavioral approach to counseling and guidance does not consist of a bag of tricks to be applied mechanically for the purpose of coercing unwilling people. It is part of a highly technical system, based on laboratory investigations of the phenomena of conditioning, for describing behavior and specifying the conditions under which it is acquired, maintained, and eliminated.

Much more knowledge of conditioning and its broad field of applicability to human behavior is available today than can be appreciated by those who have only vague recollections of the glandular and motor responses of the dogs studied by Pavlov.

It is the major purpose of this paper to describe, in a didactic way, a portion of the new knowledge that has been obtained. Starting from definitions of specialized concepts and terminology, mastery of which will permit further reading of the technical literature, an overview is given of a descriptive and explanatory system of behavior that has relevance for counseling and guidance. Although application to practical counseling problems is not made in the main body of the paper, no doubt many counselors will perceive the similarity to counseling situations of the behavior processes that are described. A briefer concluding section summarizes some of the theoretical and practical implications of the system for counseling and guidance.

It is necessary to understand at the outset that the familiar characterization of behavior as a function of the interaction of hereditary and environmental variables is accepted, not with the lip service that is sometimes given before fleeing to hypothetical constructs of inner behavioral determiners that are neither heredity nor environment, but with utmost seriousness.

The consequences of this orientation should be made explicit: Inherited genetic and constitutional determiners are not under the control of, or subject to, direct experimentation by behavioral scientists. This means that the only channel open to counselors for influencing human behavior is through changes in the environment. Additionally, certain environmental manipulations, such as separating a person from his frontal lobes or administering drugs that have psychopharmacological effects, are not available to psychologists and educators. The phenomenon with which counselors deal, then, is behavior, and the independent variable which controls behavior must be the environment. A behavioral system attempts to specify, without reference to unobservable, hypothetical inner-determining agents, the conditions and the process by which the environment controls human behavior.

A Behavioral System[1]

Respondent Conditioning

Certain physical events in the environment are related to certain human muscular and glandular activities in a relatively invariable way. A light shined in the eye elicits a constriction of the pupil. An acid solution placed on the tongue elicits secretion by the salivary gland. Such physical events are called stimuli and the muscular and glandular activities are called responses. Some of these stimulus-response relationships or reflexes are present at birth, and in humans most of them are involved in maintaining the internal economy of the body or protecting it against harmful external conditions.

A stimulus which is not a part of a reflex relationship becomes a *conditioned stimulus* for the response by repeated, temporal pairing with an *unconditioned stimulus* which already elicits the response. This new relationship is called a *conditioned reflex*; and the pairing procedure is called *respondent conditioning*.

In general, conditioning does not produce permanent effects. If the conditioned stimulus is presented frequently in the absence of the unconditioned stimulus, a procedure called *extinction*, it loses its eliciting properties.

The procedures for producing conditioning and extinction were first explored systematically by I. P. Pavlov, and respondent conditioning is an area of continued interest and active investigation.

However, if conditioning phenomena were limited in applicability to the transfer of eliciting effects from reflex stimuli to other stimuli, the field would be of little importance in understanding human be-

---

[1] The principles of the system presented here are based on data reported by a great many people. Most studies within the last 5 years were reported in the *Journal of the Experimental Analysis of Behavior*.

The statements about avoidance are based in large part on work done by Murray Sidman and his associates. Statements about punishment are based primarily on the work of N. H. Azrin and his associates. A more complete treatment of the material basic to this systematic presentation is available in J. G. Holland and B. F. Skinner, *The Analysis of Behavior* (New York: McGraw-Hill, 1961) and in B. F. Skinner's earlier work, *Science and Human Behavior* (New York: Macmillan, 1953). Similar material has been presented in several shorter papers, like the present one, addressed to some special audience. Two of these are especially valuable in their thoroughness and in their detailed discussion of practical applications of research findings. They are C. B. Ferster's "Reinforcement and punishment in the control of human behavior by social agencies," *Psychiatric Research Reports*, X (1958), 101–18 and M. Sidman's "Operant Techniques," in Arthur J. Bachrach (ed.), *Experimental Foundations of Clinical Psychology* (New York: Basic Books, 1962).

havior. Most of the behavior that is of interest to society does not fit the paradigm of the reflex. There is in general no identifiable eliciting stimulus for the broad class of "voluntary" activity called by B. F. Skinner *operant* behavior. The basic operation of respondent conditioning, however, the systematic temporal pairing of stimulus conditions, is of some significance since a portion of almost any kind of stimulus effect can be transferred to a new stimulus by the procedure of pairing the two stimuli.

Operant Conditioning

Whereas for reflexes and conditioned reflexes the event of critical explanatory importance is the eliciting stimulus preceding the response, for a large class of non-reflex behavior the critical events are the environmental consequences of the behavior. Such behavior can be said to "operate" on the environment, in contrast to behavior which is "respondent" to prior eliciting stimuli.

It is convenient to group the kinds of stimulus events which are consequences of acts into three major classes in terms of their effects on operant behavior.

Positive Reinforcers. These stimulus events are defined by the observation that the behavior which preceded them has a higher probability of occurrence under similar conditions in the future. Such events are often called rewards and described as pleasant. Some of these positive reinforcers are of biological significance to the organism such as food, water, sexual contact, and some are of acquired significance such as praise, affection, grades, money.

Negative Reinforcers or Aversive Stimuli. These events are defined by the observation that behavior which preceded their removal is more likely to occur under similar conditions in the future. The common aversive stimuli are those we call painful or unpleasant such as extreme heat or cold, blows on the surface of the body, distortions of certain inner organs as in a stomach ache, very loud sounds or very bright lights. Another class of aversive stimuli is that whose properties are acquired during our lifetimes such as social disapproval, criticism, nagging, threat.

The operation of presenting a positive reinforcer contingent upon a response is called *positive reinforcement*. The operation of removing an aversive stimulus contingent upon a response is called *negative reinforcement*.[2] Both operations are called *operant conditioning* and both increase the future frequency of the response which preceded them.

No Consequence and Neutral Stimuli. Responses continue to occur if they receive either positive or negative reinforcement. They cease if followed by no consequence or by neutral stimuli. The procedure of allowing behavior to occur without reinforcement is called *operant extinction,* and can be contrasted with *respondent extinction* which is the procedure of allowing a conditioned stimulus to occur without pairing it with an unconditioned stimulus.

It should be noted that none of the above statements constitutes postulates, axioms, assumptions or issues of theoretical controversy. The definitions are simply descriptions of observed relationships. Some events serve as reinforcers and some do not. The determination of what constitutes a reinforcer for a particular organism is an empirical problem, although of course, it is often very helpful to have studied biologically similar organisms or those inhabiting similar environments. In the case of humans, the reinforcers of biological significance are apparently very similar to those of other mammals and are fairly well known. On the other hand, the specification of the events of acquired reinforcing value for an individual human requires either a contemporary investigation or considerable knowledge of his environmental history.

Conditioned Reinforcers. Only a small proportion of the important consequences of human behavior are the unconditioned reinforcers attributable to biological characteristics. Other consequences, *conditioned reinforcers,* acquire their reinforcing properties as a function of experience. It appears that an event becomes a conditioned reinforcer in some degree simply by being paired with another reinforcer. However, most of the conditioned reinforcers that are important in human affairs are, in addition, stimuli in the presence of which further behavior is reinforced. In common sense terms, most conditioned reinforcers are means to an end which may be an unconditioned reinforcer or another conditioned reinforcer. For example, a match for a smoker will serve as a reinforcer for the behavior which

---

[2] Negative reinforcement should not be confused with punishment which is the presentation of an aversive stimulus contingent on a response.

procured it because it makes possible the further behavior of striking it and lighting the cigarette.

Some conditioned reinforcers are specific to particular unconditioned reinforcers as when signs regarding the serving of food, pictures of food, and menus, function as conditioned reinforcers for humans who are momentarily reinforceable with food. Some conditioned reinforcers, however, because they have been paired with many different unconditioned and conditioned reinforcers and because they have been means to many different ends almost become ends in themselves. Reinforcers that have this property, such as money, social approval, successful manipulation of the physical environment, affection, and others are called *generalized conditioned reinforcers*.

Common Sense, Automaticity, and Superstitious Behavior. It may seem that to emphasize the pleasant and unpleasant consequences of acts through "rewards and punishments" is nothing new. The effects described above have long been known and used in an intuitive way, but they also have long been misunderstood. The strengthening effect of a reward is commonly understood in terms of a rational process. It seems only natural that a person will repeat that which he can see will benefit him, and perform again those acts which he believes will terminate unpleasant conditions. However, the effect does not depend on a rational process at all. The foreseeing of consequences or the ability to state the relation between the consequences and the behavior which produced it is unnecessary. Any behavior which is followed by reinforcement—in all of the many species studied, and above all in man—is more likely to occur again in the same or a similar situation. This could be called the *automaticity* of the effect of reinforcement. To increase the occurrence of a particular class of behavior, it is necessary only to ensure that reinforcement occurs relatively soon after the behavior.

The automaticity effect is most dramatically demonstrated in what is called "superstitious behavior." When reinforcement follows behavior, even though the behavior did not produce or in any sense cause the reinforcement, it is called *accidental reinforcement*. Behavior which is developed as a function of accidental reinforcement was whimsically referred to as superstitious behavior in a study with pigeons (8) and the term has become a quasi-technical term in the behavioral field. Humans, probably because of their more complex environment, provide many more examples of superstitious behavior than lower animals. The verbalizations and unique motor activities of gamblers and the unnecessary postures and movements seen in sports activities are examples of the effects of accidental contingencies of reinforcement.

Shaping

Inasmuch as an operant response must first occur before it can be followed by reinforcement, one might suppose that operant conditioning cannot be used to produce new behavior. However, the detailed topography of a response—the particular muscle actions, including force and speed of various muscle components—varies from one occurrence to another. To produce new behavior then, or behavior that has not appeared in the response repertoire before, it is sufficient to selectively reinforce one of the variations in topography which resulted from the previous reinforcement, while allowing the other variations to extinguish. This has the effect of producing a further class of variations from which one may again differentially reinforce some and allow others to extinguish, and so on.

For example, in teaching a child to talk, his efforts to pronounce a particular word will at first be reinforced rather uncritically. Eventually, some of the variations will resemble accepted pronunciation more than others and receive selective reinforcement while other variations are allowed to extinguish. These events have the effect of producing a class of responses which come ever closer to the correct pronunciation than the last reinforced response, and the selective reinforcement can be applied again. This procedure for producing new behavior is called *shaping*. It is essentially the differential reinforcement of successive approximations to some complex form of behavior. It is the technique which animal trainers use to produce unusual and entertaining behaviors in their subjects, and it is the technique whereby humans acquire the complex response topographies of speech, athletic abilities and other motor skills.

Stimulus Control of Operant Behavior

Although the emphasis in describing operant behavior has been on the reinforcement occurring subsequent to the response, stimulus control is implied in the phrase concluding the principle of operant conditioning—if an operant response is followed by reinforcement it is more likely to occur *under similar conditions* in the future. The simplest principle of stimulus control is that the future probability of response is highest when the stimulus conditions resemble most closely those existing at the moment of previous reinforcement. The expression "resemble most closely" must be analyzed in some detail, but first a description is needed of a typical experimental situation in which the effects of stimuli on operant behavior are studied. A lower animal rather than a human is described as the subject in this example because stimulus control in humans is confounded by their extensive training regarding the relevance of certain classes of stimuli (see "discrimination training" below). A food-deprived monkey is placed in a small chamber containing a movable foot pedal, and reinforced with food for pressing the pedal. Suppose that the chamber is illuminated by a relatively bright overhead light, a moderately loud tone of 1000 cycles per second plays constantly, and a small translucent disc above the pedal, at eye level, is illuminated from behind with a bright green light. Although none of these stimulus conditions can be said to elicit the response, they all come to exert some control over its probability, for if any of them is changed, the tendency to respond will be temporarily lowered. Of course, if we continue to reinforce in the presence of the changed stimuli, responding will recover and the class of stimulus conditions controlling the response will be broadened. If, instead of changing only one of the stimulus conditions, we change all of them, the tendency to respond will be very low. In brief, any change from the stimulus conditions that existed at the moment of reinforcement will reduce the tendency to respond, and the greater the change, the greater the reduction.

There is, however, a vagueness in this formulation. How can the extent to which a changed stimulus condition resembles the original one be evaluated? For example, can we predict for a specific monkey whether changing the tone will reduce his tendency to respond more than will turning off the overhead light? We cannot. It is an empirical question. To some extent the similarity of different stimulus conditions will depend on the biological characteristics of the species. But in part, as in the case of reinforcers, the importance to the individual organism of the various aspects of the stimulus condition will depend on the previous history of that particular organism.

In the situation described above a change in color on the translucent disc would not be expected to change the tendency to respond very much because the disc color is only a small part of the total stimulus situation. By skilled use of the procedures of reinforcement and extinction, however, we can bring about the more precise type of stimulus control that is called *discrimination*. If we change the color from green to red, and in the presence of the red disc we do not reinforce the pedal response, it will become less frequent, i.e., extinguish. If we then restore the color and in its presence pedal pressing is again reinforced and so on, alternating the two conditions, the control of the disc color over the pedal response will become quite strong. This procedure is called *discrimination training*. If in the presence of a stimulus a response is reinforced, and in the absence of this stimulus it is extinguished, the stimulus will control the probability of the response in high degree. Such a stimulus is called a *discriminative stimulus*.

Almost all important human behavior is under the control of discriminative stimuli. Although part of the educational process involves extensive shaping, particularly for motor skills, the educator's major efforts are directed toward the development of *discriminative repertoires*, or in common terminology, knowledge. Many details regarding the building of discriminative repertoires have been discovered in the experimental laboratory, and these findings are now beginning to see systematic exploitation in the field of programmed instruction.

The development of effective discriminative repertoires for interpersonal behavior is also a topic of great importance for those dealing with the practical control of behavior, and although the principles of discrimination are the same when the stimuli to be discriminated are the behaviors of other people, the details of application remain to be worked out.

A beginning has been made in applying basic principles of discrimination to verbal behavior, language, and communication. This is presently seen to be a field composed of one discriminative repertoire under the control of the many features of the physical and social environment, with additional repertoires controlled by features of the first (9).

Schedules of Intermittent Reinforcement

Thus far discussion has centered on the role of reinforcement in simply making a response more likely to occur in the future, in shaping up novel topographies or forms of response, and in bringing a response under the control of a particular stimulus condition. But reinforcement does not lose its relevance once an adequate topography has been developed and the behavior is under proper stimulus control.

It has additional effects that may be treated according to the schedule by which reinforcement is given.

An important characteristic of much behavior is that it is repeated, either because the appropriate stimulus conditions persist or because they recur. Having learned to ask a parent for a cookie a child can immediately ask for another, and another. This behavior must eventually cease because of temporary changes in the parent's disposition to provide the reinforcer, because the reinforcer loses its effectiveness by satiation, or for other reasons, but there will be other occasions for similar behavior to occur. If every occurrence of such a repeatable response is followed by reinforcement the behavior will continue until other variables exert control. On the other hand, if reinforcement is discontinued altogether the behavior will cease.

Between the extremes of *continuous reinforcement* where every relevant response is reinforced and *extinction* where there is no reinforcement there are many situations where responses are only occasionally reinforced. Such *intermittent reinforcement* might be expected to produce an effect intermediate between continuous reinforcement and extinction, but that is not the case. The situation is much more complex. A schedule of intermittent reinforcement is actually a way of arranging reinforcement contingencies regarding the passage of time, the number of responses, or both. The complexity arises from the varied and intricate ways in which these temporal and number contingencies can be combined and interrelated in natural and laboratory environments, and from the extreme sensitivity of the behavior of organisms to such conditions.

Ratio Reinforcement. There is a large class of schedules involving solely a number contingency, and this is usually specified in terms of the ratio of responses to reinforcements. Industrial piecework pay is an example of ratio reinforcement, as is the pay-off schedule provided by the "one-armed bandit" of the gambling house. The principal characteristic of such schedules is that the more rapidly one works the more frequently one is reinforced. Behavior conforms to this kind of requirement by occurring at a high rate. Another feature of this kind of schedule is that very large amounts of work per reinforcement can be tolerated, but to avoid premature extinction the organism must approach such conditions gradually by first being exposed to less stringent requirements. A third feature is that simple ratio reinforcement does not have self-corrective properties. Any temporary reduction in the tendency to respond simply delays the ultimate reinforcement. Vicious circles can easily develop where the less one responds the less one gets, and therefore the less one responds in the future.

Interval Reinforcement. Another class of schedules involves only temporal contingencies. The most commonly studied arrangements are those where the probability of a response being reinforced increases as a simple function of the passage of time, and under these conditions the frequency of responding generally reflects the changing probability of reinforcement. An example from daily life is the behavior of telephoning someone who is not at home. One cannot hasten his return home by rapid re-dialing, as in ratio reinforcement, but the probability of making the connection and completing the call increases as time passes. If the interval varies randomly, response frequency is relatively constant over time. If the interval is constant, responding increases in frequency as the time for reinforcement approaches. In such schedules the rate of responding is directly related to the frequency of reinforcement. Only moderate response rates are generated by interval reinforcement but when the reinforcement is discontinued altogether, responding decreases in frequency very slowly compared with behavior which has been continuously reinforced. Resistance to extinction is high. In contrast to the ratio schedules described earlier, interval schedules in general are self-corrective. Any temporary reduction in response frequency is counteracted by receiving the next reinforcement after fewer unreinforced responses, and this restores the tendency to respond.

Much more complex arrangements of temporal and number contingencies occur in the human physical and social environment, and also in the behavior laboratory. Fortunately the field is somewhat systematized and it is becoming increasingly possible to predict the effects of new arrangements on the basis of what is known about their components.

Intermittent Reinforcement and Motivation. In addition to its general theoretical relevance in illuminating the effects of reinforcement contingencies, intermittent reinforcement is of considerable practical significance because of its relationship to the traditional field of motivation. The well-motivated person is one who works at some activity with persistence, even though his reinforcement is long delayed. He is also a person who can put out a very large amount of work with only an occasional reward. It is not evident, however, that these properties are *in* the person or that the behavior cannot be produced by manipulating the environment. Variable interval schedules generate great persistence in the face of non-reinforcement, and ratio schedules produce large amounts of work for the minimum number of reinforcements. Not only good motivation but the pathologically "driven" behavior that is said to characterize the gambler can be generated in the laboratory by programming the same kind of variable ratio schedule that acts on the gambler. Similarly when a child cries and begs his parents with great persistence and intensity to take him with them rather than leave him with a baby sitter, we are likely to say something like "he *wants* very much to go with them." The work on intermittent reinforcement tells us very clearly that just such a performance could be generated by acquiescing to the child's requests after only mildly intense and slightly persistent entreaties at first and then slowly raising the requirement. Whether any particular sample of behavior arose in this way is an empirical question.

Deprivation and Satiation

Not all motivational problems fit the paradigm described above. Deprivation and satiation have two major effects on behavior which cannot at present be reduced to the effects of any of the biological or environmental variables discussed previously.

Food, water, sexual activity, activity in general, and some other similar unconditioned reinforcers will serve as reinforcers only if the organism has been deprived of them. Satiation weakens and deprivation strengthens the effectiveness of these reinforcers. This is one major effect of this variable. In addition, deprivation with respect to a reinforcer results in an increased likelihood of occurrence of all the behavior that has in the past been reinforced with it.

Stated in terms of food, for example, the first effect is that as deprivation time increases, food becomes a more powerful reinforcer. As eating continues, food loses its reinforcing capacity. The second effect is seen in that food-seeking behavior becomes more frequent as time since last eating increases, and less frequent as eating proceeds. This second effect cannot at present be reduced to the first, since the increase in food-seeking behavior can be observed even before reinforcement has been received.

The study of deprivation-satiation variables appears to come closest to the traditional field of motivation, but there are many cases where these variables are *not* relevant but it is common to infer them. For example, one man may show strong persistent behavior directed toward socio-sexual relations with women, and another may show very little such behavior. The customary explanation is in terms of sex drive, with the implication that equivalent periods of deprivation affect the two men differently or that one is more deprived than the other. It is more likely in our culture that differences of this magnitude are due largely to different histories of intermittent reinforcement although again this interpretation would require independent evidence in any particular case. Laboratory studies with lower animals indicate quite clearly that variables such as frequency of reinforcement and kind of schedule can cause variations in frequency and persistence of behavior that are greater than the variations generated by deprivation.

It would also be a mistake to infer a history of specific deprivation from the knowledge that a particular event will function as a reinforcer. In the case of ordinary conditioned reinforcers this mistake would not usually be made—the fact that the sight of a telephone is reinforcing certainly doesn't suggest telephone deprivation, since a telephone is so obviously a means to an end. The generalized conditioned reinforcers, however, of affection, attention, money, because they are means to many different ends, erroneously might be assumed to be subject to the deprivation effect in themselves.

In summary then, deprivation and satiation are critical determiners of the momentary effectiveness of a number of reinforcers, and of the momentary strength of large classes of responses. But to pattern all "motivational" problems on this model would be to neglect other equally if not more important determiners.

Emotion

It is customary to consider emotion as respondent behavior, but operant aspects of emotion can also be specified. Like deprivation, emotional variables affect a large class of operant responses. For example, a person who is ordinarily described as fearful not only shows the respondent effects such as a more rapid heart rate, moist palms and dry throat, but also he shows an increased tendency to engage in all those operant behaviors which have in the past been reinforced by escape from current or similarly difficult situations. Further, those aspects of his repertoire which ordinarily receive positive reinforcement in this situation are weakened. His tendencies to run away, to hide, to seek help from other individuals, are all increased, whereas his tendencies to eat, play, and engage in normal social behaviors are decreased. These phenomena presently are not well understood.

The operations which produce behavioral changes in respondent and operant repertoires under emotion have not yielded to efforts to develop a simple classification scheme. Furthermore, the class of responses which are altered by any particular operation contain such a large component of acquired behaviors that the similarities between different individuals are of little systematic value. However, although an empirical description and ordering of the responses which change with emotion presently are limited, the principles whereby already developed repertoires can be transferred from one stimulus condition to another are somewhat better understood. The operation of temporal pairing is relevant. Any stimulus which is systematically present during an emotional condition will produce some of the respondents and some of the change in the operant repertoire that characterize the emotional condition when it is presented alone. Practical use of principles in this field has been under investigation in the U.S.S.R. ever since the earliest work of Pavlov. More recently, however, a group of British investigators have made very successful deliberate applications of emotional conditioning principles to the treatment of abnormal behavior (3).

Aversive Control

Escape and Avoidance. An environmental arrangement in which an organism's response can terminate an already present aversive stimulus is called an *escape* procedure. It is negative reinforcement, and operant conditioning of the response is the result. When behavior can prevent or delay the onset of the aversive stimulus the procedure is called *avoidance,* and this arrangement also will result in the development and maintenance of operant behavior. Avoidance cannot be considered as a simple case of negative reinforcement, however, since there is often no obvious stimulus termination immediately following the response. Turning off an alarm clock that has already begun to ring is an example of escape behavior, but pushing in the stop before it begins to ring is avoidance.

Examples of this kind of control are easily found in parent-child interactions. Children's cleanliness activities are often maintained as escape behavior where the aversive stimulus is the nagging verbal behavior of a parent. Sometimes these activities constitute avoidance behavior. Here the aversive stimulus is criticism, scolding, or being made to wash over again. Later, when children go to school their studying behavior is often maintained as avoidance behavior, where the aversive stimulus is again criticism, failing grades, or removal of privileges. The distinction between behavior for positive reinforcement and the avoidance paradigm is illustrated in the following not uncommon interchange between parent and child. The child is told to do something and asks "What will I get if I do?" whereupon the parent replies "You'll get something if you don't!"

Laboratory findings with avoidance behavior have indicated several characteristics of this kind of control which are closely related to behavior disorders of many kinds. In the first place, successful avoidance behavior will by its very nature prevent the discovery that the aversive stimulus has been discontinued, and when this is coupled with the extraordinary persistence of such behavior it suffices to explain many human activities that serve no current function.

Another finding relevant to behavior problems is the fact that occasional presentations of the aversive stimulus without respect to the organism's behavior will maintain the avoidance repertoire almost indefinitely. In this way, even though the bad thing that one is avoiding is no longer related to one's behavior, so long as it occurs once in a while the avoidance repertoire may persist.

A final point concerns the conditions under which the escape or avoidance repertoire will occur. In escape behavior the presentation of the aversive stimulus produces immediate strength in the escape repertoire and the escape repertoire is not readily seen in the absence of the aversive stimulus. In avoidance, the presentation of stimuli which have in the past accompanied that or other aversive stimuli strengthen the avoidance repertoire, but an even stronger effect is seen when the aversive stimulus itself is presented momentarily. To maintain behavior in this manner it is necessary to maintain the threat of aversive stimulation.

Punishment. Technically, punishment refers to the operation of presenting an aversive stimulus contingent upon a response, or removing a positive reinforcer contingent upon a response.[3] It is widely used in our culture to reduce the frequency of behavior, and according

---

[3] Common sense usage often has punishment synonymous with what is referred to here as an aversive stimulus or, even more broadly, as aversive control.

to "common sense" psychology is often described as opposite in effect from reward. As rewards strengthen behavior, so punishments are believed to weaken it. Considerable experimental evidence is now available regarding the effects of this operation, which turn out to be quite complex.

One kind of complexity arises because whereas the strengthening effects of reinforcement can be studied in isolation, the weakening effects of punishment can only be studied by superimposing them on preceding or ongoing strengthening effects. This is not only a methodological problem. In practical affairs the question of the efficacy of punishment seldom arises except with respect to behavior that has at least moderate probability of occurrence.

It is difficult to generalize about this competition between reinforcement and punishment since the parameters of the positive reinforcement and the aversive stimulus used are critical, as is the availability of alternative responses which are reinforced and/or punished to varying degrees. However, it is probably safe to say that when no other response but the punished one can obtain positive reinforcement, and with positive reinforcers like food, it takes very severe punishment to effectively reduce the frequency of the behavior.

Added to this complication is the fact that an aversive stimulus may have some effects because it is aversive, but it also has other stimulus effects. By the principle of stimulus control mentioned earlier an aversive stimulus can reduce the frequency of responding if the stimulus constitutes a change from the conditions which existed during previous reinforcement, regardless of its aversive characteristics. And since reinforcement often occurs in the same situation as punishment, an aversive stimulus, as a result of some systematic relation to the reinforcement, can acquire even more complex stimulus properties, such as those of a discriminative stimulus, or even a conditioned positive reinforcer.

Finally, there is a complication in interpreting the effects of punishment in human interactions that is brought about by the fact that a person who punishes may for a time be less disposed to provide any ordinary positive reinforcement. If this is the case, punishment systematically precedes a period of extinction. This arrangement results in a reduction in some behavior—but not due to the aversive effects of the punishment. On the other hand, punishers sometimes show a greater disposition to provide positive reinforcement shortly after they have administered punishment. This results in a temporary increase in some kinds of behavior, and, under proper conditions, even a future increase in the punished behavior.

Any stimulus which is paired temporally with an aversive stimulus acquires some of its properties. Such stimuli are called *conditioned aversive stimuli* or conditioned negative reinforcers. Aversive stimuli and conditioned aversive stimuli, in addition to producing the effects described above are also classed as emotional variables, because of their respondent effects and their effects on large classes of operant responses. This emotional effect enters into and further complicates various kinds of aversive control. It also appears to be responsible for various deleterious changes in certain internal organs. Because of this, and for many other reasons, aversive control is in most cases socially undesirable although it is apparently not completely avoidable.

This concludes the presentation of the basic empirical principles of this behavior system. Of course, many details have been omitted, but the major relations have been covered. Further development of this system is proceeding along two lines: workers in experimental laboratories are constantly discovering new details, improving imprecise relations, and sometimes revealing new major principles; others working in applied settings are developing a behavioral technology based on these basic principles.

IMPLICATIONS FOR COUNSELING AND GUIDANCE

General Implications

The behavior system described has the clear implication that observable behavior is the only variable of importance in the counseling and guidance process, and it is the only criterion against which the outcome of the process can be evaluated. Conceptual formulations such as ego-strength, inferiority feelings, or self-concept are not behavior but simply ways of organizing and interpreting observable behavior by referring it to an inner determiner. Such formulations may be incorrect, insufficient, or merely superfluous. They may be harmful or impeding when applied in the sense that they direct attention and effort to irrelevant variables, or they may be unessential "decorations" which do no harm but do not contribute to the counselor's efforts or the learner's behavior.

Almost all approaches to counseling and guidance are in agreement that the goal of counseling is to affect behavior and that behavior is lawful. "Pathological," self-defeating and disorganized behaviors as well as "healthy" behaviors are seen as lawful phenomena whose laws can be discovered. In addition, there appears to be general agreement that the crucial behavior of human beings is learned. Man is not at the mercy of his "unconscious" or his drives; for these entelechies, if they exist, can be expressed in many different ways. The critical questions in counseling and guidance, therefore, seem to relate to how behavior is learned and how it may be unlearned or altered.

It is here that a behavioral approach differs from other approaches in counseling and guidance practice. Present practice is to consider the sociological or psychological category to which a problem may be assigned. Is it an educational, vocational, or social problem, or is it a problem of dependency, self-conflict, or choice anxiety? Alternatively there may be some concern for the locus of the problem: Is it primarily a factual-reality problem whose locus is in the environment or is it primarily an emotional-irreality problem whose locus is in the patient? At least a portion of treatment procedures depends on the answers.

These questions and answers, however, to the extent that they reflect limited concern with the process by which the presenting behavior was learned and what must be done to deal with it, obscure rather than illuminate the problem to be solved. From a behavioral standpoint, the only relevant questions relate to behavior itself. What behavior must be created or maintained and what deficient or inadequate behaviors must be altered? Once these basic questions are answered— and an experienced counselor often can reach a diagnosis in a short time even when the client is unaware of the source of his distress— successful corrective procedures follow the behavioral principles and processes that have been described. Unquestionably, some efforts of guidance workers, counselors, and psychotherapists who use traditional approaches result in great success. They probably do so, however, because of the intuitive use of procedures that may be specified explicitly in behavioral terms.

The entire field of guidance, counseling, and psychotherapy might benefit considerably if all workers considered seriously just one behavioral principle and its corollary, namely, that behavior is controlled by its environmental consequences and that an effective procedure for producing behavioral change is the manipulation of the environment so as to create consequences that will produce the desired behavior. If then, it was desired to create, maintain, strengthen, weaken, alter, or eliminate a particular behavior or set of behaviors, attention would be directed toward the operation of the behavioral determiners outlined in the previous section. One advantage of this kind of formulation is that it is explicit, teachable, and testable. Another advantage is that it tells the counselor what has to be done and allows him to monitor progress within an objective rather than an intuitive framework.

At the beginning of behavioral counseling or psychotherapy, the counselor may have to manipulate the determinants so as to facilitate desired behavior coming under the control of "natural" behavioral consequences in the environment. Some professional workers perceive or create an ethical problem here by asking if it is moral for one person to attempt to control the behavior of another. This question has already been answered in our society and perhaps in all societies. Parents, educators, and guidance workers make no bones about their earnest intention to create and maintain the "good" behavior that is valued and approved of by the culture and to eliminate "bad" behavior to the maximum degree of which they are capable. It is not clear that the task of the counselor is, or should be, different.

Advice giving, information giving, interpretation and clarification, training and reconditioning, persuasion, encouragement and moral support, subtle direction toward some things and away from others are all frequently mentioned as currently important tools of counseling and guidance. Even in psychotherapy, "growth-inducing" and uncovering techniques did not come to be preferred to directive and controlling procedures because the therapist could not readily perceive the ineffective behavior of his clients that had to change if better adjustment was to occur. The counseling fashion changed because the crude, directive procedures then available were relatively ineffective except in those fortuitous circumstances where the individual was already under the partial control of some appropriate environmental variable.

A return to inadequate directive procedures is not advocated. Behaviorally oriented counselors agree that telling people what is wrong and what they "should" do is an ineffective procedure. The heart of the behavioral approach in counseling is that the environment must be manipulated so as to allow strong reinforcing consequences to become attached to the behavior that is desired.

This implies, of course, that almost any behavior can be manipulated, and behavior principles do not specify what behavior should be fostered. Certainly the knowledge of how to shape behavior can be misused. However, the ethics of deliberately guiding human beings to personally and socially fulfilling lives may not be a problem for any except a relatively small group of counselors committed to an inner-directed philosophy and seemingly nondirective procedures. For most of those to whom society entrusts the guidance of others, influencing or inducing people to behave in ways that society says are "good" ways is an accepted goal, and the critical question is "How can we 'motivate' a person so that he does behave, 'wants to' behave and 'enjoys' behaving in good ways?"

The principles discovered by researchers in the experimental analysis of behavior offer some direct answers now and some procedures for discovering others.

Specific Implications

There are two major ways in which a behavioral approach to counseling may be useful. One is simply to improve the effectiveness of present counseling efforts. The other is to help build a better world.

Improving Counseling and Guidance. To some degree, behavioral principles, as descriptions of how behavior is created, maintained, altered, or placed under stimulus control are neutral principles. They permit, at least for a time, various theoretical or philosophical views of the *real* nature of the human condition. If, for example, one psychotherapist believes that catharsis is a necessary condition for amelioration or correction of neurotic behavior, while another believes that healthy behavior is best achieved by "accentuating the positive," the same properly applied reinforcement principles will produce catharsis in one patient and healthy talk in the other, or a client can be led from one kind of talk to the other. To the extent that a therapist manipulates the environment so as to facilitate the expression of affect, reduce self-ideal discrepancies, or whatever behavior he believes is necessary for a patient's improvement, he is in control of a powerful tool. If he applies reinforcement principles successfully, it doesn't matter a great deal if the therapist originally believes that he is simply assisting in liberating a primordial, natural force within the person. To the extent that differential results are obtained when he deliberately uses or does not use behavioral techniques, the environmental consequences will shape his behavior also and may even change his theory.

This is not the place for a technical discussion of the origins and treatment of the grossly deviant behavior that is believed to require psychotherapy. It should be mentioned, however, that more than 30 years ago it was demonstrated that phobias, for example, could be induced, generalized, and removed by purely behavioral procedures (5, 12), and in these cases where the origin of the behavior was known, it was superfluous to look for the hidden forces or the "real" meanings which mediated the phobia. Bandura (2) gives an excellent survey of the large amount of more recent experimental and clinical studies using behavioristic psychotherapy. Many kinds of deviant behavior have been treated successfully by direct focusing on the behavior itself.

For problems traditionally assigned to counseling and guidance personnel, the relevance of a behavioral approach is even more clear cut. The great bulk of the problems here do not have disputed ethical implications. In schools, no one questions that it is better for children to learn school subject matter than not to learn it; that it is desirable to get along with other children and with adults without excessive conflicts; that more is to be gained by staying in school than by dropping out; that very early marriage of school children is unwise; that law abiding behavior is better than delinquent behavior. In brief, in great part, the behavior that children "should" engage in is known and agreed upon, and the task of the counselor is to facilitate and strengthen its emergence and maintenance. As in counseling with special populations such as the mentally retarded and the physically handicapped, the problems may be considered straightforward ones of behavioral engineering.

Although there has been little experience with these kinds of problems, it seems reasonable to believe that if a school counselor systematically learned to utilize only a small number of principles such as the behavior-influencing power of positive reinforcement, the undesirable long range consequences of aversive control and some of the details regarding shaping and the development of stimulus control, he could fulfill his job functions with greater efficiency. It is not so much that a behavioral approach would necessarily change a great deal of what the counselor did, but he would know why certain activities such as the recognition of merit are good and other activities such as grading on the curve are not. Knowing the effects of these activities, he might come to manipulate them more effectively. He would also come to ask, in each case of deficient or mal-adaptive behavior, how the behavior was linked to consequences and, instead of measuring abilities or personality, attempt to alter the consequences so as to shape up more desirable behavior.

On the other hand, a counselor who accepted the complete behavioral system and worked within it would tend to ask more radical questions about some present school practices and to initiate more radical changes in counseling functions. For example, in connection with the critical school drop-out problem, he would be less concerned with specifying the characteristics of students who drop out than in studying the kind and frequency of the reinforcements that are available for school learning in comparison with other reinforcers and with the frequency of avoidance and punishing conditions that exist in the classroom. He would experiment with introducing token reinforcers in the classroom dispensable immediately upon the occurrence of a desired response. He would analyze the conditions under which a potential drop-out could be led to emit new responses in a tight, reinforcing feedback loop so as to shape behavior that would ultimately come under the control of the natural reinforcers of the environment. For example, a student might be paid in money for working a teaching machine program in bookkeeping or algebra, or he might be given tokens that would make him eligible for earning money or some other generalized reinforcer. "What!" someone may exclaim, "You propose to pay children for learning what is good for them?" Certainly. Industry does this regularly now. Colleges and universities pay out large amounts of cash to an extent undreamed of a generation ago. We are now paying thousands of students to go to school.

Human beings do not "naturally" like what the experience of the species indicates is necessary or good for them. Drop-out students by their behavior are saying that they are not receiving the "natural" reinforcers of the classroom that influence the school-going behavior of most children, or that these cannot compete in strength with other reinforcers. The task of the counselor is to discover what is reinforcing to potential drop-outs and to make these reinforcers contingent upon school learning. If the drop-out problem is a serious one; if we really believe that our society and economy require an educated population; and if the monetary and social costs of large numbers of uneducated or undereducated persons are great; there should be no hesitancy in taking advantage of scientific principles of learning to apply effective extrinsic reinforcers to help shape desirable behavior. Some problems of juvenile delinquency and its behavioral treatment can be considered in the same way (11).

The social ramifications of this kind of approach are great, and many new kinds of counselor behavior will be required. It is apparent that many aspects of counseling and guidance work that focus on behavior and behavioral change cannot be done effectively in the traditional verbal, face to face, office situation. To a far greater degree than is presently the case, the behavioral counselor must be able to influence the consequences of behavior, as it is emitted, by personal action, by machines, and by enlisting the aid of teachers, parents, and school administrators in creating healthy behavioral environments. The principles for doing this are simple, but the techniques for application are complex, and perhaps progress in appreciable degree may have to wait on the creation of experimental, school behavior laboratories.

Building a Better World. Much, perhaps most, of the present work of counseling and guidance personnel consists of giving information and advice based on the measured characteristics, capacities, interests, and attitudes of the client and helping to resolve the conflicts that arise when there are discrepancies among them, or between any of them and the requirements of the environment.

The recognition of "individual differences" and the development of a technology for measuring them was a tremendous advance in the guidance and control of human behavior at the time these developments occurred. There is danger, however, that the increased precision with which a person can be described at a given moment of time may lead us to neglect or minimize the fact that *what is* is not identical with *what must be.*

Educators and psychologists have always been in the vanguard of those who have striven to push back the boundaries of a personal destiny determined primarily by heredity. It is almost a cliché in the behavioral sciences that inherited genetic and constitutional variables may set limits on the behavior that is possible for a human being, but environmental variables determine the behavior that a person actually engages in. In addition, educational and social experiences have shown that the limiting effects of hereditary variables have always been far slighter than was believed to be true at an earlier time.

This knowledge, of course, has been tempered by the empirical observation that other things equal—in the absence of additional knowledge and a better technology for inducing change—the past is one of the best predictors of the future.

One crucial consequence of the research that has been oriented to a functional analysis of behavior is the explicit notice that other things are no longer equal. An improved understanding of how behavior is formed and maintained, and an improved technology for inducing behavioral change now exist; and we can use this knowledge for the deliberate building of a better world. Skinner (10) has sketched the larger social implications of this revolutionary gain in knowledge. Discussion here will be limited to effects on the concept of "individual differences."

From a behavioral standpoint, most of the variation in behavior that presently is assigned to individual differences reflects the influence of unmanipulated environmental variables. Within wide limits now and even wider limits in the future, as additional knowledge is gained, desired or desirable behavior can be acquired by everyone. A large scale, if brief, foretaste of things to come occurred during World War II when, under less than optimal conditions, Rosie the housewife easily became Rosie the riveter; adolescent college boys became commanders of destroyers; and farm boys became skilled electronic technicians.

Probably few counselors would object to the statement that individual differences arise from the interrelationships among capacity, motivation, and opportunity. The last has a firm footing in the environment, but the first two are often perceived as being somehow *in* the person. It should be evident from the description of principles that this notion is unacceptable in a behavioral system. On the contrary, differences in "intelligence," for example, are reflections of some of the performances that result from differential exposure to learning experiences in a relatively chaotic environment. If intelligence can be analyzed into the behavior that constitutes its component parts, it can be taught in an orderly environment so that almost everyone can reach the same high level of performance. Similarly, motivation can be considered not as an innate function of specific drives but as a function of environmental determiners of which one of the most important is positive reinforcement. Under appropriate environmental conditions, which man can create, almost anyone can be motivated to do anything.

Human beings no longer allow themselves to be pushed around by a chaotic physical environment. We heat cold environments and cool warm ones; we fly into space and dive into the ocean depths; and we rearrange many other features of the physical environment to suit our convenience. The psychological and social environments can be manipulated in similar ways. It is no longer necessary to accept without question what a chaotic "natural" environment offers or what chance provides, but with knowledge now available we can build a better world.

REFERENCES

1. Ayllon, T., and Michael, J. The psychiatric nurse as a behavioral engineer. *Journal of the Experimental Analysis of Behavior,* 1959, *2,* 323–34.
2. Bandura, A. Psychotherapy as a learning process. *Psychological Bulletin,* 1961, *58,* 143–59.
3. Eysenck, H. J. (ed.). *Behavior Therapy and the Neuroses.* New York: Pergamon Press, 1960.
4. Isaacs, W., Thomas, J., and Goldiamond, I. Application of operant conditioning to reinstate verbal behavior in psychotics. *Journal of Speech and Hearing Disorders,* 1960, *25,* 8–12.
5. Jones, Mary C. The elimination of children's fears. *Journal of Experimental Psychology,* 1924, 7, 382–90.
6. Skinner, B. F. *Cumulative Record.* New York: Appleton-Century-Crofts, 1961, pp. 3–36.
7. ————. Pigeons in a pelican. *American Psychologist,* 1960, *15,* 28–37.
8. ————. Superstition in the pigeon. *Journal of Experimental Psychology,* 1948, *38,* 168–72.
9. ————. *Verbal Behavior.* New York: Appleton-Century-Crofts, 1957.
10. ————. *Walden Two.* New York: Macmillan, 1948.
11. Slack, C. W. Experimenter-subject psychotherapy: a new method of introducing intensive office treatment for unreachable cases. *Mental Hygiene,* 1960, *44,* 238–56.
12. Watson, J. B. and Rayner, R. Conditioned emotional reactions. *Journal of Experimental Psychology,* 1920, *3,* 1–14.

The Interpersonal Relationship:
The Core of Guidance

I WOULD LIKE TO SHARE with you in this paper a conclusion, a conviction which has grown out of years of experience in dealing with individuals, a conclusion which finds some confirmation in a steadily growing body of empirical evidence. It is simply that in a wide variety of professional work involving relationships with people —whether as a psychotherapist, teacher, religious worker, guidance counselor, social worker, clinical psychologist—it is the *quality* of the interpersonal encounter with the client which is the most significant element in determining effectiveness.

Let me spell out a little more fully the basis of this statement in my personal experience. I have been primarily a counselor and psychotherapist. In the course of my professional life I have worked with troubled college students, with adults in difficulty, with "normal" individuals such as business executives, and more recently with hospitalized psychotic persons. I have endeavored to make use of the learnings from my therapeutic experience in my interactions with classes and seminars, in the training of teachers, in the administration of staff groups, in the clinical supervision of psychologists, psychiatrists, and guidance workers as they work with their clients or patients. Some of these relationships are long-continued and intensive, as in individual psychotherapy. Some are brief, as in experiences with workshop participants or in contacts with students who come for practical advice. They cover a wide range of depth. Gradually I have come to the conclusion that one learning which applies to all of these experiences is that it is the quality of the personal relationship which matters most. With some of these individuals I am in touch only briefly, with others I have the opportunity of knowing them intimately, but in either case the quality of the personal encounter is probably, in the long run, the element which determines the extent to which this is an experience which releases or promotes development and growth. I believe the quality of my encounter is more important in the long run than is my scholarly knowledge, my professional training, my counseling orientation, the techniques I use in the interview. In keeping with this line of thought, I suspect that for a guidance worker also the relationship he forms with each student—brief or continuing—is more important than his knowledge of tests and measurements, the adequacy of his record keeping, the theories he holds, the accuracy with which he is able to predict academic success, or the school in which he received his training.

In recent years I have thought a great deal about this issue. I have tried to observe counselors and therapists whose orientations are very different from mine, in order to understand the basis of their effectiveness as well as my own. I have listened to recorded interviews from many different sources. Gradually I have developed some theoretical formulations (4, 5), some hypotheses as to the basis of effectiveness in relationships. As I have asked myself how individuals sharply different in personality, orientation and procedure can all be effective in a helping relationship, can each be successful in facilitating constructive change or development, I have concluded that it is because they bring to the helping relationship certain attitudinal ingredients. It is these that I hypothesize as making for effectiveness, whether we are speaking of a guidance counselor, a clinical psychologist, or a psychiatrist.

What are these attitudinal or experiential elements in the counselor which make a relationship a growth-promoting climate? I would like to describe them as carefully and accurately as I can, though I am well aware that words rarely capture or communicate the qualities of a personal encounter.

CONGRUENCE

In the first place, I hypothesize that personal growth is facilitated when the counselor is what he *is*, when in the relationship with his

‧client he is genuine and without "front" or façade, openly being the feelings and attitudes which at that moment are flowing in him. We have used the term "congruence" to try to describe this condition. By this we mean that the feelings the counselor is experiencing are available to him, available to his awareness, that he is able to live these feelings, be them in the relationship, and able to communicate them if appropriate. It means that he comes into a direct personal encounter with his client, meeting him on a person-to-person basis. It means that he is *being* himself, not denying himself. No one fully achieves this condition, yet the more the therapist is able to listen acceptantly to what is going on within himself, and the more he is able to *be* the complexity of his feelings without fear, the higher the degree of his congruence.

I think that we readily sense this quality in our everyday life. We could each of us name persons whom we know who always seem to be operating from behind a front, who are playing a role, who tend to say things they do not feel. They are exhibiting incongruence. We do not reveal ourselves too deeply to such people. On the other hand each of us knows individuals whom we somehow trust, because we sense that they are being what they *are*, that we are dealing with the person himself, and not with a polite or professional façade. This is the quality of which we are speaking, and it is hypothesized that the more genuine and congruent the therapist in the relationship, the more probability there is that change in personality in the client will occur.

I have received much clinical confirmation for this hypothesis in recent years in our work with randomly selected hospitalized schizophrenic patients. The individual therapists in our research program who seem to be most successful in dealing with these unmotivated, poorly educated, resistant, chronically hospitalized individuals, are those who are first of all real, who react in a genuine, human way as persons, and who exhibit their genuineness in the relationship.

But is it always helpful to be genuine? What about negative feelings? What about the times when the counselor's real feeling toward his client is one of annoyance, or boredom, or dislike? My tentative answer is that even with such feelings as these, which we all have from time to time, it is preferable for the counselor to be real than to put up a façade of interest and concern and liking which he does not feel.

But it is not a simple thing to achieve such reality. I am not saying that it is helpful to blurt out impulsively every passing feeling and accusation under the comfortable impression that one is being genuine. Being real involves the difficult task of being acquainted with the flow of experiencing going on within oneself, a flow marked especially by complexity and continuous change. So if I sense that I am feeling bored by my contacts with this student, and this feeling persists, I think I owe it to him and to our relationship to share this feeling with him. But here again I will want to be constantly in touch with what is going on in me. If I am, I will recognize that it is *my* feeling of being bored which I am expressing, and not some supposed fact about him as a boring person. If I voice it as my *own* reaction, it has the potentiality of leading to a deeper relationship. But this feeling exists in the context of a complex and changing flow, and this needs to be communicated too. I would like to share with him my distress at feeling bored, and the discomfort I feel in expressing this aspect of me. As I share these attitudes I find that my feeling of boredom arises from my sense of remoteness from him, and that I would like to be more in touch with him. And even as I try to express these feelings, they change. I am certainly not bored as I try to communicate myself to him in this way, and I am far from bored as I wait with eagerness and perhaps a bit of apprehension for his response. I also feel a new sensitivity to him, now that I have shared this feeling which has been a barrier between us. So I am very much more able to hear the surprise or perhaps the hurt in his voice as he now finds *him*self speaking more genuinely because I have dared to be real with him. I have let myself be a person—real, imperfect—in my relationship with him.

I have tried to describe this first element at some length because I regard it as highly important, perhaps the most crucial of the conditions I will describe, and because it is neither easy to grasp nor to achieve. Gendlin (2) has done an excellent job of explaining the significance of the concept of experiencing and its relationship to counseling and therapy, and his presentation may supplement what I have tried to say.

I hope it is clear that I am talking about a realness in the counselor which is deep and true, not superficial. I have sometimes thought that the word transparency helps to describe this element of personal congruence. If everything going on in me which is relevant to the relationship can be seen by my client, if he can see "clear through me," and if I am *willing* for this realness to show through in the relationship, then I can be almost certain that this will be a meaningful encounter in which we both learn and develop.

I have sometimes wondered if this is the only quality which matters in a counseling relationship. The evidence seems to show that other qualities also make a profound difference and are perhaps easier to achieve. So I am going to describe these others. But I would stress that if, in a given moment of relationship, they are not genuinely a part of the experience of the counselor, then it is, I believe, better to be genuinely what one is, than to pretend to be feeling these other qualities.

EMPATHY

The second essential condition in the relationship, as I see it, is that the counselor is experiencing an accurate empathic understanding of his client's private world, and is able to communicate some of the significant fragments of that understanding. To sense the client's inner world of private personal meanings as if it were your own, but without ever losing the "as if" quality, this is empathy, and this seems essential to a growth-promoting relationship. To sense his confusion or his timidity or his anger or his feeling of being treated unfairly as if it were your own, yet without your own uncertainty or fear or anger or suspicion getting bound up in it, this is the condition I am endeavoring to describe. When the client's world is clear to the counselor and he can move about in it freely, then he can both communicate his understanding of what is vaguely known to the client, and he can also voice meanings in the client's experience of which the client is scarcely aware. It is this kind of highly sensitive empathy which seems important in making it possible for a person to get close to himself and to learn, to change and develop.

I suspect that each of us has discovered that this kind of understanding is extremely rare. We neither receive it nor offer it with any great frequency. Instead we offer another type of understanding which is very different, such as "I understand what is wrong with you" or "I understand what makes you act that way." These are the types of understanding which we usually offer and receive—an evaluative understanding from the outside. It is not surprising that we shy away from true understanding. If I am truly open to the way life is experienced by another person—if I can take his world into mine—then I run the risk of seeing life in his way, of being changed myself, and we all resist change. So we tend to view this other person's world only in our terms, not in his. We analyze and evaluate it. We do not understand it. But when someone understands how it feels and seems to be me, without wanting to analyze me or judge me, then I can blossom and grow in that climate. I am sure I am not alone in that feeling. I believe that when the counselor can grasp the moment-to-moment experiencing occurring in the inner world of the client, as the client sees it and feels it, without losing the separateness of his own identity in this empathic process, then change is likely to occur.

Though the accuracy of such understanding is highly important, the communication of intent to understand is also helpful. Even in dealing with the confused or inarticulate or bizarre individual, if he perceives that I am *trying* to understand his meanings, this is helpful. It communicates the value I place on him as an individual. It gets across the fact that I perceive his feelings and meanings as being *worth* understanding.

None of us steadily achieves such a complete empathy as I have been trying to describe, any more than we achieve complete congruence, but there is no doubt that individuals can develop along this line. Suitable training experiences have been utilized in the training of counselors, and also in the "sensitivity training" of industrial management personnel. Such experiences enable the person to listen more sensitively, to receive more of the subtle meanings the other person is expressing in words, gesture, and posture, to resonate more deeply and freely within himself to the significance of those expressions.[1]

POSITIVE REGARD

Now the third condition. I hypothesize that growth and change are more likely to occur the more that the counselor is experiencing a warm, positive, acceptant attitude toward what *is* in the client. It means that he prizes his client, as a person, with somewhat the same quality of feeling that a parent feels for his child, prizing him as a person regardless of his particular behavior at the moment. It means that he cares for his client in a nonpossessive way, as a person with potentialities. It involves an open willingness for the client to be whatever feelings are real in him at the moment—hostility or tenderness, rebellion or submissiveness, assurance or self-depreciation. It means a kind

[1] I hope the above account of an empathic attitude will make it abundantly clear that I am not advocating a wooden technique of pseudo-understanding in which the counselor "reflects back what the client has just said." I have been more than a little horrified at the interpretation of my approach which has sometimes crept into the teaching and training of counselors.

of love for the client as he is, providing we understand the word love as equivalent to the theologian's term "agape," and not in its usual romantic and possessive meanings. What I am describing is a feeling which is not paternalistic, nor sentimental, nor superficially social and agreeable. It respects the other person as a separate individual, and does not possess him. It is a kind of liking which has strength, and which is not demanding. We have termed it positive regard.

UNCONDITIONALITY OF REGARD

There is one aspect of this attitude of which I am somewhat less sure. I advance tentatively the hypothesis that the relationship will be more effective the more the positive regard is unconditional. By this I mean that the counselor prizes the client in a total, rather than a conditional way. He does not accept certain feelings in the client and disapprove others. He feels an *unconditional* positive regard for this person. This is an outgoing, positive feeling without reservations and without evaluations. It means *not* making judgments. I believe that when this nonevaluative prizing is present in the encounter between the counselor and his client, constructive change and development in the client is more likely to occur.

Certainly one does not need to be a professional to experience this attitude. The best of parents show this in abundance, while others do not. A friend of mine, a therapist in private practice on the east coast, illustrates this very well in a letter in which he tells me what he is learning about parents. He says:

> I am beginning to feel that the key to the human being is the atti-
> tudes with which the parents have regarded him. If the child was
> lucky enough to have parents who have felt proud of him, wanted
> him, wanted him just as he was, exactly as he was, this child grows
> into adulthood with self-confidence, self-esteem; he goes forth in
> life feeling sure of himself, strong, able to lick what confronts him.
> Franklin Delano Roosevelt is an example . . . "my friends. . . ." He
> couldn't imagine anyone thinking otherwise. He had two adoring
> parents. He was like the pampered dog who runs up at you, frisking
> his tail, eager to love you, for this dog has never known rejection or
> harshness. Even if you should kick him, he'll come right back to you,
> his tail friskier than ever, thinking you're playing a game with him
> and wanting more. This animal cannot imagine anyone disapprov-
> ing or disliking him. Just as unconditional regard and love was
> poured into him, he has it now to give out If a child is lucky enough

to grow up in this unconditionally accepting atmosphere, he emerges as strong and sure and he can approach life and its vicissitudes with courage and confidence, with zest and joy of expectation.

But the parents who like their children—if. They would like them if they were changed, altered, different; if they were smarter or if they were better, or if, if, if. The offspring of these parents have trouble because they never had the feeling of acceptance. These parents don't really like these children; they would like them if they were like someone else. When you come down to the basic fundamental, the parent feels: "I don't like *this* child, this child before me." They don't say that. I am beginning to believe that it would be better for all concerned if parents did. It wouldn't leave such horrible ravages on these unaccepted children. It's never done that crudely. "If you were a nice boy and did this, that and the other thing, then we would all love you."

I am coming to believe that children brought up by parents who would like them "if" are never quite right. They grow up assuming that their parents are right and that they are wrong; that somehow or other they are at fault; and even worse, very frequently they feel they are stupid, inadequate, inferior.

This is an excellent contrast between an unconditional positive regard and a conditional regard. I believe it holds as true for counselors as for parents.

THE CLIENT'S PERCEPTION

Thus far all my hypotheses regarding the possibility of constructive growth have rested upon the experiencing of these elements by the counselor. There is, however, one condition which must exist in the client. Unless the attitudes I have been describing have been to some degree communicated to the client, and perceived by him, they do not exist in his perceptual world and thus cannot be effective. Consequently it is necessary to add one more condition to the equation which I have been building up regarding personal growth through counseling. It is that when the client perceives, to a minimal degree, the genuineness of the counselor and the acceptance and empathy which the counselor experiences for him, then development in personality and change in behavior are predicted.

This has implications for me as a counselor. I need to be sensitive not only to what is going on in me, and sensitive to the flow of feelings in my client. I must also be sensitive to the way he is receiving my communications. I have learned, especially in working with more disturbed persons, that empathy can be perceived as lack of involvement; that an unconditional regard on my part can be perceived as indifference; that warmth can be perceived as a threatening closeness, that real feelings of mine can be perceived as false. I would like to behave in ways, and communicate in ways which have clarity for this specific person, so that what I am experiencing in relationship to him would be perceived unambiguously by him. Like the other conditions I have proposed the principle is easy to grasp; the achievement of it is difficult and complex.

THE ESSENTIAL HYPOTHESIS

Let me restate very briefly the essentially simple but somewhat radical hypothesis I have set forth. I have said that constructive personality growth and change comes about only when the client perceives and experiences a certain psychological climate in the relationship. The conditions which constitute this climate do not consist of knowledge, intellectual training, orientation in some school of thought, or techniques. They are feelings or attitudes which must be experienced by the counselor and perceived by the client if they are to be effective. Those I have singled out as being essential are: a realness, genuineness, or congruence in the therapist; a sensitive, empathic understanding of the client's feelings and personal meanings; a warm, acceptant prizing of the client; and an unconditionality in this positive regard.

SOME LIMITATIONS

I would like to stress that these are hypotheses. In a later section I will comment on the way these hypotheses are faring when put to empirical test. But they are beginning hypotheses, not the final word.

I regard it as entirely possible that there are other conditions which I have not described, which are also essential. Recently I had occasion to listen to some recorded interviews by a young counselor of elementary school children. She was very warm and positive in her attitude toward her clients, yet she was definitely ineffective. She seemed to be responding warmly only to the superficial aspects of each child and so the contacts were chatty, social and friendly, but it was clear she was not reaching the real person of the child. Yet in a number of ways she rated reasonably high on each of the conditions I have described. So perhaps there are still elements missing which I have not captured in my formulation.

I am also aware of the possibility that different kinds of helping relationships may be effective with different kinds of people. Some of our therapists working with schizophrenics are effective when they appear to be highly conditional, when they do *not* accept some of the bizarre behavior of the psychotic. This can be interpreted in two ways. Perhaps a conditional set is more helpful with these individuals. Or perhaps—and this seems to me to fit the facts better—these psychotic individuals perceive a conditional attitude as meaning that the therapist *really* cares, where an unconditional attitude may be interpreted as apathetic noncaring. In any event, I do want to make it clear that what I have given are beginning formulations which surely will be modified and corrected from further learnings.

THE PHILOSOPHY WHICH IS IMPLICIT

It is evident that the kind of attitudes I have described are not likely to be experienced by a counselor unless he holds a philosophy regarding people in which such attitudes are congenial. The attitudes pictured make no sense except in a context of great respect for the person and his potentialities. Unless the primary element in the counselor's value system is the worth of the individual, he is not apt to find himself experiencing a real caring, or a desire to understand, and perhaps he will not respect himself enough to be real. Certainly the professional person who holds the view that individuals are essentially objects to be manipulated for the welfare of the state, or the good of the educational institution, or "for their own good," or to satisfy his own need for power and control, would not experience the attitudinal elements I have described as constituting growth-promoting relationships. So these conditions are congenial and natural in certain philosophical contexts but not in others.

EMPIRICAL STUDIES

This raises some questions which I have asked myself, and which you too must be asking. Are these characteristics which I have described as essential to a helping relationship simply my personal opinion, preference, and bias? Or do they represent simply a bias growing out of a generally democratic philosophy? Or do they in *fact* promote constructive change and development?

Five years ago I could not have answered these questions. Now there are at least a dozen well-designed research investigations which, approaching the matter in a variety of ways, throw light on the issues (1, 3, 6a through 6j). To report each of these studies would be confusing rather than helpful. Let me try to describe their methods in general terms and then report on the findings.

The studies deal with two rather different classes of clients: students and community members who voluntarily come to counselors for help; and on the other hand, schizophrenic individuals in a state hospital who have been there for periods ranging from a few months to many years. The first group is above the socio-educational average, the second below. The first group is motivated to gain help, the second is not only unmotivated but resistant. The over-all range in adjustment is from well-functioning individuals through varying degrees of maladjustment and disturbance, to those who are completely unable to cope with life, and who are out of contact with reality.

In the different studies there have been three ways of measuring the attitudinal elements I have described. The first method is based on brief segments, usually four minutes in length, taken in a randomized way from the tape-recorded interviews. Raters, listening to these segments, judge the degree to which the counselor is, for example, being accurately empathic, and make a rating on a carefully defined scale. The raters have no knowledge of whether the segment is from an early or late interview, or whether it is a more or less successful case. In most of the studies several raters have made ratings on each of the qualities involved.

A second method of measurement is through the use of the Relationship Inventory (1), filled out by the client at different points in time. The inventory contains statements regarding the degree to which the counselor is acceptant, empathic, and congruent, and the client responds by evaluating the statement on a six-point scale from "strongly true" to "definitely untrue." Examples concerning empathy are: "He generally senses or realizes how I am feeling"; "He understands my words but does not realize how I feel." In relationship to congruence some items are: "He behaves just the way that he is in our relationship"; "He pretends that he likes me or understands me more than he really does." The Inventory is scored for each of the four attitudinal elements, and there is also a total score.

The third method is also based on the Relationship Inventory, but this time filled out by the therapist or counselor. The items are identical except for a suitable change in pronouns.

In the various studies different criteria are used for assessing the degree of constructive personality change which has taken place over the course of the interviews. In all cases the criteria of change are independent of the measurement of attitudinal conditions in the relationship. Some of the measures of change are: changes in various Minnesota Multiphasic Personality Inventory scales and indices; changes in projective tests as analyzed "blind" by clinicians having no knowledge of the research; changes in Q-sort adjustment score; changes on a measure of anxiety; therapist's ratings of change in personality and in adjustment.

THE FINDINGS

Let me now give some of the general findings from these studies:

The counselor is the most significant factor in setting the level of conditions in the relationship, though the client, too, has some influence on the quality of the relationship.

Clients who will later show more change perceive more of these attitudinal conditions early in the relationship with their counselor or therapist.

The more disturbed the client the less he is likely to (or able to?) perceive these attitudes in the counselor.

Counselors or therapists tend to be quite consistent in the level of the attitudinal conditions which they offer to each client.

The major finding from all of the studies is that those clients in relationships marked by a high level of counselor congruence, empathy and unconditional positive regard, show constructive personality change and development. These high levels of conditions are associated with: positive change on MMPI scales and indices, including ego-strength; positive change from the pre- to post-test battery as rated by clinicians working "blind"; decrease in anxiety scores and in a self-consciousness score; a higher level an Process Scales designed to measure process in therapy; and positive change in counselor's ratings.

Clients in relationships characterized by a low level of these attitudinal conditions show significantly less positive change on these same indices.

In studies of clinic clients the correlation between the client's perception of the conditions offered early in the relationship and the degree of change at the conclusion of the interviews is somewhat higher than that between the counselor's perception of the conditions offered and the degree of change. The client's perception is, in other words, the better predictor of change.

This finding does not hold for the schizophrenic client, whose inner disturbance makes it difficult for him accurately to perceive the conditions offered by the therapist. With our schizophrenics, the rating of the conditions made by unbiassed raters is the best predictor of change.

An unexpected finding with the schizophrenic clients is that low conditions in the relationship are associated with *negative* change in several respects. The clients not only fail to show constructive change but become worse in the judgment of clinicians rating their pre- and post-test batteries; show an increase in anxiety; are worse off than their matched no-therapy controls. Whether this finding holds for clinic clients who come for help has not yet been determined.

A finding which seems to lend validity to the studies is that, as might be expected, more experienced counselors, when compared with inexperienced counselors, offer a higher level of these conditions, and are more successful in communicating these to their clients. Thus they are perceived as offering higher conditions, and their clients show more change over the course of the interviews.

IMPLICATIONS

What are some of the implications of these hypotheses and of these findings for the field of counseling psychology and guidance? I would like to mention four which occur to me.

In the first place, these studies indicate that perhaps it is possible to study cause and effect in counseling and psychotherapy. They are actually, so far as I know, the first studies to endeavor to isolate and measure the primary change-producing influences in counseling. Whether they are still further confirmed by later research, or whether they are contradicted or modified by future studies, they represent pioneering investigations of the question, "What really makes the difference in counseling and psychotherapy?" And the answer they give is that it is the attitudes provided by the counselor, the psychological climate largely created by him, which *really* makes the difference, which really induces change.

There is another highly practical significance to these studies. They indicate quite clearly that, by assessing a relationship early in its existence, we can to some degree predict the probability of its being a relationship which makes for growth. It seems to be quite within the range of possibility that in the not too distant future we will acquire an increasingly accurate knowledge of the elements which make for constructive psychological development, just as we have in the realm of nutrition acquired an increasingly accurate knowledge of the elements which promote physical growth. As this knowledge accumulates, and as our instruments grow sharper, then there is the exciting possibility that we may be able, relatively early in the game, to predict whether a given relationship will actually promote or inhibit individual psychological growth and development, just as we can assess the diet of a child and predict the extent to which this diet will promote or inhibit physical growth.

In this connection the disturbing finding that an inadequate interpersonal relationship can have a negative effect on personal development, at least in the case of highly disturbed individuals, makes such early assessment of a relationship an even more challenging possibility and responsibility.

Another significant meaning for the counseling field is that we now have the beginnings of a theory, and some empirical facts supporting the theory, as to the specific elements in an interpersonal relationship which facilitate positive change. Thus we can now say with some assurance and factual backing that a relationship characterized by a high degree of congruence or genuineness in the counselor, by sensitive and accurate empathy on the part of the counselor, by a high degree of regard, respect and liking for the client by the counselor, and by an absence of conditionality in this regard, will have a high probability of being an effective, growth-promoting relationship. This statement holds, whether we are speaking of maladjusted individuals who come of their own initiative seeking help, or whether we are speaking of chronically schizophrenic persons, with no conscious desire for help. This statement also holds whether these attitudinal elements are rated by impartial observers who listen to samples of the recorded interviews, or whether they are measured in terms of the counselor's perception of the qualities he has offered in the relationship, or whether they are measured by the client's perception of the relationship, at least in the case of the nonhospitalized client. To me it seems to be quite a forward stride to be able to make statements such as these in an area as complex and subtle as the field of helping relationships.

Finally, these studies would, if confirmed by further work, have significant implications for the training of counselors and therapists. To the extent that the counselor is seen as being involved in interpersonal relationships, and to the extent that the goal of those relationships is to promote healthy development, then certain conclusions would seem to follow. It would mean that we would endeavor to select individuals for such training who already possess, in their ordinary relationships with other people, a high degree of the qualities I have described. We would want people who were warm, spontaneous, real, understanding, and nonjudgmental. We would also endeavor so to plan the educational program for these individuals that they would come increasingly to *experience* empathy and liking for others, and that they would find it increasingly easier to be themselves, to be real. By feeling understood and accepted in their training experiences, by being in contact with genuineness and absence of façade in their instructors, they would grow into more and more competent counselors. There would be as much focus in such training on the interpersonal experience as on the intellectual learning. It would be recognized that no amount of knowledge of tests and measures, or of counseling theories, or of diagnostic procedures could make the trainee more effective in his personal encounter with his clients. There would be a heavy stress upon the actual experience of working with clients, and the thoughtful and self-critical assessment of the relationships formed.

When I ask myself whether the training programs I know, in guidance, in clinical psychology, in psychiatry, approach this goal, I come up with a strong negative. It seems to me that most of our professional training programs make it *more* difficult for the individual to be himself, and more likely that he will play a professional role. Often he becomes so burdened with theoretical and diagnostic baggage that he becomes *less* able to understand the inner world of another person as it seems to that person. Also, as his professional training continues, it all too often occurs that his initial warm liking for other persons is submerged in a sea of diagnostic and psychodynamic evaluation.

Thus to take the findings of these studies seriously would mean some sharp changes in the very nature of professional training, as well as in its curriculum.

CONCLUSION

Let me conclude with a series of statements which for me follow logically one upon the other.

The purpose of most of the helping professions, including guidance counseling, is to enhance the personal development, the psychological growth toward a socialized maturity, of its clients.

The effectiveness of any member of the profession is most adequately measured in terms of the degree to which, in his work with his clients, he achieves this goal.

Our knowledge of the elements which bring about constructive change in personal growth is in its infant stages.

Such factual knowledge as we currently possess indicates that a primary change-producing influence is the degree to which the client experiences certain qualities in his relationship with his counselor.

In a variety of clients—normal, maladjusted, and psychotic—with many different counselors and therapists, and studying the relationship from the vantage point of the client, the therapist, or the uninvolved observer, certain qualities in the relationship are quite uniformly found to be associated with personal growth and change.

These elements are not constituted of technical knowledge or ideological sophistication. They are personal human qualities—something the counselor *experiences*, not something he *knows*. Constructive personal growth is associated with the counselor's realness, with his genuine and unconditional liking for his client, with his sensitive understanding of his client's private world, and with his ability to communicate these qualities in himself to his client.

These findings have some far-reaching implications for the theory and practice of guidance counseling and psychotherapy, and for the training of workers in these fields.

REFERENCES

1. Barrett-Lennard, G. T. Dimensions of therapist response as causal factors in therapeutic change. *Psychol. Monogr.* 76, 43, 1962, 1–36.
2. Gendlin, E. T. Experiencing: A variable in the process of therapeutic change. *Am. Jour. Psychother.* 15, 1961, 233–45.

3. Halkides, G. An experimental study of four conditions necessary for therapeutic change. Unpublished doctoral dissertation, University of Chicago, 1958.

4. Rogers, C. R. The necessary and sufficient conditions of therapeutic personality change. *Jour. Cons. Psych., 21,* 1957, 95–103.

5. ————. A theory of therapy, personality, and interpersonal relationships as developed in the client-centered framework. In S. Koch (ed.), *Psychology: A Study of a Science,* Vol. III. New York: McGraw-Hill, 1959, 184–256.

6. Wisconsin Psychiatric Institute: Research Reports (unpublished)

  a. Spotts, J. E. The perception of positive regard by relatively successful and relatively unsuccessful clients.

  b. Truax, C. B. Comparison between high conditions therapy, low conditions therapy, and control conditions in the outcome measure of change in anxiety levels.

  c. ————. Constructive personality change in schizophrenic patients receiving high conditions therapy, low conditions therapy, and no therapy.

  d. ————. Effects of therapists and effects of patients upon the amount of accurate empathy occurring in the psychotherapeutic interaction.

  e. ————. Effects of therapists and effects of patients upon the level of problem expression and experiencing occurring in the therapeutic interaction.

  f. ————. The relationship between the patient's perception of the level of therapeutic conditions offered in psychotherapy and constructive personality change.

  g. ————. Liccione, J., and Rosenberg, M. Psychological test evaluations of personality change in high conditions therapy, low conditions therapy, and control patients.

  h. Van der Veen, F. The effects of the therapist and the patient on each other's therapeutic behavior early in therapy: A study of the beginning interviews of three patients with each of five therapists.

  i. ————. Perceived therapist conditions and degree of disturbance: A comparison of conditions perceived by hospitalized schizophrenic patients and counseling center clients.

  j. Wargo, D. G. The Barron Ego Strength and LH4 Scales as predictors and indicators of change in psychotherapy.

ADRIAN VAN KAAM

Counseling from the Viewpoint
of Existential Psychology

COUNSELING IS ESSENTIALLY a process of making-free, a humanizing of the person who has lost his freedom in sectors of his existence where he can no longer transcend his life situation by freely giving meaning to it. He behaves there more or less as a lower form of being, as a dehumanized, determined existence. It is the aim of counseling to assist the person in regaining his freedom in these areas by creating insight into the meanings he attributes to these situations, by starting the extinction of the responses which the counselee— after gaining insight—no longer likes to retain, and by the conditioning of other responses corresponding to his new free evaluation of reality. In order to make the counselee free we have to make the counseling session an existential situation where he can be present with his whole being spontaneously and prereflexively.

We know the person from his phenomenal universe, not from his isolated and interior world. Therefore from the very beginning the attention of the client is oriented towards himself as moving in a vivid universe of events and encounters. He moves in the present, in the "here and now" of his actual world as a human existence—as "consciousness that is involved." The counselee is not encouraged to escape his present by a flight into a past, where there are no decisions to make and where there is no necessity to shape freely a world of "here and now," where existence seems determined and explained by inescapable needs. Instead of forcing the client to revise the fixed history of his past, the counselor invites him to face his situation today, not to excuse himself but to return to his world in a new mode of being, to accept its challenges.

The aim of existential counseling is to make the client feel at home in his real world by reshaping his phenomenal world, to make his real situation bearable by making it bearable phenomenologically. The counselee reconditions his behavior in his real world by reconditioning his behavior in his phenomenal universe.

The counselee who transcends his barriers and who learns to conquer the regions at the other side will know how to move with a new freedom in his world of everyday reality. Only he can cope with anxiety who calls the real world his dwelling place, the whole world from high to low and from right to left, not only the bright side of the world but its shady side as well; the mature person says yes to the whole universe.

The Embodiment of Objectives in Attitudes and Behavior

The counselor translates these objectives of existential counseling into attitudes which he in turn embodies in word, posture, facial expression and movement.

The attitudes of the counselor are determined not only by his purpose but also by the situation of his client. He must clarify the existence or modes of standing-out of the counselee who exists in a personal world, which has to be explored and expressed by means of the therapeutic relationship. In order thus to understand the attitudes in which we must embody our objectives we should first of all gain an insight into the existential world and into the kind of relationship which can induce the counselee to explore and express the realms of his existence. The insight gained in these considerations will enable us to describe some desirable attitudes which may embody the objectives so that they are communicated to the counselee within this relationship.

The Existential World of the Client

The main characteristic of the human existent is that he exists, literally stands out in a world of meaning. Subject and world, self and world are correlatives. When we know the world in which a person lives we know *him*; the counselee is best understood from his personally lived and experienced universe. His feelings, desires, hopes and ideas are embedded in a world of meaning, and consequently every experience explored by him has somewhere a place in this system of meanings. This structure as a differentiated whole explains partly the meaning of every single experience which belongs to it. Each single experience in turn colors all meanings which make up the world of the counselee as a whole. When he is able gradually to express the main lines of his existential world, the counselee will be able to understand the precise meaning of his problem within this system.

RELATIONSHIP AND EXPRESSION OF EXISTENTIAL WORLD

Relationship is the principal means for bringing to expression the world of meaning in which the client lives. The quality of the relationship determines to what degree the personal existential world will find genuine expression. The first task of the counselor is, therefore, to establish a relationship which leads to optimal communication. People learn to hide the personal world in which they live in order to protect themselves from being misunderstood, humiliated, condemned or abused. To reveal my personal world is in a sense to surrender my very being, to expose my sensitivity, my project of life, and to unveil my vulnerability when certain meanings which I cherish are at odds with the values appreciated by my environment. This fear of disapproval limits the free admission not only of base inclinations but also of sublime aspirations. It is difficult for many to verbalize their finer sentiments. They fear that the communication of refined feeling would sound ridiculous in the world of functional meaning which they share with contemporary man. This repression of the personal world under the pressure of the shared social world may be so effective that the client himself is not aware of the deepest meanings which constitute his personal existence. The counselor may make himself mistakenly the ally of this social world by lightly joking about noble sentiments in order to give the client the reassurance that counselors are regular fellows like the rest of the population. If he does so he can be sure that the personal world of experience of the counselee will remain a closed book. Some counselors may cherish the illusion that such "open-mindedness" may break barriers forgetting that an exclusive open-mindedness for the cultural-social scene may mean a closed-mindedness for the personal world of the individual in its unique, most revealing features.

THE IMPOSITION OF ONE'S OWN EXISTENCE

Every one of us has his own project of existence which implies among other things the style in which we embody our strivings in daily behavior. Such a style of existence has been formed in the light of individual experiences of the attitudes of the surrounding culture in which we are inserted by birth and education. This cultural component of our style of behavior and perception is mediated by the image of "ideal" behavior as held by the people of our home, neighborhood and society. This ideal style of life permeates our human relationships, being particularly pervasive in the meetings between us as counselors and the counselee who presents himself to us with his problems. The secret influence of this personal and cultural norm may be harmful. Existence as embodiment in space and time necessitates that we be present to others in some style of life. However, our personal embodiment of existence is not the only possible or desirable one for everybody else. The unconscious identification of our personal way of life with "the" way may limit our therapeutic relevance to that part of the population which is spontaneously in touch with our style of being while it averts others.

Therefore, the counselor should grow daily in the awareness of his prereflexive attitudes. Of course he cannot do away with a personal style of existence; as a human being he must embody his mode of being in concrete behavior, which is always limited in space and time and therefore necessarily one-sided. But he can increasingly free himself from the identification of existence as such with his personal-cultural style of being. This inner freedom will enable him to sense the unique potentialities in those counselees who differ from him in expression and perception. When the counselor is deeply aware that his own modes are incidental and transient, he will distinguish what is essential from that which is accidental. This self-awareness will enable him to transcend the temporal to become aware of his cultural and subcultural stereotypes, of his antipathies and sympathies; his emotional blocks will become manifest to him in this maturity. He may discover, for instance, that he *a priori* does not like people with esthetic inclinations because the good farmers at home confused artistry with frivolity. Or he may realize that he one-sidedly prefers "regular guys" because as a high school or college student he disliked some pale companions who were delighted more by books than by baseball. Another may find that he is unconsciously enamored with scholarly types because he is fed up with his more pragmatic colleagues who make great fun of him. Or a counselor may discover during this process of growing up that he unconsciously favors a certain compulsiveness because he has identified the compulsive mode of being with sound strictness and consequently distrusts spontaneity in himself and others.

The counselee in turn may be tempted to identify the counselor with his parents, teachers, administrators, supervisors or school friends. These identifications may harm the effectiveness of counseling, for such daily relationships usually imply some withholding of one's personal world in order to function smoothly within the frame of daily life. The counselor is usually an unknown alien for the candidate. He seems different from the people in authority whom he meets in school, family and society. His function is vague and unusual; he comes from a strange, faraway world. This relative strangeness can be an advantage. If the counselor were identified with the authorities in the environment of the candidate, the client's daily mode of existence towards those people would be immediately adopted towards him. The interview would then structure itself in terms of this mode of existence; the formal, casual, dependent or superficially friendly features which characterize daily interactions would determine this new relationship and keep it on a level which may generate pleasantries, polite caution or formal respect but no experience in depth.

When the client, however, cannot experience the counselor as he does his daily associates, then no stereotyped mode of existence towards him is available. Moreover, the candidate faces this ambiguous situation alone and not in the company of his friends or classmates. Therefore he cannot fall back on a mode of existence which he could share with others towards this new person; he has to handle this interaction all by himself. Such a situation is conducive to responses which will reveal his unique way of being in the world and which are less contaminated by socially shared modes of existence.

On the other hand, if the ambiguity is too much to bear it will evoke too much anxiety in the client and paralyze communication. The effective counselor, therefore, should not make himself known too much by being too friendly and jovial and by removing all social distance. For in that case he and the client will act out superficial social roles which usually prevent communication on a deeper and more personal level. Neither should he be so distant, alien and withdrawn that his counselee freezes in anxiety. The counselor should not maneuver himself into a situation in which he will be forced to do most of the talking; yet he must avoid sitting there like a sphinx which would prevent the possibility of spontaneous communication. This attitude of professional composure and serenity may be inspired by an unauthentic, false image of the "wise," "mature" man without emotion, which is a neurotic imitation of real wisdom and maturity.

Ideally the counselor should be experienced by the counselee as a deeply interested, wise friend whose only interest is to help me in finding myself in relation to my possible project of existence. However, the counselor may have his own unconscious needs which may make it difficult for him to establish such an interested and at the same time detached relationship. Therefore he should explore his motivations after every session. Does he need to sound like an oracle, is he in love with his sonorous voice or clever verbalizations, does he feel that he "knows" people already through and through, is he authoritarian, domineering, does he need to be popular, to be liked or exalted as a "nice chap" by his counselee, is he afraid of depth in himself and others, does he repress his own feelings and paralyze his spontaneity, is he afraid to verbalize or to hear the verbalization of certain experiences? This list could be expanded indefinitely. It is only after a period of growth and experience that a counselor is able to approximate the ideal attitude which makes the relationship itself his most efficient instrument. A mature and experienced counselor is indeed a precious gift for a community.

THE STRUCTURE OF THE RELATIONSHIP

The relationship itself which should be established by the counselor —from the first moment of the initial meeting—differs from the structure of other relationships. First it is different because of its objectives, which we have discussed earlier, and second, it is different from other relationships because of the specific attitudes of the counselor.

The attitudes of the counselor aim at the expression of the personal existential world of the counselee. At the base of these attitudes is a genuine unconditional acceptance of the client regardless of what world of meaning he will reveal. Any trace of explicit or implicit disapproval diminishes the ability of the counselee to unveil his personal existence. On the other hand, the expression of this personal world can also be arrested by too great a personal involvement of the counselor in one or another aspect mentioned by the client. Such emotional concentration on one aspect prevents the narration of other dimensions of the world of meaning which may be just as important for full understanding. The counselor must encourage the client by his patient and accepting attitude to express spontaneously all vague and confused feelings, attitudes and motives which he may have in regard to this project of existence.

The counselor should be emotionally involved to the extent necessary to keep the client interested and alive in the exploration of his world. But this interest should be tempered with a distance which enables him to accept all aspects of existence expressed by the counselee without reacting to them favorably or unfavorably. Either reaction may encourage a positive or negative concentration on some particular aspect of the counselee's world at the expense of the revelation of other ones. The counselor must be a participant in the existential world of the client while being at the same time its respectful observer.

ATTITUDES OF THE COUNSELOR IN THIS EXISTENTIAL RELATIONSHIP

The description of the counseling relationship implies the desirability of certain attitudes.

Creativity

The counselor should be creative. His counseling should not be a rigid application of rules which he has learned from books or formed for himself on the basis of experience with former clients. On the contrary, he should be convinced that every world of meaning is unique. Everything that the counselor says and does should be the creative outgrowth of his participation in this individual existence. This presupposes that the counselor is a mature person free from threat and therefore free from rigidity. Rigid behavior is a defense against the possible challenge of an unexpected world, a world which is communicated to us and which may expose us to our own repressed regions of being. The counselor who is not at home in his own existential world is unable to risk the full revelation of another world of meaning. There are two main forms of rigidity; one leading to a stiff formal attitude in order to escape communication in depth, the other leading to a compulsively "jolly good fellow" attitude which may be an even more effective defense against a truly existential encounter. Both defenses may be based on some neurotic insecurity in the counselor. Sometimes we find a curious combination of both defenses in the same insecure, anxious person; in the fulfillment of functional and administrative obligations he may be formal and rigid, while in his personal relations compulsively joking, gay, and funny. The mature person can be serious, gay, or detached according to the challenge of the situation. He adopts none of these attitudes compulsively; his behavior is not identical in different situations. Existential creativity implies flexibility of attitude, feeling, and behavior in authentic response to the real situation.

Acceptance

Another fundamental attitude in this relationship is acceptance, an attitude which generates in the counselee an experience of really feeling understood in his own existential world. The counselee feels that he really shares this personal world with the counselor, and this feeling enables him to explore this world further and to communicate the outcome of this exploration with less embarrassment. When the candidate perceives that the counselor co-experiences what things mean to him and still accepts him, he gradually feels a safe experiential communion with the counselor and with the world which the counselor represents.

That the counselor co-experiences what people and things mean to the client does not imply that he agrees with this meaning or that he approves of it. Acceptance of a person does not imply personal agreement with his thought or feeling as such. The co-experience and acceptance of the counselor implies only a non-judgmental attitude. His whole attitude communicates to the person: I do not judge at this moment whether or not your feelings and attitudes prove that you are personally guilty for maintaining them; I leave that to your own conscience for this moment. My special function here is not to judge how far you personally are responsible for those attitudes and feelings but to understand what region of your existence they reveal. Basically I respect and like you because deep down your nature is a gift of being; this gift is fundamentally good and, therefore, lovable no matter how it may be overgrown and veiled by attitudes, feelings, and opinions with which I could not agree personally.

The attitude of acceptance is so fundamental for effective counseling and at the same time so different from our usual mode of encounter that it may be fruitful to go somewhat deeper into this matter. The views, feelings, and behavior of the counselee can be accepted under various aspects. For example, the counselor might consider expressed views, feelings, and behavior as isolated abstract norms of human conduct, in which case he can accept or reject them as such. When a client mentions, for instance, that he thinks that certain races should be exterminated, the counselor cannot accept this personally as a highly commendable norm for human existence. Or, he might consider those views, feelings, and behavior under the aspect of their usefulness for the counselee himself. For instance, the counselor may personally dislike poetry and would not accept and cultivate this interest in his own life; he may sense, however, that the poetical mode of existence may be very important for this specific person and he may accept it under this aspect. At the same time, he would reject under this aspect a suicidal interest of the counselee. However, he does not openly express the acceptance or rejection of those judgments as isolated judgments. For, regardless of his acceptance or rejection of those particular views, feelings, or behavior as isolated absolute expressions, the counselor always accepts and respects the client himself as a worthwhile human person dynamically present in those communications. For the same attitudes are not only categories of socially or personally acceptable or rejectable behavior but are also manifestations of a fellow human being. They manifest that the client is not an animal or an inanimate being; their specific content reveals that this human being has adopted certain modes of existence in the world.

The counselor *as counselor* experiences primarily in all these views, feelings, and behavior a wrestling, suffering, sometimes victorious, sometimes defeated human being who tries desperately to find his existential position within this world. It is in this last way that the understanding counselor experiences and accepts the views, feelings, and behavior of the client, namely, under the aspect of their being manifestations of the coping human person, desperately looking for a meaningful project of existence. He shows, therefore, deep genuine interest in those communications. It is this acceptance which opens up the client who becomes actively involved in the process of self-discovery and its expression when he senses that the counselor really cares about what he thinks and feels; a climate is created in which the flow of communication is not halted by the anxious expectation of disapproval, rejection, criticism or other negative responses which the counselee expects on the basis of his past experience in family, school or society. Acceptance lessens considerably defensiveness and therewith the compulsion to rationalize, deny, or distort existential attitudes and inclinations in order to prevent disapproval.

If the counselor himself has deeply buried in himself some aspects of his personal existence he should become aware of it. The same anxiety which made him bury the awareness of regions of his own existence may close him when he senses the slightest indication of the same threatening reality in another. The implicit communication of this anxiety will prevent the free exploration of this specific area of existence. This danger points to the necessity for the counselor to evaluate himself continuously and thoroughly. Every session with a candidate should be a source of self-reflection. What did I say? How did I respond? What did I feel? How did this communication affect me? Was I uneasy, excited, threatened, at ease, uncomfortable? Why was I so? The personal existence of the counselor is his main tool. In order to keep it refined and sensitive he should work through his inhibitions, anxieties, and insecurities with a therapist whom he trusts. He should keep refining this instrument that he himself is. For, no amount of literature, study, or oratory can replace the crucial impact of his very being upon the relationship with the counselee.

Gentleness

The counselor should maintain mildness in his approach. We do not mean anything sentimental, effeminate, or soft. Gentleness reveals itself in sensitive, considerate, and tolerant modes of existence. The counselor should be able to manifest this amenity spontaneously; it will be difficult for the counselee to express himself fully if this atmosphere of gentle consideration is absent. For some counselors it may seem nearly repulsive to be gentle. Sometimes a male counselor in a high school may believe that he should ideally give the boy he is counseling the impression that he himself is just another boy, one who is bigger, taller, heavier, and more muscular, yet a boy, an enlarged version of an adolescent who speaks and acts big, very big. This attitude was perhaps deeply rewarded by his friends in college or high school who looked up towards him as the real tough guy. For some it may take time to realize that the same behavior will be ineffective in their new adult role when they like to go beyond the peripheral and reach the core of human existence. Others may not have worked through their anxious concern about being a real man and the unconscious occupation with their manliness may paralyze their gentility. Others again have not worked through the loneliness of existence and

remain unconsciously in search of a tenderness which fulfills sentimental needs. Their gentility lacks spine and strength; it has a sticky,
slimy quality which repels certain people. Some counselors may develop unauthentic friendliness which does not originate in the depth
of existence but is calculated and carefully added to behavior in those
situations in which the good counselor should be pleasant. It is practiced as a tour de force, a feat of strength, a stunt of psychology.
Such a forced gentility remains superficial and will not open up the
deeper layers of existence.

Sincerity

Finally the attitude of the counselor should be straightforward,
honest, and sincere. The counselor should be aware that he has been
compelled in daily life to develop a social façade in order to protect
himself against obliteration by the demands of the crowd. He cannot
get involved in everyone's problems. He has had to develop a smooth,
easy way of dealing with large numbers of people who accost the counselor with their questions, neuroses and venerations. Moreover, the
population at large demands from him that he be "nice" regardless
of his mood, his toothache or the troubles with his principal. The
effective functioning and the serenity of the school community to
which he belongs requires a smooth interaction between faculty and
counselor which implies certain social niceties. How tempting it is to
fall back on these habits when meeting the counselee. However, such
habits, no matter how useful in the community at large, if introduced
into the counseling session will prevent effectively that deeper communication which is the aim of this encounter.

Existential Counseling and Theories of Psychology

We described the openness of the existential counselor, and considered attitudes of his that foster optimal communication with the
counselee. The final question to be dealt with is that of the relationship between existential counseling and theories of psychology. Does
the openness of the existential counselor imply that psychological
theory is superfluous; if not, what is its role?

The Avoidance of a Premature Use of Theoretical Concepts

Existential counseling fosters a self-understanding in the counselee,
which is free from subjectivistic influences; it attempts to uncover the

real structures and meanings of experience; it means a purification of the naïve knowledge of self by a search for real self-experience beyond the subjectivistic explanations of everyday life. If the counselor, however, brings uncritically theoretical categories to naïvely experienced behavior he may be caught in another sophisticated form of subjectivism, which might distort the given phenomena. He may unwittingly substitute for the experience of daily life an artificially made up "scientific experience." He immediately "perceives," for example, in the counselee inferiority feelings, projections, archetypes, repressions, reinforcements, resistances, Oedipus-complexes, transferences, sublimations and the like. This artificial scientific *experience* is the abortive result of two sources: one is the naïve experience of everyday life, the other the immediate interpretation of this naïve natural experience by established scientific theories. Such an interpretation—when prematurely indulged in—prevents a respectful attention for the inner structure and meaning of experience itself in this unique situation. Consequently, established intersubjectivistic theoretical influences are substituted for or added to the subjectivistic distortions which are already present in the naïve experience itself. This impoverished, made-over experience is then considered as *the* full real experience, substituting for the experience in everyday life. This scientific experience is called fact and this fact is then hailed as the first primary original experience of the counselee. Out of the collection of enumeration of these facts one should come by induction to the establishment of laws which should govern the activities of counselors and clients alike. This process leads to a system of counseling autonomous and closed in itself, an empty game with splendid ideas irrelevant to real experience of people in vital situations, a mythology of behavior which claims to explain everything while it explains nothing.

Obviously much harm can be done by a counselor when his perception is distorted by the premature introduction of theoretical explanations. The existential counselor will penetrate first into behavior as it manifests itself and only then ponder how existing scientific theories may illuminate this behavior without distortion, or how scientific theories should be corrected, expanded, or renewed in order to keep in touch with behavior as given in reality today. Theories of personality and psychotherapy should supplement rather than supplant existential understanding. The existential counselor should draw on the rich fund of insight called science of psychology which is a collection of intellectual contributions by numerous enlightened theorists of behavior. But, his prudent selection from this treasure-trove of theoretical explanations should be illumined by real behavior as it manifests itself in his clients. His primary commitment is to existence, not to a theory about existence, even an existential theory. His existential openness for the communications of his counselee will enable him not only to spot the relevant theoretical explanation but also to adapt it to the concrete situation or even to improve it on the basis of his observation. In the last case he may possibly enrich the treasury of psychology so that others after him may have more knowledge available. It should be his wish, however, that his successors will neither abuse his ideas for the distortion of data nor substitute his observation for their own existential perception. It should be his hope that they may be more sensitive to behavior than to his explanations about behavior, that their ears may not be deafened by the noise of theories, and that their eyes may not be blinded by expositions in journals, books, and papers, even if they happen to be his own.

Language Habit

Language habit in this context refers to the embodiment in our language of psychological theories. The language may be scientific or pre-scientific; likewise psychological theories embedded in the language may be scientific and pre-scientific. English, for instance, is a pre-scientific language; the psychoanalytic idiom is a scientific language. Language is not the experience itself of the counselee but an expression of this experience. Many words may communicate more than the pure experience of the client. They express, for example, also the pre-scientific view of his experience, which he has received from his culture in the package of his language. In that case the language habit implies not only the expression of experience but also the pre-scientific view which created this biased and selective expression. By the same token it conceals other real aspects of experience which fall outside the scope of the pre-scientific theory, which dominates the mood of his civilization, and therewith the cast of its language.

An example of the influence of theory on language is the term "experience." The German word for experience is "Erlebnis"; the Dutch word is "beleving." The German "Erlebnis" is derived from "erleben" which literally means "to live an event," for, "erleben" connotes "leben" which means "to live." "Experience" denotes thus in both languages the actuality of a lively presence of the subject to a reality here and now. The term "experience" in the English language, however, has lost this meaning under the impact of empiricism. "Experience" instead of indicating an awareness in the present points to an awareness in the past. Consequently, this language habit may obscure or falsify the perception of the counselor and of the client. They may—misled by the language—overlook or misinterpret behavior which embodies an actual "lived" presence of the subject to reality without reflection. An open perception, however, that momentarily suspends the language habit may rediscover this reality of behavior which was lost in the language. The rediscovery of such a reality may force the counselor or counselee to enrich the language with a new expression which covers the forgotten phenomenon. They may speak, for instance, of "lived" experience, or "lived" awareness. Language is thus the treasure-trove of accumulated theories, insights and observations uncovered by a people in the current of its history; the fascinating history of a-standing-out-together in certain ways towards reality. This shared ex-sistence towards reality reveals itself in peculiar ways to the cultural co-existents. The resulting insights are conserved in the constituted language of a people. This constituted language should be a help, not a hindrance, towards further discovery of reality; it should not suppress but support living language, not fossilize but foster vision, not limit but expand perception.

Constituted *scientific* language presents a similar problem. Psychoanalytic, behavioristic, or organismic terminology should not paralyze but nurture the openness of observation, should not limit but expand perception and vision. The counselor might profit fully from the treasure of scientific language if he frees himself temporarily from its influence on perception. For perception unadulterated by theoretical tenets prepares him for a new appreciation of what other theorists have seen before him. Yet, his previous open perception of "behavior-as-it-is" liberates him from the limitations inherent in the position of every theorist.

The existential openness with its attitudes of suspension and vigilance is fundamental in the counselor who should encounter people beyond theory and classification. Only afterwards may he see in what sense and to what degree he may characterize their behavior by constructs *about* behavior. Theoretical psychology becomes then a light that enlightens, not a veil that dims, the perception of the counselor.

SELECTED REFERENCES

1. Buytendijk, F. J. J. "The Phenomenological Approach to the Problem of Feelings and Emotions." In M. L. Reymert (ed.), *Feelings and*

Emotions, Mooseheart Symposium. New York: McGraw-Hill, 1950, pp. 127–41.

2. Dondeyne, A. *Contemporary European Thought and Christian Faith.* Pittsburgh: Duquesne University Press, 1958.

3. ———. *Geloof en Wereld.* Antwerpen: Patmos, 1961.

4. Frankl, V. E. *From Death-Camp to Existentialism: A Psychiatrist's Path to a New Therapy.* Boston: Beacon Press, 1959.

5. Kwant, R. C. *Encounter.* Pittsburgh: Duquesne University Press, 1960.

6. Lopez, Ibor, Juan. "The Existential Crisis." In J. Braceland (ed.), *Faith, Reason and Modern Psychiatry.* New York: P. J. Kennedy and Sons, 1955.

7. Luijpen, W. *Existential Phenomenology.* Pittsburgh: Duquesne University Press, 1960.

8. May, R. "Freedom and Responsibility Re-examined." Unpublished paper read at the 1962 meeting of the American College Personnel Association, Chicago, April 18, 1962.

9. ———. "The Meaning of the Oedipus Myth," *Review of Existential Psychology and Psychiatry,* I, 1 (1961), pp. 44–52.

10. Perquin, N. *Paedagogiek.* Roermond-Maaseik: J. J. Romen & Zonen, 1952.

11. Rogers, Carl R. "The Loneliness of Contemporary Man," *Review of Existential Psychology and Psychiatry,* I, 1 (1961), pp. 94–101.

12. ———. *On Becoming a Person.* Boston: Houghton Mifflin Company, 1961.

13. Van Kaam, A. "The Nurse in the Patient's World," *The American Journal of Nursing,* LIX (1959), pp. 1708–10.

14. ———. "Freud and Anthropological Psychology," *The Justice* (Brandeis University), May 1959.

15. ———. *The Third Force in European Psychology.* Greenville, Delaware: Psychosynthesis Research Foundation, 1960.

16. ———. "Assumptions in Psychology," *Journal of Individual Psychology,* XIV, 1 (1958), pp. 22–28.

17. ———. "Phenomenal Analysis: Exemplified by a Study of the Experience of 'Really Feeling Understood,'" *Journal of Individual Psychology,* XV, 1 (1959), pp. 66–72.

18. ———. "The Impact of Existential Phenomenology on the Psychological Literature of Western Europe," *Review of Existential Psychology and Psychiatry,* I, 1 (1961), pp. 63–92.

19. ———. "Clinical Implications of Heidegger's Concepts of Will, Decision and Responsibility," *Review of Existential Psychology and Psychiatry,* I, 2 (1961), pp. 205–16.

20. ———. *Religion and Personality.* Englewood Cliffs, N. J.: Prentice-Hall, Inc., 1964.

21. ———. "Humanistic Psychology and Culture," *Journal of Humanistic Psychology*, I, 1 (1961), pp. 94–110.
22. ———. "The Fantasy of Romantic Love." In *Modern Myths and Popular Fancies*. A series of lectures given at the community college, sponsored by the Duquesne University Alumni Association, Oct. 6 to Oct. 27, 1960. Pittsburgh: Duquesne University Press, 1961.
23. ———. "Will and Religion," *Academy Newsletter of Religion and Mental Health* (Summer, 1962).

Ego-Counseling in Guidance

EGO-COUNSELING is uncomfortably elusive to define, i.e., to distinguish from generic concepts of counseling and psychotherapy. Then why the distinctive label? And the hyphenated term? May not any counselor who accepts psychoanalytic conventions claim a primary attention to ego process? We note but defer answer to such questions, hoping to deal with them, at least implicitly, in the ensuing presentation.

This article is directed mainly to counseling as *method*, to the general principles and strategies with which a counselor might guide his conduct. It is lacking on two counts: first, because many of its intricacies still remain to be worked out, the theory of ego development which underlies the counseling method is treated only sketchily; second, space requirements restrict illustrative case materials. It is hoped, nevertheless, that ego-counseling will be recognized as a distillation of psychological theory and counseling method with a distinctive character and with a special promise for the work of guidance.

THE EGO

The progress of a human life normally is accomplished by slow, uncertain but vitally significant increases in *control* over inner impulse and over the conditions of external reality. Such control is conceived to be exercised by a (hypothesized) structure within the personality of dynamically interrelated capacities and dispositions. This structure is called the *ego*. The structure of the ego changes continually as an individual matures and learns from experience. Over any given segment of time, however, the ego is the principal and most stable agency through which a human being adapts to his life circumstances.

During its history as a psychological concept, the term "ego" has been given varying and somewhat contradictory meanings. Before attempting to establish the place of ego in ego-counseling, it may be useful briefly to review both its traditional meaning and the peculiar perspective in which it is viewed by certain modern critics of ego psychology. In traditional psychoanalytic thought, the ego was construed mainly as a passive, uncertain agency of defense against the memory of early painful experiences and against the imperious demands of the id, a term which Freud used to denote the individual's biologically rooted instinct life. To attain stability for the individual, the ego was seen both to repress disordering memories and fantasies and to delay or divert irrational impulses to act in the external environment. The ego was also a mediator of the conflicting demands from the id and from external reality. Any stability attained by the ego, however, would always be temporary, uncertain, never complete; repression and mediation would be ever imperfect; conditions arise in every human life which, at varying times and to varying degrees, will weaken or overwhelm the ego defenses, leaving the individual vulnerable to painful affect and predisposing him to act tragically in a world which requires certain kinds of human order and control.

The traditional psychoanalytic view of the ego has been extended dramatically by certain modern critics of ego psychology. Brown (5) revisits the "dark underworld" which Freud discovered in each of us, where cosmic possibilities for living and for dying hang on the interplay and resolution of unconscious drives. Brown finds the source of a universal neurosis in the ego's efforts to repress natural libidinal aims and energies in order to meet the requirements of organized society. To achieve a civilized ego, says Brown, one must become unconscious of his real desires; spawned in each of us by repression of fundamental psychic needs is an elaborate complex of disguised hostile urges which, because we are unconscious of them, dispose us to destroy ourselves and the lives of those around us. Since repression (by the ego) is universal in modern civilization, so, according to Brown, is neurotic stupidity. Watts (21), examining psychotherapy from the perspective of Oriental philosophy, objects to the dualism which assumes a fictitious ego to be a controlling agent behind our acts, thoughts and feelings; to conceive of, to value and to attempt to strengthen the ego, Watts believes, is to nourish within each of us the dangerous illusion that we are autonomous in the world, and to blind ourselves to the continuous, inseparable relation between man and all of nature.

Marcuse (14) shares Brown's antagonism toward the role of repression in human development and toward modern ego psychology in general. His more technical analysis of the problem, however, distinguishes the necessary guidance and restriction of the instinctual drives from what he calls "surplus-repression." Some degree of repression is required to advance the welfare of the individual and to preserve his society. But the modern human condition is characterized more by *surplus-repression,* a process in which, from infancy onward, each individual is made unconscious of his own instinctual tendencies. The essential aim of surplus-repression is not the happiness of the individual, nor the welfare of society, but the domination of individuals to preserve a *particular* social system. The person whose ego is civilized by surplus-repression is more likely to be faithful to a *particular* organization of family living, of government, of work or of religion. In Freudian terms, repression supposedly enables an individual, in guiding his conduct, to replace the pleasure principle with the reality principle. Surplus-repression, however, according to Marcuse, enforces not a reality principle but a *performance* principle. As a function of repression, an individual will be coerced to experience reality only in ways which a particular social system will tolerate, and to conduct himself accordingly. A relevant instance here is the intolerance which educators and parents may feel toward an "incorrigible" academic underachiever. In the conventional view, he is refusing to "face reality." Or might he merely be unable to affirm by academic *performance* a view of reality which (consciously and/or unconsciously) is alien to his own?

The writers cited above offer no program with practical alternatives to repression; it is likely to continue to be a key mechanism for civilizing our young. Marcuse's interests are in the "philosophy" of psychoanalysis; Brown is a self-described utopian; and Watts would contradict a key lesson in Eastern thought were he to advocate a program for social action. Yet these writers merit a respectful hearing. In their pungent commentary on the human situation, they reveal the unintended misery which parents and educators would inflict on the young by efforts, too simply conceived, to foster their ego development. Self-control and responsibility may be hallmarks of an integral ego; but controlled and responsible behavior may also characterize, depending upon the conditions under which such qualities are acquired, a life vulnerable to guilt and anxiety, and compelled by obscure urges to destroy itself, or at least to defeat its possibilities for happiness.

THE EGO IN COUNSELING AND TEACHING

All formal education inevitably influences ego development. Thus follows an essential dilemma: to teach each individual what is known and valued in his culture while enabling him to remain maximally aware of his inner nature, and while guiding and strengthening him to act ultimately in terms of his own purposes and on his own responsibility. The dilemma may be approached, at least in concept, by defining teaching and counseling as distinct but complementary processes. The teacher represents the main values and achievements of the culture; teaching pivots around problems which the culture already has defined and around solutions already reached. The teacher promotes standards; he criticizes and evaluates a learner's performance against norms established in advance. The learner may be encouraged to criticize and to reject certain viewpoints; but ultimately, however liberal and benign his relationship with his teacher, he must submit to the latter's authority.

In the counseling relationship, at least in its ideal conception, authority is uniquely absent. Counseling is a specially conceived way for one human being to help another. The help is psychological; it derives predominantly from the quality of the relationship and of the communication between counselor and counselee. The counselor is permissive, unconditionally accepting of the counselee, however unlovely may be some of the latter's personal qualities; the counselor strives to understand how the world may be experienced and consciously perceived from the counselee's "internal frame of reference" (18); he strives to avoid prejudice—he refrains from imposing judgments—out of respect for the counselee's freedom and (postulated) inherent capacity to work out himself the most appropriate solutions (for him) to the problems which are identified in their discussions. Out of his experience in such a relationship, the counselee derives a heightened understanding of his own human nature. More concretely, the counselor helps him to appraise certain observations and information about himself and about his surrounding circumstances;

he is helped through such appraisal to make decisions and to plan how he might act on his own responsibility to implement his decisions. The observations made in discussion between counselor and counselee are directed typically to the latter's abilities, interests and values in relation to the requirements for action which confront him in his immediate or predictable future environment. The outcomes of counseling may be said to have been helpful if the counselee has achieved a fuller awareness of his "real" feelings and abilities and has increased his power to choose and to act adaptively in his environment.

Teaching and counseling influence ego development in complementary ways. The teaching process begins typically by communicating to the learner what a society determines its members at various ages ought to know. Teaching strengthens the ego, among other ways, by informing the individual about "reality"—about ideas, objects and people (mainly *other* people) as the culture comprehends them. Counseling, however, begins with questions the individual construes to be relevant to his own space and time; and moves, mostly spontaneously—the counselor does not plan a curriculum—toward solutions which satisfy the counselee's own values. Given a confluence of favorable societal conditions with fortunate individual circumstances, teaching, complemented by other socializing influences may be sufficient to foster "optimal" ego development. But the vast, accelerating social change which each of the past several generations has experienced makes pure teaching and socializing strategies increasingly inadequate.

One social trend with critical implications for ego development has been characterized by Peters (16) as ". . . the rise of the fatherless society." In the emerging "brotherly" sort of society, each of us has gained remarkably in the freedom and opportunity to control our own development and destinies. But this freedom is accompanied by a great intensifying of personal responsibility and a loss of the old certainties. For the population as a whole, repression has become a less formidable developmental mechanism; but repression is still experienced by each individual, at various stages of his life, in haphazard combination with extremes of free choice. The monistic authority of the father and his surrogates is replaced by a plurality of uncertain and ambiguous authorities. The individual increasingly needs guidance to clarify for himself what is opportunity and what is restriction; what is option and what is necessity. It is in this context that counseling, ego-counseling in particular, is seen to strengthen the individual ego and to advance the individual human career.

The Ego in Ego-Counseling

Despite his startling wisdom and his personal courage, or perhaps because of these qualities, there is throughout Freud's work (11) a disturbing theme of futility concerning the human condition. This theme is echoed in the writers cited earlier, especially by Brown. Freud could not envision a civilized society which did not perpetuate itself by repressing libidinal drives and, thus, suffer its consequences. Marcuse's distinction between necessary and surplus-repression, however, provides a way to incorporate (selectively) the wisdom of psychoanalytic thought in our theories and methods for counseling and guidance, and for educational practice in general. Marcuse does not sink to a simple-minded distinction between good and bad repression; he criticizes such neo-Freudians as Karen Horney and Erich Fromm severely, in fact, for what he perceives to be their naïve tendency to seek an optimistic balance between good and bad in life. But Marcuse's concept is reconcilable with recent contributions to ego theory, especially those of White (23) and of Erikson (8), which acknowledge the tribulations of an ego created through repression, but emphasize as well the active, exploratory character of ego processes.

In White's view, at least, the ego is not merely a passive uncertain monitor of a chaotic impulse life, but actively engages objects in reality, seeking through such engagements to expand for the individual his "competence" (White's term) to guide and to govern his actions in accord with what is real. White adduces evidence for the existence of basic ego energies and satisfactions which are independent of and just as fundamental to human life as the libidinal energies. The ego develops not merely as the individual responds defensively to instinctual drives but as he curiously explores his environment, attempts novel actions and assesses their consequences. The ego does not merely, through repression, learn to adopt the reality principle; more precisely, as the human organism's capacities to exercise perception, thinking and motor control mature, his ego gradually formulates and organizes *his* meanings for what is *real*.

A view which features each of us as an active explorer and organizer of our own reality is likely to be more congenial with current concepts of counseling and guidance than is the image of a repressed, uncertain, self-defeating life being lived mainly in our own unconscious underworld. For one thing, the former is optimistic, and optimism, as Adelson (1) observes, has been a salient quality in the American view of the human condition. American optimism has too readily tamed or slighted the "raging, oceanic" power of Freud's instincts. Prevalent theories for counseling and guidance have preferred to envision a human organism with infinite growth potentials engaged in "actualizing" itself. Such theory has attended mainly to conscious, peripheral attitudes toward self and reality. In such a framework, counseling outcomes have frequently been measured by the rules of a superficial matching game between attitudes toward a hypothetical "real" self and an imagined ideal self. Underlying much counseling theory as it has been influenced by the ideas of self-concept and of self-actualization is a near-moral belief that man can make and remake himself as he grows toward perfection (1).

Views such as White's and Erikson's are persuasive not for their optimism but for their greater comprehensiveness. They share Freud's regard for the persistent powerful grasp of instinct and its derivatives, a regard which self-theorists have not joined. And they analyze more systematically than have self-concept theorists, events—both normative and pathological—which occur across the human life span. In self-concept theory most reference is to adults who seem to have emerged full-blown at that stage in life and whose repressed experiences (18) await only the right kind of relationship with another human being to be brought to awareness. The intimate, cumulative, tenacious relationship among all life experiences from conception to death may be assumed within self-concept theory where it describes life to be a "process of experiencing." But in self-concept theory, the personality "structures" through which developmental experiences are related, and the manner in which they might influence human choice and action at any moment in time, have hardly been conceptualized.

The Ego in Guidance

A persuasive rationale for counseling might be deduced from any of the great religious or ethical systems. Such principles of the counseling relationship as "unconditional acceptance," whether or not they can be validated through science, seem inherently appropriate in a helping relationship between one human being and another. It is assumed here, however, that the theory and practice of counseling can be strengthened significantly by relating it *through a theory of guidance* to a science of human development. It is hoped, eventually, to develop a theory of guidance rooted in the psychology of ego development. An ideal theory of this kind might contain propositions to govern the guidance practitioner's efforts to foster in human beings at any developmental stage what Erikson (8) might call a sense of ego-identity. We shall not try to specify here what ego integrity might mean operationally; and for obvious reasons, we shall beg the question of what values, if any, such a guidance process should implement. We personally look to a confluence of ego psychology, existential philosophy and the liberal tradition as a source of wisdom in this regard. But a treatment of philosophical issues at this point would be an intolerable distraction.

The effort to employ ego concepts in counseling is neither novel nor lonely. It has been anticipated in part by Bordin (3), who suggests that the primary aim of the counselor be to foster growth and integration as against his secondary efforts to resolve immediate situations. With Bronfenbrenner (4) and with others who have attempted to formulate an eclectic dynamic theory of personality, a dominant place is given to the concept of ego. An analogy suggests itself between the idea of ego and that of an internal guidance system. Guidance starts not with the counselor, but with the individual's efforts through his ego to guide himself. The ego-counselor joins the individual as his collaborator in these efforts. He is not concerned with the interests, the values and the capacities *per se* of the counselee. It is with the efficacy of the ego as a guidance system—with ego strength—with the maturing capacity of the individual to perceive reality in more accurate terms, to differentiate and impose more complex meanings on reality and on his own fantasy (and to comprehend the difference)— yet to control impulse in the light of anticipated consequences, to mediate conflicting dispositions, to employ rational considerations in solving problems, to pursue more remote goals in a dependable way, to achieve a dynamic balance among psychic dispositions—it is to foster *qualitative* aspects of ego organization such as these that the ego-counselor participates in the life of the counselee.

In its typical aspect, guidance has subsumed a loose set of principles and techniques intended to assist an individual's educational and vocational decision-making. To reconstrue guidance in terms of a guidance psychology may require a radical switch in perspective and a simple-minded faith that ideas really do change educational practices. Such faith stems from a vision of a guidance profession, rooted in education, but with its own career line, whose functions, counseling included, are rationalized by an applied science of guidance psychology. It is from an applied science of guidance (ego) psychology and

from the work of a guidance profession whose attention is directed
to the process of ego development, that counseling, as perhaps the
most important of the guidance functions, would derive its rationale.
Were such a framework to become real, then the process under discussion could be called simply *guidance counseling.*

EGO-COUNSELING AS METHOD

The term "method" is to be construed loosely here. It implies, not a
set of prescriptions and techniques, but a complex of preferred counselor attitudes and strategies to be implemented flexibly and with
utter respect for the counselee's ultimate freedom—and responsibility—to be himself. Where the counselee has reason to perceive a
counselor's approach as coercion, we would attribute this to tactical
error, not to a deliberate denial of the counselee's freedom. The
method has been developed on the basis of tryout with secondary
school students, mainly with "bright but underachieving" high school
boys. Following a series of pilot studies, a formally designed inquiry
(10) was conducted; the research will be reported in a separate monograph. In addition to the use mainly with underachieving high school
boys, two special conditions applied in the conduct of ego-counseling
during this research: First, the counseling was conducted in a short
series of interviews: five were considered modal, staged once weekly,
beginning about the middle of the academic year. The decision to
limit the number of contacts was made as a deliberate condition. It was
felt that if ego-counseling is to be useful in educational institutions,
it ought to be effective within the limits of educational practice. One
can only agree with Bordin (3) that educational institutions are unlikely ever to support even five-interview counseling for more than a
small percent of the case load. Apart from economic grounds, it
seems foreign to the concept of a counseling process intended to
further normal (ego) development to commit this process to extensive
efforts at personality reorganization.

The second condition is concerned with limits in a different way.
Here the limits concern the scope of the topics which are to be considered. In this sense, the notion of *sector* coined by Felix Deutsch (7)
has been applied: Deutsch used the term to refer to a strategy with
patients in brief psychoanalytic psychotherapy; to define a sector
Deutsch would focus on the underlying meaning of a psychosomatic
symptom for a patient and on the particular meaning of words used

by a patient to describe his symptoms. In ego-counseling usage, the term is somewhat modified. It means that the counselor influences the counseling deliberations as early as his assessment of a counselee warrants so that a gradual focus is made on a particular encounter the counselee experiences in relation to some (significant) role or situation in reality. The likely sector is initially determined by the setting (here the secondary school guidance program), by situational problems such as the reason for referral, e.g., vocational concerns (here underachievement), and increasingly as the counseling progresses, by idiosyncratic features of the counselee's life situation. The gradual centering on a sector is fostered by an often implicit transaction in which the counselor reflects, questions, and interprets in such a way that examination by the counselee of the meaning of certain events and the consequences of certain decisions seems to him to be a natural course of action.

Hopefully, the definition of a sector, the examination of alternative modes of thought and action, the making of choices—hopefully, such steps lead to mastery by the counselee of particular roles or situations. The sector may be defined broadly, e.g., the purposes and values of the counselee to be served by attending college; or it may be particular, e.g., his inability to do work for a certain teacher; it may center on a concrete incident, e.g., the commitment by a shy boy to appear in a school play; or it may be relatively abstract, e.g., whether one can trust the future—and adult values—enough to justify hard work on school subjects which seem to have no utility. As isolated instances, these examples may sound pedestrian; yet any one could be of transcendent importance to a single case.

A COUNSELEE'S PERSPECTIVE

Let us examine a description by a counselee of his experience with counseling. His testimony is not intended to prove that the process works; the statements of satisfied clients, however encouraging to their counselors, must always be suspect as evidence. But the counselee's observations may reveal how he experienced both his relationship with the counselor and the process of analyzing and reorganizing his own attitudes. The excerpts below were taken from an assessment interview with S.X.B., a very bright high school senior whose marginal academic performance would have him classified as an underachiever. His counseling had consisted of five interviews with a person other

than the assessment interviewer. In the comments excerpted, the counselee is referring mainly to his heightened motivation to improve his
academic work.

1. Counselee's perception of the counselor's ambiguity:

... I mean, he wouldn't, he never told me to do anything; and I
don't know, he just, he never had, he never said anything. ...

2. Counselee's sense of being challenged (to examine the consequences of his behavior):

... He didn't make it a challenge to me to try and not just get by,
I mean he didn't make the challenge to me, he made me make it a
challenge to myself.

3. Counselee's "ingratitude":

... It did help me a little, I didn't think I would have, it probably
would have been about two weeks ago that I would have decided
that I had to study. ...

Whether in evaluating this case an investigator would agree or not
with the counselee's claim that he would have improved anyway, it
is significant that the counselee can acknowledge being helped, yet
still credit his own capacity to help himself. A counselor might be
well pleased by the counselee's effort here to preserve his sense of
personal responsibility.

4. Counselee's feeling that he was "pushed," but not coerced:

... If he hadn't pushed me on, and actually he wasn't doing any
at all, but he was, I know he was pushing me, he knew he was pushing me, but I, but he wouldn't admit it; he was doing it, I mean,
he was making me do it, but in a way he wasn't even telling me
to do it, he wasn't even asking me to do it and he wasn't even
suggesting that I do it. ...

5. The counselee perceived that he was influenced to consider alter-
nate modes of action:

... He was just saying two things: You do this, or you do this.

6. Note counselee's perception that, as he examined alternatives,
he had been influenced to consider the consequences of his behavior:

... He'd say, where do you go when you do this, where do you go
when you do that. Of course, then I'd tell him and then he'd say
'eh.' ...

7. Counselee perceived that the counselor was fostering something in him:

. . . The seed was planted; he planted the seed, he kept working on it and so—it did help me; I'm sure.

8. Prior to counseling, S.X.B. both disliked and failed to carry out academic tasks:

. . . I was bound to have to wake up, not wake up that I had to study, but wake up that I had to study stuff that I didn't want to study.

. . . Yeah! I haven't actually changed my attitude but I've just changed my—my method.

The counselee has not been influenced to change his opinion about studying: he still dislikes it. He has changed, however, his "method" —his behavior in relation to tasks that he knows must get done if he wants to realize larger aims.

9. S.X.B. has not really liked his part-time jobs, but he has done the work anyway. Since counseling, he has come to see a parallel which had not been apparent to him before.

There were things I did that I didn't want to do, such as work! But I never felt that way about studying. Actually, I still don't feel that way, but . . .

. . . It's really a funny thing; it never occurred to me, but things I didn't like to do at work . . . If you can't beat it, you've got to do it, so I did it. . . .

He implies that the counselor has helped him to generalize his approach toward paid work to his approach toward academic study.

One might consider the counselee's new strategy toward academic study to be a poor payoff. Where is an intrinsic commitment to learning, to self-education? Is he not merely learning a strategy of manipulation to a new situation while missing the essential values of academic study? Such questions, bearing on larger issues in education, must unhappily, in this paper, be slighted. For the present, it will be observed that the counseling interview is a poor medium in which to dramatize a new viewpoint or to persuade someone to revise his basic values. A lifetime of learning will have determined the counselee's awareness and beliefs with relation to the value of academic study. Even if he were inclined, the counselor of S.X.B. is unlikely to have the leverage in a few hours of conversation to win a basic new commitment to academic study. He derives part of his special power, in fact, by dampening his (normal) tendencies to direct or to exhort the counselee. S.X.B. is in counseling partly because efforts to motivate him by other means had failed to win his commitment.

Assuming the validity of S.X.B.'s observations about his experience with counseling, it might be inferred that his attitudes and his actions toward academic study are now less arbitrary and more effectively controlled. He might, in addition, have become more aware of his own responsibility for choice and for the consequences of his actions with reference to school and to other sectors of his life. He will be thus in a better position to cope with the demands of formal education and to capitalize on its opportunities. Perhaps no less a Philistine at this time than before counseling in his attitude toward a liberal education, he seems at least to be in a better position to examine and to revise his attitudes and academic performance, and to *educate himself*, should he eventually make the commitment.

A Paradigm of Ego-Counseling

A paradigm of the ego-counseling process as it is experienced by both counselee and counselor involves: (1) setting; (2) relationship; (3) analysis; (4) synthesis; (5) action.

Setting

The behavior of counselor and counselee is structured to some degree by general precedents about the purpose of their meeting. A counselor is expected to be aware of the opportunities and limits inherent in his function; the counselee clarifies for himself these opportunities and limits as part of the treatment process. In schools where program planning and college application are a major concern of guidance counselors, where guidance services often seem to serve mainly administrative efficiency and parents' anxieties, the student appearing for an interview at the guidance office is not typically prepared to engage in searching examination of his aims and his dilemmas. Although the regular guidance services in the school attended by S.X.B. were reasonably flexible in their organization, his initial conception of counseling was still overly determined by an image of the guidance office as a place where you "find out how you did on the tests" and where you make plans to apply for college.[1] In the case of S.X.B., the counselor was apparently successful in creating a setting, a "climate," in which the counselee found it appropriate to explore the purposes which might underlie his decisions and actions.

Relationship

The main characteristics of the counselor-counselee relationship, already intimated, can be conveyed only in generalities; out of concern that the concept and practice of ego-counseling remain flexible and subject to revision, the method may never be specified to the degree that its potential users would like. It is surely not intended to train a breed of "ego-counselors." When used in this paper, the term "ego-counselor" refers to any qualified counselor during the period of time when he is making deliberate use of the method. Any counselor may employ the main features of the method and modify it to the degree warranted by his conception of appropriate practice. The thresholds beyond which the method no longer would have identity or efficacy are not clear or arbitrary. The tolerance for flexibility in the behavior of the counselor seems, at this point, to be quite wide; this is partly because the method is still undeveloped and partly because in any form of psychological treatment, we have not arrived—nor ought we necessarily ever to arrive—at a scaling of procedures so refined as to warrant a technician's cookbook.

The above implies that the counselor should be encouraged to modify his approach in accord with his assessment of the needs of a particular counselee and of his own competencies and limits. Yet the quality of the counseling relationship *qua* human relationship cannot be wholly dictated by formal rules. The extent to which the counselor discloses to a particular counselee the love and empathy presumptive in all his work, and encourages analogous expression from the counselee, will be importantly determined by the counseling setting and by the counselor's continuing reassessment during their transactions

---

[1] Much of the increased institutional support for school guidance services stems from the counselor's purported competence to assess pupils more efficiently for program selection, college admissions and occupational entry. Ironically, the more emphasis placed on his role as manpower distributor, as gatekeeper for college and occupational entry, the more the "school guidance officer" is likely to become alienated from his function as counselor and educator. To the degree that a student perceives a counselor to be an arm of school administration, a surrogate of society's demands and parents' expectations, he is less likely to perceive in him those qualities of trustworthiness and of freedom from prejudice which are so vital to a frank discussion of personal concerns.

of counselee needs and strengths. Attention in this paper is directed mostly to short-contact proceedings with counselees who are assessed to be sufficiently mobile and autonomous to make and to implement decisions within significant sectors of their life-space during the relatively early future. Should the counselor find early or late in the counseling series that his counselee does not meet these criteria, he will modify his approach accordingly. He would be ready to modify such aspects as the number and scheduling of treatment sessions, the settings in which he meets his client and the kind of relationship he encourages. The main features of the method are believed to have an integrity which will survive a variety of modifications.

Counselor as Collaborator.   In his relationship with a counselee, an ego-counselor is characteristically unassuming. His main attention, unless the counselee's feelings about him and about the conditions of their relationship become a distraction to either of them, is directed as early as possible in their interviews to the counselee as "investigator," as potential analyst of certain aspects of his personal condition. An ego-counselor is unassuming about the personal relationship in that he initially approaches the counselee as if the latter is ready to analyze some of the circumstances which underlie his presence in the interview. He assumes "unassumingly" that such analysis is natural and useful to do. He offers to collaborate with the counselee, to deliberate with him about the "meaning" of these circumstances and to attempt to help him to reconstrue them in ways that might lead the counselee to their more effective control. Whether a counselee in pain and bewilderment eagerly requests help, or whether he is referred against his will for behavior which is recognized as a problem only by someone else, or whether he is scheduled as part of a school or college counselor's effort to become acquainted with students who are assigned routinely to his case load, this general approach would seem to be still appropriate. A creative practitioner, of course, whatever his reliance on "method," meets each new person to some degree in unique, spontaneous ways.

An ego-counselor respects the power and the subtlety in the counseling relationship; his love for the counselee is implicit. He and the counselee may come to feel deeply for one another; and purely from their affiliation, the counselee may derive substantial comfort and strength. Yet in an ego-counselor's philosophy of practice, love is not enough. Beyond the counseling hour are circumstances in the counselee's life which require analysis and resolution. There are facts to be surveyed, feelings to be clarified, alternatives to be considered, decisions to be made and acted upon. One decision may be more appropriate than another; some actions promise consequences more desirable to a counselee than their alternatives.

Out of fearfulness, or shame, or loneliness, or other powerful feelings, a counselee may postpone or avoid analysis of his personal condition, finding sufficient value in his affiliation with a permissive counselor. The counselor has, of course, no prerogative to stipulate how the counselee ought to construe and to feel about their relationship. He does not, like a Balinese mother, deliberately thwart a counselee's feelings. He will not "correct" a counselee nor will he respond with disappointment or dissaffection should the counselee refuse his offer of collaboration. He cannot know whether the counselee really loses anything by construing the counseling process differently from him. To the degree that he is guided by the method of ego-counseling, however, a counselor will himself construe the counseling relationship primarily as a means or a vehicle. Although he respects the counselee's sentiments, he is likely to give more pronounced attention to the counselee's questions and choices than to his satisfaction in their relationship.[2]

The counselor-counselee collaboration in ego-counseling assumes a helping relationship; collaboration can be maintained, I believe, with no necessary contradiction to the client-centered principles which have been enunciated so eloquently by Rogers (18). An ego-counselor accepts a counselee nonevaluatively, i.e., he offers his collaboration, initially at least, without conditions; the counselee is free to reject his offer, without hazarding the counselor's disaffection. It is a premise of

[2] I hope not to seem to slight the enormous subtlety and importance of personal relationship, especially of its complex affective elements, in all psychological treatment processes. Can we not develop more fruitful theories of counseling, however, by striving to include in our models some better balance between concepts of cognition and of affect? Bordin (3) makes some beginning effort to consider a "cognitive-conative balance" as an aspect of counselor focus and skill. The attempt to comprehend counselee behavior partly as "analysis" or "thinking activity" may seem alien to some counseling practitioners. They might worry, with reason, that such a theoretical focus would lead to oversimplification and pseudo-objectification by the counselor in relating himself to his counselees. But there is too much fruitful promise for counseling theorists to ignore in the work of Piaget, Bruner, Rapaport, George Kelly and of other investigators into the nature of thinking. In addition to the vital realm of impulse and affect, can our perspective on the counselee also comprehend the rational pathways which he might pursue to achieve personal control and an enhanced sense of personal responsibility? Can we have our cognitive processes and relationship too? Still only a vague promise in the present paper is a framework for ego-counseling which will open hospitality to both kinds of constructions.

the method that he can, in Tyler's (20) sense, "accept" the counselee unconditionally as a person and convey his acceptance sincerely, while still making judgments concerning the counselee's readiness to use his collaboration within such limits as time and the counselor's competence. Concomitant with his communication of acceptance, the counselor makes an unremitting effort to understand the counselee and to impart back his understanding.

Communication as Technique. How does a counselor communicate to a counselee that he is making an effort to understand him? To tell him so explicitly is merely a conversational gambit; the counselee must still experience for himself that what the counselor says is valid. Rogers (18) suggests that if the counselor *is* genuinely accepting and understanding, whatever he *says* to the counselee will convey these attitudes. He implies that there is no answer at the level of technique.

It can be agreed that the counselor is likely to defeat his purpose if he communicates with the counselee in the form of mechanical conversational devices. Yet there are still constructive reasons to describe and to analyze counselor behavior in terms of style and technique. At a psycholinguistic level of analysis, for example, it is possible to identify "reflection" as a powerful technique for communicating understanding; in reflecting, the counselor tries actively to restate the meanings he perceives to be implicit in the utterances of the counselee. In a study employing data derived from content analysis of assessment interview protocols, this writer (10) demonstrated that interviews characterized by a high ratio of interviewer reflection statements were also those in which the interviewee was more responsive throughout the interview conversation; reflection statements seemed to act in these interviews as a catalyst to encourage interviewee participation. Reflection responses seem to foster the counseling process in several ways at once: the very linguistic form of the counselor's restatements communicates, in addition to whatever truth the counselee perceives in his remarks and without the counselor needing to express this attitude directly, that what the counselee has to say is of first importance; that the thoughts and feelings of the counselee are to constitute the main object of their deliberations; and that he respects the capacity of the counselee to carry on the process of self-inquiry.

Transference. It was indicated earlier that the counselor offers his help without initial conditions. This cannot mean, of course, that there are no limits to the counseling relationship. The setting in which counseling occurs defines important limits. For yet another reason, rooted in social psychology, a counselor will attempt to abridge the counselee's investment in their relationship. He will do so to minimize *transference*. Responsive and understanding, yet ambiguous[3] about his own attitudes, the counselor is quite likely to be attributed qualities and intentions which are not objectively "real." The counselee, for example, may redintegrate from the counselor's empathic responsiveness toward him the pattern of an earlier primary relationship; he may then reincarnate in the counselor stereotyped fragments, distorted in recall, of qualities he had perceived to be salient in the other party to the original relationship. Responding in accord with these distorted perceptions, he may display exaggerated feelings of love, of dependence, of hostility toward the counselor.

In psychoanalytic practice, such perceptual distortion is heightened not merely by the ambiguity in the analyst's role but by his efforts to interpret to the patient the meaning of his repressed conflicts.[4] The patient may attempt to ward off painful awareness by misperceiving the therapist's intentions; he may develop a "transference neurosis" within the treatment relationship, coming to perceive the therapist as an agent in his neurotic conflicts. In classic psychoanalytic practice the therapist permits a transference neurosis to run its course. As treatment progresses, he "interprets the transference," attempting to help the patient to differentiate neurotic recrudescenses of earlier behavioral patterns from those responses which are appropriate within their relationship and in other current situations in the patient's life.

Whatever its worth in psychoanalytic therapy, the deliberate utilization of the transference relationship has no place in ego-counseling. Apart from its subtle and hazardous aspects, such a tactic seems inappropriate to the conditions of treatment, usually short-term, with persons who are assessed to be relatively free of crippling neurotic defenses. In a typical ego-counseling relationship, the counselor assumes that the counselee is willing and capable to analyze and to cope with those concerns which brought him into counseling; gradually and

[3] Bordin (3) has given considerable attention to the function of "ambiguity" as a therapeutic variable.

[4] In their treatment of psychosis, Rosen (19) and Whitaker and Malone (22) use treatment strategies so radical that they may be said to "provoke" transference reactions. Alexander and French (2) on the other hand, represent probably a growing minority of psychoanalysts who question the efficacy of transference manipulation as a standard unexceptionable treatment activity. Perhaps the issue splits primarily in terms of the strength of the ego and the particular symptomatology as assessed in each case.

implicitly (in the ideal case!) he offers his collaboration[5] in the analysis.[6] Whenever resistance to his collaboration or to the strain of self-analysis heightens in the client, the counselor may respond to it on an immediate, experiential level; he may say, for example, "You probably find it difficult to talk about these things." Or he may divert the topic to less stressful topics. He is most unlikely, however, to interpret out of personality theory why the counselee may be talking or acting, or relating to him, in a certain way.

Despite a counselor's even highly sensitive and skillful efforts, a counselee may become unwilling to continue their relationship or he may be unable to use the counselor's collaboration effectively. In part, this may derive from a considered defense of his privacy—from an inherent resistance to reveal personally significant aspects about himself to another person. It may also derive from the counselee's reluctance, which all human beings evidence at some moments in their lives, to take responsibility for solving his own problems.

The counselee is free to construe the counselor's offer of collaboration in any terms he wishes. He may perceive the counselor as snoop, as repairman, as menace, as deliverer, or as some combination of archetypes such as these. A counselor would estimate to what degree such apperceptions might be an obstacle to the counseling process. If he judges them to be serious barriers, he may then choose to discuss more explicitly with the counselee the conditions which might guide their collaboration. In cases of firm counselee resistance, he may conclude that termination or referral to another kind of treatment service is the only appropriate procedure; naturally, the counselor will be alert to refer for reasons other than resistance.

Analysis

There seems to be, unfortunately, no term not already preempted and given special meaning in dynamic psychology to comprehend the notion of analysis in counseling. In the sense of perceptual learning, the process might be subsumed by the term "differentiation"; but this would slight the complex cycle of separation and combination of constructs in which the counselee becomes actively engaged as he makes new sense out of his experience. Earlier sections of this paper have

[5] Perry and Estes (15) propose the concept of collaboration in a most evocative discussion of the counseling relationship.

[6] "Analysis" is used here in a general rather than in its special psychoanalytic sense. The term is employed deliberately to suggest an important place for cognitive processes in the conceptual framework for ego-counseling.

alluded to the special usage for ego-counseling of the term "analysis." More rigorous explications must await additional time and thought. But the idea of analysis can be suggested once again by posing the kinds of questions with which a counselee might confront himself in this phase of ego-counseling. As a sector emerges from the deliberations between counselor and counselee, for example, concern about qualifying for college, the latter may ask: "What's expected of me? Do I have sufficient capacity to meet these expectations? What do I myself want? Am I really interested in this or that idea, object or activity? How do I compare with others? What am I really like? What am I doing, denying, distorting, avoiding? What are the consequences? What are the alternative ways to regard . . . ? What goals make sense as my own? In what respects do my present efforts promise to realize or to fail them?"

How tempting for a parent or friend or teacher to respond to such questions with his own insightful judgments! What a ready opportunity to portray to this young person a future with exhilarating visions and noble ends! The counselor, however, will offer his advice and solutions only by rare and thoughtful exception. He resists the temptation to substitute his own "mature" judgment for the counselee's. His essential aim is to foster understanding and to guide decisions for which the counselee will take responsibility and which he will be competent to implement himself.

Yet the counselor does not remain outside the analysis. A certain unfortunate orthodoxy deriving from Rogers' (18) persuasive principles [see Porter (17)] would have him do so. The counselor would be constrained to respond mainly to clarify what the counselee construes his dilemmas to be and how he feels about them. Such a position, however, is unlikely to stimulate most counselees to conduct as comprehensive and as candid an examination of self-in-reality as that for which they may, with encouragement, be ready. Elusive but potentially significant meanings—hunches only vaguely perceived— may not be brought into counselee awareness in deliberations where the counselor remains unyieldingly reflective. To argue from the premise that the counselee is ready to deal with only that which he introduces himself or to which he responds in the reflections of the counselor assumes too confining a model of how one person learns about himself when in relationship with another person; more broadly, it seems also to slight the capacity of a human being to overcome inherent anxiety associated with new awareness and to employ a variety of media and strategies to attain new concepts of self and nonself.

Assuming that he is perceived to be a genuine collaborator, a counselor can interpret[7] and confront[8] what the counselee says and does without necessarily undermining the counselee's sense of personal responsibility. Conversations in which the counselor's style embodies reflection, questioning, interpretation and confrontation may actually make the counselor's role in the dialogue seem to the counselee less artificial than a style which is characteristically reflective. There are clinical indications, for example, that adolescent delinquents tend to construe permissive, ambiguous, persistently reflective behavior by a therapist to be either naïve or dangerously seductive. It is crucial, of course, that interpretations be perceived to emanate from a well-intentioned collaborator, not from a mere critic; the counselor introduces new information and hypotheses into their discourse as one who is trying not to convert the counselee but to join him in a mutual effort at understanding. An ego-counselor will accept a counselee's possible disinclination to examine certain aspects of self-in-environment and to seek solutions to his "real" problems. But he will attempt to bring the counselee's attention to those requirements for choice and for action which may confront a counselee in his "real" environment.

In a research on ego-counseling to which this paper is related (10), the subjects were selected initially because their academic performance failed to meet the expectations implicit in the standard measures of intelligence used by investigators. It was later found that the counselees felt, painfully in many cases, that they were failing to satisfy their own standards. Thus a natural sector in counseling with high school boys who are classified by academic authorities and by themselves as "underachievers" concerns the counselee's capacities and interests, decisions and actions (and their consequences and alternatives) with relation to the conditions of academic work. The questions raised above would then take more specific form as the counselor and counselee focused on the sector of academic study.

---

[7] "Interpretation" is used to refer to counselor statements which propose a construction of events in the experience of the counselee which the latter has not already himself formulated. Interpretation does not refer here to its technical psychoanalytic usage, in which the datum is given meaning by an already formulated general theory.

[8] "Confrontation" is a particular form of interpretation in which the counselor proposes that contradiction exists between two aspects of client thinking or overt behavior.

The following are a series of steps which a counselor and counselee might pursue in analyzing academic study as a sector:

1. As he comprehends the setting and finds in the counseling relationship that the responsibility for analysis and solution is to be his, the counselee begins to describe and to examine the manner in which he construes his school life, his role as a student, his current academic performance, the extent of his mastery over school tasks, etc.

2. The counselee is encouraged to project himself into the future, to discuss his conception of career and his general life aims, to portray his image of self and ideal self. Where these are poorly differentiated, he is encouraged to consider the implications of being vague and planless about such matters. The counselor refrains from "promoting" planfulness; he attempts to couch his observations to the counselee in terms of probable consequences as he—imperfectly—perceives them. (Does the emphasis on consequences in itself "promote" a value for planfulness? Maybe, but the connotation is not the same.) The counselee is encouraged to consider the connection between means and ends, the relation of his present actions to the realization of his personal aims.

3. Both parties consider obstacles to the counselee's aims and aspirations and the ways in which these obstacles might be resolved. The obstacles may be both personal and external: They may reside in the counselee's current attitudes and actions and in the form of limits to capacity and to skill. Obstacles may also be perceived in certain of the counselee's primary relationships, for example, with a demanding, rejecting parent, or with a rigid, punitive teacher; or obstacles may exist in the form of practical limits to financial support.

4. As obstacles are considered, the counselee will be encouraged to engage in systematic appraisal of self and of external circumstance. The counselor, from his observations during the interviews, and from other information, has been making inferences continually about the counselee's capacities, dispositions and ego qualities. Using care and discretion, the counselor conveys certain of his inferences in the form of hunches and tentative hypotheses. As in traditional vocational counseling, the counselor may report the counselee's test scores themselves, together with background information to enable the counselee to make useful comparisons of his performance with his peers; and the counselor may, as "expert" on certain sources of information for the counselee's use, relate his hypotheses to facts about education and the occupational world.

5. In his conversation, the counselee will have been revealing the

degree to which he feels independent, competent, personally responsible, with reference to the requirements of academic study. An ego-counselor is likely to hypothecate about such qualities, about their "connectedness" with other aspects of the counselee's problems in the sector of academic study. In analyzing the possible causes and consequences of his underachievement, for example, a counselee may deny the value of school, accompanying his denial with unrealistic images of the success which he might obtain without continuing his education; or he may merely promise himself that things will be different next semester without attempting to make explicit what he will do to make a difference; or he may project blame for his difficulties on teachers and others without analyzing his part in what may be often vicious circles of retribution in his relationships with other persons. Where a counselee continues to deny or to postpone dealing with certain implications or likely consequences from his actions, the counselor, as his collaborator in his self-analysis, may offer his interpretations. The counselee may choose to reject the interpretations, but he is encouraged first to weigh their relevance and then to reject or to accept them for considered reasons.

In all counseling dialogues, a counselor must be alert to signs in a counselee of what Bordin (3) has called "an undulating curve of resistance." Perry and Estes (15) observe similarly that ". . . the central technical problem of education and reeducation is the problem of resistance" (p. 100). A counselee is inevitably threatened, however valid he may perceive them to be, by a counselor's observations and interpretations. Even a most trusted friend and collaborator, if he calls into question one's private meanings and beliefs, is at least a temporary intruder. Unless or until the counselee has incorporated an observation by the counselor to be his own view as well, and this often requires much more than a moment, he is likely to continue to defend the only private world he knows. A counselor remains alert to resistance and aware of the pain which may accompany self-analysis; he knows that the search for self-understanding has, in pain and pleasure, twin companions. He encourages the search, nevertheless.

Synthesis

The notion of analysis is joined intimately with that of synthesis. The thought processes of a counselee may be depicted in terms of endless cycles of analysis and synthesis. There is no ready system of concepts, however, to represent these processes adequately. Each investigator into the psychology of thinking tends to create different labels and different size units. Klein (13) suggests that in studying cognitive attitudes one may slice the behavior to be observed ". . . into any segment, gross or minute, of long or short duration, which shows the boundaries of an intention on one side and a behavioral change experienced as attaining the intention on the other" (p. 96). One who would conceptualize thought processes is thus confronted with the task of defining *de novo* his units and classes.

In cognitive terms, ego-counseling may be said to help the counselee to attain a revised set of intentions, of "concepts" (6), of "personal constructs" (12) with reference to specified sectors. It should be noted that in the term "cognitive attitudes," Klein (13) is referring to "organizing principles" which guide both action and the actor's decision that the result he achieves is "adequate." The outcomes of ego-counseling cannot be known sufficiently merely by observing changes in the counselee's performance, for example, the increased allocation by an underachiever of time to study, his achievement of higher grades, or his more cooperative behavior in class. Such actions can be judged to be adequate outcomes only if consistent with the counselee's organizing principles—with what he values and intends. Successful counseling with underachievers may, in most instances, lead to higher school grades; but it is conceivable that some students who are underachievers may decide *responsibly* to reduce their efforts in certain courses, or to drop out of school. If they have clarified their reasons for doing so, and if these reasons can be judged to be integral with their long-term interests, the aims of ego-counseling may be sufficiently realized. The point bears repeating: ego-counseling is intended to foster within each counselee a more integral relation than formerly among his values, intentions and actions. (The parallel here with Marcuse's definition of surplus-repression is deliberate.) It is not to be employed to promote a *particular* set of values, intentions and actions which may be sanctioned by a *particular* society. The contribution of ego-counseling to the welfare of a society can be substantial; but the contribution will be indirect. It will be realized in the accomplishments of those members who will have been helped through counseling to achieve some better quality of ego integrity, each in his own life.

Action

In long-term psychotherapy, the client has opportunity to test the relevance of emerging insights, to determine whether in direct confrontation he can control his anger or his fearfulness, to engage in tasks in which he can judge whether his performance has improved. In treatment which is characteristically short-term, such between-interview experimentation by the counselee is necessarily limited. It is possible that school counselors, who can remain in contact with their cases over a long span of time, can also stage these contacts so that the counselee may have opportunity between interviews to test, by action, decisions he has made in the course of counseling. In the interest of systematizing counseling practice, the concept of the academic year as a time grid over which a half dozen counseling interviews might be spread planfully, merits a tryout. The opportunity to transplant and to develop newborn intentions and concepts as they emerge is typically denied the counselee in short-term treatment.

The term "rehearsal"—for action—might more appropriately denote this aspect of ego-counseling. The counselor attempts to help the counselee envision how he will act, given particular situations, for example, how he might plan his study schedule, or how he might respond when he confronts a nagging parent or a demanding teacher, or how he might obtain certain information critical to his plans. The concern with action—with practical decisions and solutions—has been a natural one in counseling. It has distorted, in fact, the conventional view of counseling, one which tends to confuse counseling with practical advice-giving. Interviews with school counselors often become overly concerned with the details of planning programs, with the transmission of information about colleges, with the "tracking" of a student's academic performance in an effort to keep him on the road to graduation. Counseling may be said to occur in such interviews only derivatively: to the extent that discussion of these topics helps to clarify the counselee's own bases for judgment and to see the implications and consequences of his actions.

Ego-counseling includes rehearsal and action, in part, because the institutional settings in which counseling has typically been practiced —high school guidance services, college centers, rehabilitation services—are concerned with practical effects. Educational institutions have a palpable interest in the quality of academic performance and vocational planning, in valid selection of students, and in the mature use by students of their extracurricular time. They might reasonably expect their counselors to assist students to act more effectively in such matters. Essentially, however, action and rehearsal are included in a paradigm for ego-counseling not to make ego-counseling a more suitable function to practice in these institutions, but because action, feedback and rehearsal for action are natural phases of a guidance and, thus, an educative process. A resolve during a counseling interview to repair a failing grade, for example, may become another mere New Year's resolution when the counselee confronts, one evening after another, the lonely vigil of study. The counselee needs to experience a connection between what he intends and construes during the interview and what he experiences in "natural" circumstances.

The entire paradigm set forth in the preceding pages is, of course, notional—a crude representation of the great variety of conversations which take place in counseling interviews. The concepts of setting, relationship, analysis, synthesis and action may separate out and fall in sequence to a small degree in certain cases. For the most part, however, all these concepts may be relevant to any excerpt of a counseling dialogue. They have been discussed separately in an effort to stimulate study and understanding of a process whose strength, paradoxically, may lie in part in its resistance to systematic abstraction.

CONCLUSION

Adequate definition eludes us still. Ambiguity and incompleteness seem inevitably to accompany labor in "applied fields." A method for educating intelligent beings can never be fully specified. The burden of doubt is common to educators, physicians, politicians and others who would apply behavioral principles to human problems. Yet one must continue to gnaw at ambiguity.

Still to be clarified are the distinctions between ego-counseling and generic conceptions of counseling and psychotherapy. Also problematic is the relation of ego-counseling to the classic image of instruction: Is this not how a teacher in the liberal tradition typically approaches a learner? We also have fenced only sketchily with the outcome problem: What is construed to happen as a product of successful ego-counseling? Finally, the relation of ego-counseling in guidance to psychoanalytic theory and to the larger traditions of educational thought and practice remains only suggestive. A fuller analysis of guidance and of ego-counseling (as ideal but realizable processes) will reveal, I believe, that they are concerned fundamentally and not at all naïvely with human freedom. They ought thus to be considered integral, not merely adjunctive, to the thought and practice of education.

REFERENCES

1. Adelson, J. Freud in America: Some observations. *Amer. Psychologist,* 1956, *11,* 467–70.
2. Alexander, F. and French, T. M. *Psychoanalytic therapy.* New York: Ronald Press, 1946.
3. Bordin, E. S. *Psychological counseling.* New York: Appleton-Century-Crofts, 1955.
4. Bronfenbrenner, U. Toward an integrated theory of personality. In R. R. Blake and G. V. Ramsey (eds.), *Perception: An approach to personality.* New York: Ronald Press, 1951, pp. 206–37.
5. Brown, N. O. *Life against death.* New York: Vintage Books, 1959.
6. Bruner, J. S., Goodnow, Jacqueline J. and Austin, G. A. *A study of thinking.* New York: Wiley, 1956.
7. Deutsch, F. *Applied psychoanalysis.* New York: Grune & Stratton, 1949.
8. Erikson, E. H. Identity and the life cycle: Selected papers. *Psychol. Issues,* 1958, *1,* 18–171.
9. Hummel, R. C. Interviewee responsiveness as a function of interviewee method. Unpublished doctoral dissertation, Columbia University, 1958 (University of Michigan Microfilm).
10. ———. An evaluation of a model for guidance counseling. Research proposal submitted to Commissioner of Education, U. S. Department of Health, Education, and Welfare, 1960.
11. Jones, E. *The Life and work of Sigmund Freud.* Abridgement by L. Trilling and S. Marcus. Garden City, N. Y.: Doubleday (Anchor Books), 1963.
12. Kelly, G. A. *The psychology of personal constructs,* Vols. I, II. New York: W. W. Norton & Co., 1955.
13. Klein, G. S. Cognitive control and motivation. In G. Lindzey (ed.), *Assessment of human motives.* New York: Holt, Rinehart & Winston, 1958.
14. Marcuse, H. *Eros and civilization.* Boston: Beacon Press, 1955.
15. Perry, W. G., Jr., and Estes, S. G. The collaboration of client and counselor. In O. H. Mowrer (ed.), *Psychotherapy: Theory and research.* New York: Ronald Press, 1953, pp. 95–119.
16. Peters, R. S. *Authority, responsibility and education.* London: George Allen & Unwin, Ltd., 1959.
17. Porter, E. H., Jr. *An introduction to therapeutic counseling.* Boston: Houghton Mifflin, 1950.
18. Rogers, C. R. *Client-centered therapy.* Boston: Houghton Mifflin, 1951.
19. Rosen, J. M. *Direct analysis.* New York: Grune & Stratton, 1953.

20. Tyler, Leona E. *The work of the counselor* (2nd ed.). New York: Appleton-Century-Crofts, 1961.
21. Watts, A. W. *Psychotherapy east and west.* New York: Mentor, 1963.
22. Whitaker, C. A. and Malone, T. P. *The roots of psychotherapy.* New York: Blakeston, 1953.
23. White, R. W. Ego and reality in psychoanalytic theory. *Psychol. Issues,* 1963, *3,* 1–210.

EDWARD JOSEPH SHOBEN, JR.

Guidance: Remedial Function
or Social Reconstruction?

THE CURRENT PUBLIC AND PROFESSIONAL STATUS OF GUIDANCE

THERE IS A SENSE in which guidance services as a part of the American educational enterprise are in their heyday. The major policy statement about educational matters that fails to assign a prominent place to guidance is a rarity, and as an explicit beneficiary of the National Defense Education Act, along with only a tiny cluster of the currently most valued subject-matter fields, guidance has enjoyed strong financial support. According to the U.S. Office of Education, for example, nearly 8,000 people have been enrolled under N.D.E.A. auspices for short-term guidance training institutes, and more than 1,700 have been supported in regular-session institutes. In 1960, 30,000 persons were concerned with "scheduled guidance activities" in secondary schools across the nation, although only about one-third of them were functioning as full-time guidance personnel. Similarly, in the same year, the number of students studying for advanced degrees in guidance and counseling exceeded the combined total in physical education, business education, industrial arts education, and music education, and the figure closely approximated the numbers majoring in such standard programs as administration and curriculum. The American Personnel and Guidance Association has a dues-paying membership of well over 13,000, owns its own building in Washington, operates the highly successful *Personnel and Guidance Journal,* and exercises a not inconsiderable influence in the governmental and private circles where issues of policy and finance for education are decided.

At the same time, however, the pattern of ebullient expansiveness is drawn taut by tensions, criticisms, and ambiguities. Wrenn (19), in examining the field in 1958, noted three disturbing signs of the times that still persist: (1) Among psychologists, counseling psychology enjoys the lowest prestige of all the specialties requiring the doctorate; (2) no one has yet developed an adequate theory of vocational choice and development; and (3) various lines of research into the learning process, including Skinner's (13, 14), make it hard to ignore the possibility that the counseling process may be so conceived as to reinforce the least integrative of the behaviors displayed by its clients. Banesh Hoffmann's recent attack (7) is only the most recent of a long series of assaults on the psychometric arsenal of guidance, and *The Brain Watchers* (5, 6) has only made highly articulate the troubled objections of many to what they regard as an invasion of the personalities and psychodynamics of the children in the school's charge. In much the same vein, Barry and Wolf (2) have documented the extent to which "myths"—assumptions and undemonstrated principles—are shot through the literature of guidance, making it less than either a firmly based discipline or a logically coherent profession.

At the very time, then, that guidance commands the greatest public favor, it is also under public fire. At the moment of its greatest expansion, it can show little in the way of solid research to demonstrate its merits or its achievements. At a peak of its influence, its basic techniques of testing and counseling evoke a marked degree of mistrust. With the best of intentions, generally if rather dimly perceived by the public and the rest of the educational fraternity, guidance is animated neither by a clear philosophy of why people should be given its special kind of service as a part of their school experience nor by a demonstrably effective core of methods by which such help can be provided.

To make this charge is by no means tantamount to a condemnation of particular guidance practices. Rather, it is a way of underscoring the place of guidance among the practical arts—in this case, the practical arts of human relationships. Pragmatically, guidance workers are undoubtedly each day doing much to assist large numbers of youngsters to cope more effectively with the business of growing up in a complex and often mystifying world. Such, at least, seems to be a reasonable article of faith, quite consonant with the common experience of those whose fate it is to visit schools and to talk frequently with the counselors and personnel officers who ply their trade there. But guidance aspires to professional status and lays claim to systematic and specialized membership within the complex educational family of occupations and disciplines. Presumably, therefore, guidance has its roots in the behavioral sciences and is watered by the springs of philosophy from which come the constant redefinitions of the role of the school in the total process of socialization. It is on this basis—the ground of its own understandable ambitions—that it is vulnerable and exposed. The gap between successes and pretensions, when one looks hard, is not only apparent; it is wide.

Nor, on reflection, is this state of affairs especially puzzling. One of the primary tensions within the guidance movement is simply a reflection of a fundamental tension in Western social thought. The societies of the West have been built essentially on the conviction that persons are free and responsible—see, for example, the whole tradition of Anglo-Saxon law.[1] Increasingly, however, the technique used for the investigation and reconstruction of those societies and the men who compose them has been that of science; and science carries the implication that human conduct, like any other proper object of scientific inquiry, is predictable and determined. Since this contradiction in basic assumptions has rarely been dealt with in any persuasive fashion anywhere, one cannot fairly blame guidance workers for not resolving it, but it has, for them, consequences of considerable moment. Not the least of these entailments is that of making guidance the unwitting smuggler of certain values that are not entirely explicit.

THE SMUGGLING OF VALUES

This proposition is worth examining for several reasons, one of which is its demonstration of the complexity of the guidance worker's job. In general, he supplies (or is supposed to supply) a highly individualized dimension to the pupil's experience of mass education. In contrast to the teacher, who is responsible for drawing students into

[1] Two instructive references here are Felix S. Cohen's *Ethical Systems and Legal Ideals* (Ithaca, N. Y.: Cornell University Press, 1959) and the popular British paperback, *Justice at Work*, by James Avery Joyce (London: Pan Books, 1957). Two books also of particular interest to educators are those by Judge Jerome Frank, *Fate and Freedom* (New York: Simon and Schuster, 1945) and *Courts on Trial* (Princeton, N. J.: Princeton University Press, 1949).

the traditions of society and inviting their membership in it, the guidance worker furnishes the information, the recommendations, and the impetus that are likely to move *particular* children in *distinctive* directions on the basis of their *special* characteristics and potentialities. The business of influencing another human being is almost always touchy and edged with uneasiness, and it certainly requires justification. In the case of school guidance work, it requires justification to parents and the community at large as well as to administrators and school board members. That justification comes most readily from science—the corpus of knowledge about tests, psychological development, and the prediction of performance in college or on a job from previous experience, including academic experience. One may grant, however, the cogency and power of science in this connection and still remain impressed by two stubborn facts: (1) Guidance remains an effort to influence particular youngsters in particular directions, and (2) those directions are not given by whatever scientific data or principles that may in other ways be relevant to the enterprise.

To put the case more concretely, if a guidance counselor is attempting to help a child develop a greater sense of personal responsibility, that aim does not emerge directly from whatever psychological knowledge the counselor may have available. Behavioral science may in some fashion indicate how the goal may be achieved; it neither defines it nor establishes its desirability. Because "responsibility" in this context is a word that carries rich positive connotations, this kind of statement of objectives is likely to evoke little opposition. But we come rapidly to more troubled waters when we discuss other such common desiderata as "spontaneity" or a "trust of one's own feelings." It seems quite probable that spontaneity and a trust of their own feelings would entail for Negro adolescents, for example, a powerful tendency to hate one's parents, to damn the school as irrelevant, and to attack society for its inequities. Despite the fact that such attitudes are by no means incomprehensible on scientific grounds, they are not likely to be encouraged by guidance workers. Even the matter of vocational choice may involve some pronounced restrictions on grounds other than those provided by psychological or sociological knowledge. Barry and Wolf (2, pp. 92–93) give an example: In Las Vegas and other gambling resorts, there is a pressing need for dealers at the gaming tables; there is even a school to train them. Pay is good, hours are short, and the working environment is, from at least one point of view, quite comfortable. For a youngster with a taste for probabilities, a suitable temperament, and an interest in games of chance, such a career may be a thoroughly "realistic" one. Yet there is ample room to doubt that any guidance counselor would condone this kind of preference, let alone raise it as an appropriate possibility.

The examples could easily be multiplied, but the point is that guidance workers, as smugglers of values, are in a position almost the reverse of that which Szasz (16) has recently described as the lot of psychiatrists. Taking the issue of legal abortion for therapeutic purposes as his test case, Szasz is more widely concerned with the question of how self-determined are the controls exercised over one's body. Abortions are illegal, of course, unless certain conditions obtain. While there is some variation from state to state in the nature of these conditions, mental illness is usually one of them. As a matter of fact, wherever such therapeutic abortions are legally performed in large numbers, justification is given most frequently on psychiatric grounds. At the Mt. Sinai Hospital in New York, for example, 39 per cent of legal abortions since 1952 have been done on the basis of psychiatric judgment as against only 10 per cent because of malignancies and only 11 per cent because of cardio-renal disease. But for Szasz, himself a psychiatrist of some prominence, mental illnesses are not diseases at all. Far from being entities like tuberculosis or hypertension, they are simply strategies for coping with life that have consequences which include quite genuine misery (17). The misery, however, is not like that of medically defined pain; it is the suffering associated with anxiety and interpersonal ineptness. In short, it is a *moral* suffering. In consequence, the psychiatric justification for therapeutic abortion is a moral justification, used to circumvent a legal restriction on the right of the individual to exercise whatever controls he wishes over his own body. In this sense, the psychiatrist is the bootlegger of certain moral values (mercy and self-determination) under the guise of a medical diagnosis in order to circumvent the limits set on these values under the social sanctions of law. While the psychiatric judgment here may have the appearance of science, it is in reality a camouflaged vehicle for the implementing of an inarticulate moral choice at variance with the codified rules.

In the case of the guidance worker, the appeal to science is equally in evidence, but the smuggled values are those of the dominant middle class, those that tend to reduce individual variability and autonomy rather than increase it. Viewed from one angle of regard, this state of affairs is not at all shocking. The school is, after all, a social agency,

charged with the preservation of society through the transmission of
the culture. Certain of its ends, therefore, are inherently and necessarily conservative, and conservatism—even in a pluralistic social context—always puts a premium on a degree of homogenization, a fitting
of particular cases to the modal pattern. Perhaps the most straightforward pronouncement on this score is that of Robert Maynard
Hutchins:

> I do not ignore [the argument that the most important thing about
> men is that they are different]; I deny it. I do not deny the fact of
> individual differences; I deny that it is the most important fact about
> men or the one on which an education system should be erected.[2]

One need not be a subscriber to Hutchins's doctrines to find a certain
descriptive accuracy in his statement. Whatever else it does, the school
—of which guidance activities are an integral part—must as a societal
institution build commonalities among people. It must lead them into
a common tradition, equip them with common skills, and disseminate
among them a core of common standards. While the construction of
commonality is not all that the school does, this task is one that it cannot neglect. Indeed, in the eyes of acute foreign observers like Denis
Brogan (4), the effectiveness of the school at turning a huge and
diverse population—the children of immigrants, children from strik-
ingly different regions, children of divergent familial backgrounds,
etc.—into recognizable Americans is one of the chief glories of our
educational system. It would be immensely difficult and possibly immensely disruptive for guidance *not* to participate in this fundamentally conservative responsibility which schools in the United States
must carry.

But there is another factor somewhat more covertly at work here.
School personnel are overwhelmingly middle class in their status. If
they do not derive from middle-class origins, they have achieved
middle-class membership through upward mobility and are vigorous
in the consolidation of their new social position.[3] There is strong evidence that such teachers—and guidance workers have almost uni-

---

[2] John Maynard Hutchins, *The Conflict in Education* (New York: Harper &
Row, 1953), p. 89.

[3] On such scales as the Warner Index of Status Characteristics, teachers are
almost without exception and, indeed, almost by definition members of the American
middle class. For an interesting example of studies of teacher-pupil perceptions, see
Hilde T. Himmelweit, "Socioeconomic Background and Personality," *Internatl. Soc.
Sci. Bull.,* VII (1955), 29–35.

versally come out of the classroom—perceive youngsters of lower-class status as sullen, defiant, dirty, aggressive, given to the erotic and the overtly sexual in their language and manner, intellectually inferior, and inadequately and improperly oriented to books and study. Children so perceived are unrewarding to work with, and the probability of their being rejected is high. Hollingshead (8) and Opstad[4] have even shown that the distribution of low and failing grades among lower-class youth is substantially greater than would be predicted from indices of intelligence.

Perhaps a significant kind of light is cast on these observations by still another finding. A great deal of attention has been paid recently to the notion of "creativity," a term endowed with highly positive connotations. Surely, there can be no argument about the degree to which we want our youngsters to be creative! Yet Torrance (18) is not the only investigator to document the fact that creative children are by no means well liked by teachers and other school officials. By definition, creative pupils challenge some of the basic rules, resist the pressure toward commonality, and behave in unpredicted and idiosyncratic ways. Such a pattern of response not only puts a strain on the corporate structure of the school; it frustrates in some degree one of its fundamental purposes. In consequence, even though the notion of increased creativity as an educational objective is an appealing one, it is not without its own sources of conflict and disturbance.

What all this means is that the school provides a setting which necessarily defines a significant part of the frame of reference within which guidance workers must operate. If the tendency is less now than it was in former years for school people to regard nonconformity, aggression, and individual self-assertiveness as "the most serious behavior problem a child can have" (3), they still view with mistrust and irritation any youngster or any event that departs from the orderly, the "nice," or the "healthy" as one segment of society defines the healthy. To the extent that a guidance worker accepts as referrals those children who are perceived by teachers as disruptive, disorderly, or discordant with the classroom group, he accepts in some degree the definition of his job as that of fitting children to the dominant patterns of the school. This task may be an essential one, and on occasion, it may be quite harmonious with that of aiding an individual child to actualize his distinctive potentialities. The fact remains that there

---

[4] Quoted in Boyd R. McCandless, *Children and Adolescents* (New York: Holt, Rinehart & Winston, 1961), p. 469.

are other times when the two enterprises are certainly different and may be in opposition to each other. Even more important is the institutional derivation of the guidance counselor's objectives; they come less from a particular corpus of knowledge or from the independent point of view of an autonomous profession than from the particularities and immediacies of the school in which he works. To make this observation is not necessarily to utter a negative criticism; it is simply to underscore a state of affairs which is usually quite inexplicit and which could productively be made the direct focus of more articulate discussion and study.

FACILITATING THE EXAMINED LIFE—THE FAILURE OF SCHOOL AND GUIDANCE

One of the problems on which discussion and study of this sort could usefully concentrate is that of specialization in education generally and in guidance particularly. The present growth of knowledge is, as we have now been often reminded, no less than awesome. In the natural sciences, knowledge doubles in slightly more than a decade; in the behavioral sciences, it doubles about every thirty years. The mass of information and the complexities of its application to modern society force specialization and therefore a narrowness that is incompatible with the basic educational aim of producing an informed and responsibly participant citizen in a democratic community. In education, teachers must specialize in one or another domain of subject matter. In guidance, most workers are inclined to think of themselves as specialists of one type or another—in testing, in counseling, in the development and utilization of occupational information, etc. Yet there is a sense in which the guidance movement arose as an effort to combat the tendency of mass education, interacting with the inevitable demands of specialization, to become impersonal and confining, to lose sight of the individual and his significant role in the free state. The result is the paradox of guidance workers' becoming specialists in the overcoming of specialization's undesirable effects.

Paradoxical or not, this emphasis on individual growth and on helping individual students to find socially appropriate ways for the expression of their distinctiveness is one of the primary wellsprings of the guidance enterprise. One way to conceptualize this aspect of things is an attempt to facilitate an active search for values among students. So conceived, guidance is the systematic encouragement of students to live what Socrates called the examined life. The examined life is one in which values are constantly being made articulate, subjected to criticism, and revised in the light of experience and thought. At one level, this process is sophisticated and intellectual; at another, it may be naïve and both unenlightened and unencumbered by a tradition of ideas. At all levels, however, it can be authentic. The constant defining and redefining of one's self in relation to one's work and one's family, for example, entails nothing less than an on-going appraisal of one's aspirations and obligations, of the progress made by one human being in the human search for contentment and self-esteem. So presented, the examined life is as serious and as possible—even as necessary—for the plumber or the gardener as for the physicist or philosopher. Knowledge is deeply relevant to it, but a clarity about values and an ability to think of oneself in valuational terms is still more so.

To what extent does the school, including its guidance services, contribute to the cultivation of the examined life? There is a wealth of evidence that suggests the somewhat wry and grim answer of "Not much" to be the appropriate one. Leaving aside the happy exceptions, the main conclusion that offers itself is that our schools and colleges serve, first, to consolidate middle-class students in their middle-class ways and, second, to provide a route to the acceptance of middle-class norms for about one-fourth of the lower-class children who originally enroll. About 75 per cent of lower-class pupils in the first grade, including those whose class membership is related to ethnic status, drop out before finishing high school, most of them before beginning their eleventh year. Aside from these observations, there is little in the way of a systematic or persuasive demonstration that education in the United States concerns itself methodically and effectively with the development of values in its charges.

THE CONCEPT OF INSTITUTIONAL POTENCY

This state of affairs is a strange one in the light of our strong consensus that the schools, at least through the secondary years, *should* be occupied with such matters as citizenship, character, moral development, and social growth. While there may be dissent, often of a heated kind, over the priorities to be given to such objectives in relation to more intellectual and academic ones, there is little doubt about their appropriateness. The teaching of plastic bits of protoplasm to become contributory and integral members of a viable community *requires* a concern for values and the non-intellective side of the child's progress toward adulthood.

But the over-all lack of evidence of success in studies of the school and college as agents of attitudinal and characterological change is relieved occasionally by signs that particular institutions seem to possess what Philip Jacob (9) has called a "peculiar potency" on this score. Although the directions of change vary from school to school, attendance at these "potent" institutions seems to matter, to result in graduates who are different people from what they were at the time of their first enrollment, to entail some jarring of original values and some re-examination and reformulation of them during one's time in residence.

The nature of institutional potency, however, has proved elusive and hard to identify. Yet it is possible that some insight into its basic dimensions can be obtained by looking freshly at an educational tradition somewhat different from our own. In the process, we may win some helpful collateral perspectives on the American system and on the potentialities of guidance within it.

To begin with, we would expect the American "whole-child" outlook in education, reflecting the humanitarian and egalitarian themes in our history (which, incidentally, provide undergirding for the guidance movement itself), to contrast sharply with, for example, the ideas bound up with such institutions as the select and elite "public" schools of Britain. It is quite true, of course, that the English public schools were and are primarily concerned with the development of leaders, not with providing a universal pattern of education. It is equally true that their curricula were and are centered on subject matter—predominantly the classics and mathematics—rather than on children. But so observant and critical an interpreter of British life as J. D. Scott puts it this way: "The *real* object of the English public school is not to teach you Latin and Greek, but to turn you . . . into a true-blue Church-of-England country gentleman."[5] The point is underscored by the famous passage in Thomas Hughes's insightful old novel where Squire Brown is musing on sending his son Tom to Thomas Arnold's Rugby:

"Shall I tell him to mind his work and say he's sent to school to make himself a good scholar? Well, but he isn't sent to school for

[5] J. D. Scott, *Life in Britain* (New York: William Morrow, 1956), p. 171.

that. . . . I don't care a straw for Greek particles or the digamma, no more does his mother. . . . If he'll only turn out a brave, helpful, truth-telling Englishman, and a gentleman and a Christian, that's all I want," thought the Squire.[6]

Let us acknowledge at once that this conception of how the school may develop leaders through dealing with the whole personality had a corrupt and brutal side. The harshness of bullying, flogging, cold dormitories, bad food, and a compulsory indiscriminate participation in games has often been documented, perhaps most dramatically in George Orwell's essay, "Such, Such Were the Joys" (11). But as the oft criticized educators of the United States have only too much reason to know, one can hardly judge a total enterprise by its perverted examples. The rational, sensible element in the British system included and still includes, in Scott's words,

> the setting of spoilt, rich mothers' darlings to make tea and clean football boots for their fag masters, and the idea that for the average boy to be hounded out to run for a few miles, even on a sleety winter afternoon, was fortifying. And one of the things which made public schoolboys easier to work for . . . than the products of most ruling-class systems of education was the fact that they had at least had a glimpse of hardship, a menial position, and "unfairness."
>
> The value set upon the public school system is that it produces leaders, but *leaders who are responsible and humane* [italics added]. . . . And there is a great deal in this. The Victorian and Edwardian public schools *did* produce out of their material a reasonable proportion of young men of character and principles, accustomed to the idea of leadership and so taking it unfussily, fair-minded, not too painfully serious, but with an idea about serving their country and a contempt for money-grubbing and pot-hunting. Commonly, they had high-spirited good manners which pleased most people who were capable of being pleased.[7]

There is more than ample room here, of course, for those of a systematic and empirical turn of mind to wonder about the adequacy of this evaluation. Nevertheless, strong suggestions have recently appeared in the research literature[8] that those American independent

---

[6] Thomas Hughes, *Tom Brown's School-Days* (London: Macmillan, 1857), p. 141.

[7] Scott, *op. cit.*, p. 173.

[8] This material is well reviewed in an unpublished research report by David Winter, Richard Alpert, and David McClelland of the Department of Social Relations, Harvard University, under the title of "The Classic Personal Style."

schools that are cut from English cloth in their purposes and program have more of an impact on the personalities of their students—possess more "potency"—than do the majority of our public schools. In what does that potency consist?

One can only raise hypotheses here, but it seems quite possible that two broad factors account for much of an institution's power to evoke change of a valuational sort in youngsters. The first has to do with the frequency and intimacy of contacts that pupils enjoy with both older students and with teachers whom they perceive as "omnicompetent" in Fritz Redl's (12) terms. School children, as Allinsmith and Goethals (1) have shown, are active in their search for character models, and there is every reason to suspect that this kind of quest, like most other forms of behavior, is strengthened by reinforcement and weakened by neglect or non-reward. What is proposed here is that the child who, regarding a particular adult as able and admirable, not only encounters him in the classroom, but also on the tennis or basketball court, at tea in the older person's home, and in the relatively frequent context of informal talks on a campus bench, is being much more intensively exposed to a model than when the relationship is limited to the classroom or counselor's office.

Similarly, if he must deal with older youngsters, more senior than he in the school's status system, then he forms a clearer sense of just what behavior patterns, attitudes and values are expected of him as he develops under the school's tuition. Obviously, this arrangement need not imply any form of coercion into a fully predetermined and restrictive mould. Self-reliance, critical thought, and initiative can be authentic objectives in this context just as readily as other-direction or the acceptance of definite and imposed norms. The central point is that the process of self-exploration and the cultivation of the examined life are likely to be facilitated by the child's relatively intimate exposure to a variety of models; the opportunity, provided by the school, to identify with several relatively diverse persons, or with some composite that he may create from their diversity, may have much to do with the flexible development of a distinctive life-style.

The second large factor that may contribute to a school's potency may be its character as a community. Assume that teachers, administrators, and guidance workers share common educational aims which are genuinely operative in their work, and that they represent differences in other domains like politics and asthetics—differences that can be openly discussed with enjoyment in the presence of and with stu-

dents. Then it is probable that the child, holding a membership proper
to his age and development in the community, will be responsive to
its values, will interiorize its ideals, and will form the habit of reflecting on the relevance and importance of diversity among people who
still participate in the attainment of other broad goals that they pursue
in concert. The main question is one of whether a school has a distinctive climate within which a boy or girl virtually breathes healthful
expectancies.

To the extent that these two sets of variables, the accessibility of
suitable models and the degree of actual community represented by a
school, account for educational potency, it is clear that the effectiveness of the educational enterprise is based bluntly in the quality of
the adults participating in it and in the character of a school's or college's *de facto* social organization. In the worry about present-day
priorities in education and in the discussion of changing curricular
structures and a newly developing educational technology, it may be
well to keep these possibilities in mind. Lip-service and teaching machines will hardly be sufficient if it truly turns out that potency is
dependent, after all, on these fundamental human elements in the
educational adventure.[9]

MORE POWERFUL FUNCTIONS FOR GUIDANCE

And what place does guidance distinctively occupy in this conception of the potent school? The position taken here suggests a radically
different and more important one than the traditional role of the counselor of the obstreperous, the adviser on college selection and vocational matters, and the purveyor of tests and occupational information.
It is not that these functions are irrelevant or lacking in vital merit.
It is only that they are subordinate to something else. That something
else is twofold in its nature: First, it is a human feedback mechanism
by which the impact of the school is assessed and made available for
the consideration of its official personnel; second, it is a catalyst for
the clarification of the character of the school as a community and as
a source of appropriate models for developing youngsters. The task
may be a delicate one; it is not one to be avoided lightly.

With respect to the feedback function of the guidance worker as it

[9] In this discussion of educational potency, I have drawn heavily on my editorial
on "Potency in the Schools" in the *Teachers College Record* for April, 1962, 63,
548–50.

is envisioned here, it must be noted that counselors, far more than either teachers or administrators, have an opportunity to hear from children themselves the extent to which their schools are disappointing or lack cogency for them. Obviously, youngsters rarely possess the fluency and insight to state their cases in terms that are immediately useful to those responsible for a school's program. But by virtue of their special training, guidance officers know, at least in some significant degree, how to elicit and to interpret the necessary material to form relevant hypotheses. If they so structure their jobs as to see a relatively large number of reasonably representative children, they have an opportunity to evaluate if not to test those hypotheses. What is important is that the hypotheses be less concerned with the personalities of the pupils and more concerned with the functioning realities of the school. Are sufficient opportunities being provided for students to identify with an adequate range of useful adult models? Are children developing any sense of what it means to be a person as a result of their acquaintance with their teachers? Are they getting any conception of an ego-ideal from the curriculum?[10] Do they have any awareness of the diversity within the faculty or of the way that individuality of a responsible sort is prized in the adult society? Are they evolving any such concept through their contact with student leaders and the exemplars in their peer group? Have they any sense of participant membership in a community that is valuable to them and that is supportive of them even while it makes demands on them?

If the guidance worker's hypotheses are pertinent to questions of this kind, and if they are based on the poignant realities of interviews and supplemented by the inventive use of analogues to the industrial morale survey and sociometric assessments, then he can feed his information helpfully into the school's over-all operations and provide a vigorous leadership in promoting the kinds of functioning that contribute to increased potency. In other words, the guidance counselor functions less as a remedial resource than as a prime agent in the continuous reconstruction of the school culture. Basic to this notion is a lesson recently learned from the administration of mental hospitals (10, 15).

[10] One of the major justifications of the classical curriculum was the degree to which it held up to the student a model of desirable and commendable manhood. The same idea animates the study of literature today and the introduction of much of the biographical and historical material that enters the school program in other disciplines. A striking oddity of our educational life is that this plausible assumption has neither been systematically exploited nor intensively studied!

When mental hospitals are examined as microcosmic cultures, they frequently are found to operate as social structures that are all but explicitly designed to reinforce pathological behavior. Professional personnel are relatively inaccessible; the day-to-day emphasis in management, exercised primarily through nurses and attendants, is on docility and the avoidance of behavior that would be disruptive of routines. Opportunities for privacy are curtailed at the same time that much of intramural living—meals, recreation, occupational therapy, etc.—is stringently regimented and dominated by the group. Because expectancies are low, few chances are provided for achievement and fewer still for the evolution of a distinctive life-style that could be generalized to the world outside the institution. The "good patient" is essentially one who adapts to this milieu, becoming a chronic but bland and unobtrusive psychotic. If the hospital is to fulfill its rehabilitative purpose, however, it is less important for it to provide more psychotherapeutic hours (although this provision is far from of no consequence) than to restructure itself as a community. In such a restructuring, a prime consideration is that of making available relatively enduring and intimate relationships. In their context, the patients can generate functional new concepts of what it means to be "normal"; they can be confronted with expectancies which they are encouraged to meet with courageous efforts and confidence in their ultimate success, and they can examine their lives productively in a quest for new meaning and new directions for the future. There is no reason to anticipate miracles, of course, and the cost of this kind of cultural revision is occasionally high. Patients at times test their new freedom in destructive ways, abuse their physical environment in a fashion that can be expensive, and put heavy strains on the people who serve them. Nevertheless, these tendencies have their positive aspects as efforts toward the rediscovery and reassertion of meaningful selfhood, and they are worth tolerating for the gains that can be registered in humane terms when the mental hospital reconceives itself as a therapeutic culture.

The problems of the school, of course, are quite different from those of the psychiatric hospital, but there are important areas of overlap. Some basic principles—the fundamental utility of the human model, the developmental value of diverse relationships of some intimacy and intensity, the stimulus to growth of membership in a genuine community, and the facilitation of the examined life through explicit forms of encouragement and example—apply in common to both. Willy-nilly, the school represents a society-in-little. The challenge before it is whether it can transform itself into a developmentally productive one on an articulate and informed basis and, by a regular and planful process of self-appraisal, maintain itself as a true growth-enhancing community. In such an effort to sharpen the impact of the school and to give it greater cogency for individual students, guidance workers can play a key role, forging, in the course of it, a genuine new profession for themselves. To reconstruct the school as an integrated and humanly significant little culture requires that creative consideration be given to a number of topics—the grouping of pupils, the contributions of the academic curriculum to the encouragement of the examined life, the diversification of teacher load, the ways in which student government can be meaningfully related to the specific objectives of the school, and a host of others—but leadership can properly be expected from guidance workers. Because of their grounding in behavioral science, their familiarity with the techniques of testing and counseling as ways of identifying human needs, and their orientation toward the individual pupil, they have the opportunity to define new horizons in our educational aspirations and to explore novel ways of approaching them. The task, attempted in a setting of universal education and the widest possible range of individual differences, will hardly be an easy one. But part of the American educational tradition has entailed finding ways to do for the many what other nations have done only for the few.

REFERENCES

1. Allinsmith, Wesley, and Goethals, George. *The Role of the Schools in Mental Health.* New York: Basic Books, 1962.
2. Barry, Ruth E., and Wolf, Beverly. *Epitaph for Vocational Guidance.* New York: Teachers College, Columbia University, Bureau of Publications, 1962.
3. Beilin, Harry. "Teachers' and Clinicians' Attitudes toward the Behavior Problems of Children: A Reappraisal," *Child Developm.,* 1959, *30,* 9–26.
4. Brogan, Denis. *America in the Modern World.* New Brunswick, N. J.: Rutgers University Press, 1960, pp. 64–86.
5. Dollard, John. "Answers Unproved," *New York Times Book Review,* October 21, 1962, p. 6.
6. Gross, Martin. *The Brain Watchers.* New York: Random House, 1962.

7. Hoffmann, Banesh. *The Tyranny of Testing.* New York: Crowell, 1962.
8. Hollingshead, A. B. *Elmtown's Youth.* New York: John Wiley, 1949.
9. Jacob, Philip. *Changing Values in College.* New York: Harper & Row, 1957.
10. Jones, Maxwell. *The Therapeutic Community.* New York: Basic Books, 1953.
11. Orwell, George. *A Collection of Essays.* Garden City, N. Y.: Doubleday, 1954, pp. 9–54.
12. Redl, Fritz. "What Do Children Expect of Teachers?" Address to the Bank Street College of Education. New York, N. Y., 1955.
13. Skinner, B. F. *Verbal Behavior.* New York: Appleton-Century-Crofts, 1957.
14. ———. *Science and Human Behavior.* New York: Macmillan, 1953.
15. Stanton, A. H., and Schwartz, M. S. *The Mental Hospital.* New York: Basic Books, 1954.
16. Szasz, Thomas. "Bootlegging Humanistic Values Through Psychiatry," *Antioch Rev., 22,* 341–49.
17. ———. *The Myth of Mental Illness.* New York: Harper & Row, 1961.
18. Torrance, E. Paul. *Explorations in Creative Thinking in the Early School Years.* Minneapolis: Bureau of Educ. Res., University of Minnesota, 1959.
19. Wrenn, C. Gilbert. "Editorial Comment," *J. Counsel. Psych.,* 1958, *5,* 242.

DAN C. LORTIE

Administrator, Advocate, or Therapist? Alternatives for Professionalization in School Counseling

THESE ARE DAYS of high excitement for those engaged in school counseling. A new recognition of the import of counseling services prevails: extensive assistance to guidance is a significant feature of the National Defense Education Act, strong endorsement for increased counseling service occurs in that potent source of legitimation, the Conant Reports, and programs directed toward assisting the urban disadvantaged—programs of increasing moment—place heavy emphasis on augmented guidance activities. Small wonder that members of the counseling field show heightened self-awareness and concern for their occupation and its future. Small wonder that counseling leadership seeks to seize the moment to attain professional status for their timely work.

The sociologist who is invited to comment on these trends is likely to find himself, like the late arrival at a lively party, in a somewhat ambiguous situation. He can, of course, jump in and join the festivities, but this line of action contributes no special benefit. Yet should he stand aside, calm and detached, his sobriety may simply inhibit the vitality of others. Permit me to make one point early in the hope that subsequent observations will not appear to be anticonvivial. The continued development of counseling services is, in my opinion, crucial in the construction of a more specialized, rational order in the public schools—a kind of order which will be more and more necessary in the years ahead. The issues involved in refining counseling activities are too critical to set aside; of the questions pressing for scrutiny, few are more urgent than the professionalization of school counseling.

To professionalize an occupation is to crystallize it in specific, formal, and even rigid ways. Careless decisions can "freeze" inappropriate solutions to problems in organizing a complex field of work. Serious risks are involved—an inadequate structure can result in the unwitting sabotage of earnestly sought goals. Counselors could, in short, organize their work in such a way that future years will see them doing things they never intended in ways they never planned.

Indications are that guidance does face serious problems in professionalization. McCully, in a review of major writers in the field, can find no consensus on what are the essential and primary services offered by counselors.[1] In the pages that follow I shall argue that without such a consensus—without a clear image of core services and skills—effective professionalization of guidance will not occur. I shall attempt to demonstrate that the current position of the counselor contains diverse, contradictory functions and that members of the occupation will be forced to resolve thorny issues in moving toward the professional model of work organization. The analysis, however, is not exhaustive; logical rather than empirical, it seeks to isolate issues which require attention from the professional group. It should become clear, however, that resolution of these issues will require extensive and thorough research into the current work reality of counselors and others working in schools. I hope that the ideas put forth here will prove to be hypotheses capable of empirical confirmation, rejection, or amplification.

I

To make a profession of an occupation requires monumental efforts of those so committed.[2] It calls for the development and diffusion of

[1] C. Harold McCully, "The School Counselor: Strategy for Professionalization," *Personnel and Guidance Journal*, April, 1962.

[2] Although there is no one definition of profession which is commonly accepted, certain elements found in established professions can be used effectively in analysis of the process of professionalization. Good illustrations can be found in Myron Leiberman's *Education as a Profession* (Englewood Cliffs, N. J.: Prentice-Hall, Inc., 1956) and Howard S. Becker's "The Nature of a Profession," in Nelson B. Henry (Ed.), *Education for the Professions,* The Sixty-first Yearbook of the National Society for the Study of Education, chap. ii (University of Chicago Press, 1962).

collective beliefs, it involves patterning relationships the practitioners will have with persons inside and outside the profession, and it permeates the personalities of members of the colleague group. It is, in fact, the construction of a subsociety within the larger community, for it features a unique culture, peculiar modes of interaction, and an apparatus for the socialization of would-be members. Some of this effort is informal and emerges spontaneously in the course of day-to-day activities, but an enterprise of such scope also requires formal political work—a working constitution must be hammered out. Constitution-making is a sequential process in which alternatives which are selected early constrain later decisions; the cumulative effect is not only something new and unique but a structure in which many logical alternatives have been ruled out. In a sense, we can describe professionalization as a "narrowing" process—a narrowing process, however, which rests on basic agreements hacked out over the years.

Although we cannot engage in a complete analysis of professionalization processes here, we can illustrate some of the typical mechanisms by a brief review of three problems which face every profession. (1) Who will be admitted for training? (2) How will candidates be prepared for practice? and (3) How can members of the profession be induced to comply with its standards of conduct? The answers selected to these questions become the structure within which individuals are shaped to the professional ideal. Conversely, perhaps without awareness, the answers chosen reflect the group's conception of what its members seek to become.

Modern professions must come to terms with the university system, and the latter has much to do with the answers given to the admission question. The casual entry of an earlier era gives way to a controlled, single route of specific educational requirements which frequently imply allied characteristics. The age of entrants, for example, usually goes down, for university regulations and/or facilities frequently proscribe participation in later periods of the life cycle. Beginners are truly beginners who come to the field without previous experience and specific commitments to given ways of doing things. The newly formalized requirements are usually longer, and greater time demands increase the direct costs of education and such indirect costs as income foregone; the social class background of students, often linked to financial resources, may change as a result. The sex balance of the occupation may shift as rigidly specified training makes it more difficult for women to combine the career with family responsibilities. Thus does insistence on new academic qualifications introduce social homogeneity that was absent before the new requirements; unintended but significant consequences can flow from any one of these alterations in the social composition of entrants to the field.

Occupational leaders find that as they construct a system of professional preparation, many difficult issues require resolution. What should the balance be, for example, between scientific and intuitive components in the curriculum? If fact, what sciences are relevant to their profession? In assessing a given candidate, how should they weigh his demonstration of practical skills versus his performance in academic work? How do they test those elusive personality characteristics they feel are so important in practice? Those preparing professionals seem almost compelled to find standard answers to such questions and to apply them to institution after institution; perhaps this drive for standardization stems from the professional's insistence that his special preparation is so significant—it is chiefly the training, after all, which separates the legitimate practitioner from the quack. Established professions have, however, managed to develop complex curricula featuring a surprising amount of internal consistency, of unity in socialization experiences. But such a standardization is possible, after all, where there is consensus on what the practitioner should do and how he should do it. Where the image of the practitioner's future work is diffuse or ambiguous or controversial, educators and senior practitioners have no criteria to assist them in arbitrating the many decisions they must make in building a system of professional preparation. Not knowing what kind of man they wish to produce, they cannot design a program with repetitive, consistent experiences intended to personify the professional ideal; lacking just such a unifying theme, the impact of their program is never quite strong enough.

Inducements for compliance in the established professions are many and subtle, and they range from the internalization of ethical principles ("professional conscience") to controls built right into the career system and the distribution of rewards. Law and medicine, for example, test the young practitioner's technical competence and moral qualities at crucial points in the career—professional success is gained or lost largely in the context of colleague judgments.[3] A long period of socialization follows the university period—young doctors and

---

[3] For medicine, see Oswald Hall, "The Stages of a Medical Career," *American Journal of Sociology*, LIII (March, 1948), 327–36. For law, see Dan C. Lortie, "Laymen to Lawmen: Law School, Careers and Professional Socialization," *Harvard Educational Review*, XXIX, 4 (Fall, 1959).

lawyers learn much, technically and otherwise, from the senior colleagues who oversee their early years in practice. This system of instruction, however, rests upon the consensus felt by those who rule the profession and influence the fates of young aspirants to high position. It also requires a highly effective system of communication to implement the values which underlie the judgments and influence the allocation of money, prestige and power rewards. The system defines who is in and who is outside the professional group; one knows, in short, who one's colleagues are.

This brief discussion may suggest some of the complexity connected with answering the questions cited earlier—the questions of entry, preparation and control which face every group seeking professional status. Many specific questions and issues must be resolved and similar answers adopted by members of the professional group; adoption implies a willingness to accept rules of the game which affect one's career and life fate. The group must agree on what is important to do and how it should be done in specific terms.

Where does school counseling stand in regard to these problems of professionalization? The current role of the counselor combines several different functions which are difficult to project into a unitary professional model. We shall examine the counselor's role in terms of three clusters of tasks which focus on different functions within the school's social organization. Scrutinizing each in turn (we shall begin with administrative functions in the counselor's role), we shall find that selection of any one of the three components as the core would lead in a different direction and would result in a distinctive type of professionalization.

II

The duties of guidance counselors generally include some activities which are administrative in function. Among these are situations where counselors route students to specific teachers or specific departments of the school. In so doing, they are performing an important executive function—using Parsons' phrase, they are allocating primary materials.[4] Few matters influence a teacher's work or a department's status more deeply than the operation of the assignment system. Such decisions, by exerting an important influence on the technical level of

---

[4] Talcott Parsons, "Some Ingredients of a Theory of Formal Organization," in Andrew W. Halpin (ed.), *Administrative Theory in Education* (Chicago: Midwest Administration Center, University of Chicago, 1958).

work, are clearly managerial in nature, and since they require choices among members of that level, they must be made by persons either above it or apart from it. The counselor's decisions, unlike those made by most administrators, may be accompanied by esoteric techniques and special psychological knowledge, but the *functions* of such decisions, from the organizational point of view, are essentially administrative in nature.

Counselors may also engage in another administrative activity of some consequence—the maintenance of the school's system of order and discipline. The counselor who works with "behavior problems" referred by teachers and principal deals with an individual at any given moment; in acting with a succession of deviations from the school's normative order, however, counselors give that cultural system significant support. The techniques used do not matter very much; strong sanctions or subtle suasion, the ends served are the same. To uphold the school's norms is more than a simple police function. Problem behavior and its control invariably raise judicial issues, and judicial decision-making requires the counselor to diagnose the likely effects of alternative decisions not only on the child but on the school as an organization. Continued concern with the viability of the organization is executive's work.

Schools and counselors differ in the importance they attach to these and other administrative aspects of the counselor's role. Some school districts, for example, consider the counselor's position the first rung on the administrative ladder; in these schools, the counselor is an administrator-in-training. (We find the same thing in some colleges and universities where the dean of students position is clearly linked with an administrative career.) Although many counselors may scorn the "administrative trivia" of their jobs, some spokesmen for guidance assign great weight to the administrative function. Shoben, for example, advocates a position for the counselor akin to that of the pathologist checking the surgeon's work, for the implementation of his suggestions would require the counselor to report, and therefore appraise, the effect of teachers and others on the climate of the school.[5] The Michael and Meyerson viewpoint is more dramatically administrative, for their depiction of the counselor as a master pedagogical engineer leaves administrators little by way of educational leadership in the school.[6] Administrative functions are more than accidental elements

[5] See pp. 110–26.
[6] See pp. 24–48.

in the counselor's role if school systems and professional spokesmen are prepared to give administration the central place in guidance work.

It seems reasonable, in light of what we know about men and their work, to expect that a man's outlook will be heavily influenced by the repetitive problems and interactions he encounters on a day-to-day basis.[7] Much time spent in allocating students, for example, could lead to preoccupation with balancing the often conflicting values of fairness-justice and individual appropriateness. The assignment of students to a vocational program versus a college preparatory course, for example, is not a private affair—it involves the vital interests of students, their families, local employers, colleges, etc. The public nature of these decisions increases the decision-maker's concern with their legitimation and the result is that he places greater reliance on "objective" indicators of capability, interest and the like. Since such modes of thought require categories (bright versus dull, high versus low motivation, etc.), the counselor, no matter how profound his dedication to individuals, must constantly classify individual students into relevant groups. Such categorical considerations, although intended to clarify single decisions, introduce their own constraints. Once used and announced, any objective basis for allocation may be cited by others as justifying a similar decision. Willy-nilly, the counselor finds himself enmeshed in a round of precedents and judicial decisions; his actions, far from being free in each new instance, are constrained by an ever more complex set of policies and rules.

The counselor can become a man deeply committed to solving a recurrent series of complicated interpersonal as well as individual problems. As is true of the general school administrator, the counselor finds that he must become skilled in suggesting as well as in implementing policy and that he acts for the organization as it classifies and routes students into potentially different life careers. In all these matters, he must heed his official position, the wishes of legal superiors and the consequences decisions may have for the organization's ability to help future students. He is not only, as an employee, committed to working toward the goals of the organization, but his tasks make it difficult for him to deviate from the organization's means for meeting those goals. The counselor who allocates students has a relationship

---

[7] This assertion has, of course, become a central thesis of the sociology of work. Perhaps the most significant article in granting it formal attention was that written some years ago by Everett C. Hughes—"Institutional Office and the Person," *American Journal of Sociology*, XLIII (November, 1937), 404–13.

to the individual student which is not a pure dyadic transaction free of other entanglements. It must be filtered through a complex set of policies, relationships to various publics and organizational loyalties.

Protracted engagement in the work of order maintenance is also likely to lead to preoccupation with administrative issues. In this instance, the goals and means of the organization are especially important—the counselor is acting to protect them, in fact, against the incursions of deviating students. It need not be true that the organization's interests and those of the student be always in conflict for this to be problematic; it is enough that where such a conflict arises, the counselor cannot disregard established school ways. The latter alternative is frequently ruled out by considerations of justice or expediency stemming from the visibility of disciplinary decisions. Furthermore, those responsible for upholding any established order sense the need for some minimum predictability in its rules if those rules are to have validity. School counselors know full well that continued "bending" of established school rules will, after a period of time, undermine the very relevance of the rule system. The law may need changing, but until changed, it is the law.

How would counseling be effective were it to professionalize around such administrative functions? This definition of the role would, of course, fix it clearly as an official position—it would place counselors as specialized administrators, sub-officials within the school hierarchy. Their special expertise might include such unique knowledge as recent advances in psychology and measurement and peculiar skills (diagnosis, test administration and interpretation, the psychology of persuasion, etc.). The work, however, would not feature unique ends for the counselor's proximate goals would not differ, in any appreciable way, from those of other functionaries in the school system. As with other administrators, one would expect him to demonstrate his loyalty to the organization by showing enthusiasm for its goals and respect for its ways. He would act inappropriately were he to put a personal conception of counseling (or one asserted primarily by the professional colleague group outside the organization) ahead of established school policy. He would, of course, work for changes he considered desirable, but at any given moment, his decision would necessarily flow from pre-existing policy.

Research might reveal that counselors engaged in administrative functions vary in their relationships with general administrators and teachers, but I believe that priority to this function necessarily involves distance in the counselor's interactions with students. The student, at least the perceptive student, will recognize the role the counselor plays and his possession of power to affect him, the student; rational behavior on his part, therefore, would dictate caution in relating to the counselor. (Where a student has a clear and specific purpose, in fact, rationality would include efforts to manipulate the counselor to assist in realization of that purpose.) The shrewd student would, at the very least, seek to make a "good impression" on the counselor, and such an orientation would generally discourage revelatory outbursts which might put him in an unfavorable light and tarnish the image he is attempting to project. The counselor, for his part, could not adopt the nonjudgmental stance recommended for therapists. As a school official charged with implementing specific policies, he could only pretend to no prior commitments were he willing to engage in hypocrisy. Holding power and authority, he would find it impossible to be "buddy" and "boss" simultaneously. Counselors playing administrative roles no doubt differ in some of the ways in which they interact with students, but like all who possess power, they sooner or later know the toughness of the boundary which separates those on different sides of an authority relationship.

Some may question the usefulness of counseling if it is primarily administrative in nature—why differentiate it at all under these circumstances? There is at least one answer to this query, although that answer does not dictate, in any way, the choice counselors should make in the years ahead. There seems little doubt that the advance of school administration will require some effective link to the world of applied psychology and will need persons skilled in the use of such knowledge in those areas where it is most relevant. Someone, no doubt, will play this role if school counselors do not; schools will not be able to ignore a large and important area of substantive knowledge in making rational provision for allocation, order maintenance and allied matters. Those leading guidance may or may not choose to organize the field around administrative core tasks. Whatever their decision, there is a positive contribution of specialized knowledge and ability that rests in the application of modern psychology to the governance of public schools.

III

Wrenn and others have remarked that counselors currently perform many administrative and clerical duties.[8] Yet we know better than to leap from this fact to the conclusion that the counselor's role

[8] McCully, *op. cit.*

is identical with that of the principal or any school official. Among the special attributes of the counselor's role is the private nature of his relationship with students and the dyadic setting within which it takes place; although the outcomes can be highly visible, the processes usually take place under conditions of greater privacy than found in principal or teacher dealings with students. Teachers may employ the rhetoric of individual instruction, but the ecology of their work offers them small opportunity for private interaction with students. Principals may see students privately, but the context is usually special and often involves "trouble." The counselor, however, routinely spends many hours in face-to-face conversation with students. The regularity of these private encounters has important repercussions for his role and could lead to a definition quite distinct from that we have been examining.

No social system works perfectly—all, to at least some extent, sacrifice individual interests in the operation of the whole. Schools are no exception, and as quasi-bureaucracies they promulgate and enforce rules which do not always fit the individual's needs. The privacy and access which the counselor has in relating to students make it likely that he will become aware of such disjunctions more frequently than will other professionals in the school. In fact, the counselor's job title encourages students to define him as the logical person to hear their dissatisfactions. Undistracted by thirty other students needing attention, the counselor can more readily react by empathizing with the student before him; furthermore, counseling, as a position, probably attracts more persons who wish to "help" individuals than does teaching or administration. This combination of factors—privacy, dyadic relationships, students frustrated by the organization, and counselors oriented to helping youngsters—can readily lead to counselor identification with beleaguered students. Such identification, were it to occur on a large scale, could bring about another logically possible formulation of the counselor role. Lacking a prior term, I shall call this function "advocacy."

The counselor who acts as advocate (specifically, as defendant's attorney) treats a given substantive complaint presented by a student as a serious matter. Where convinced that the complaint is valid, his inclination is to act, to press for a change in the situation which is problematic for the student. His eye is on reality problems, not on the emotional turbulence and distorted perceptions of the psychologically troubled student. Where this type of counselor finds a problem needing action, he is willing "to go to bat" for the student even where such attention might cause embarrassment to other professionals in the school. Although he needs and uses diagnostic skills in discerning valid from invalid complaints (in terms of *his* criteria), his is not the therapist's stance. His interest is in helping individual students cope effectively with the sometimes impersonal juggernaut of the school.

Significant changes in the organization of our schools would be necessary before the advocate function could become the central activity of school counselors. Though current role arrangements may permit the counselor to "battle" for some individual students, there is little evidence that regular conflict of this kind has become institutionalized in our school structure. If counselors are to engage in strenuous, prolonged advocacy in the interests of individual students, they will need protection to do so and a clear set of rules guiding their behavior and that of those with whom they debate. Fighting the cause of the individual student could easily put the counselor in direct conflict with administrators and teachers. He would need a special "license" to perform this function, a license which defined his actions as professional, not personal, and which made it clear that he was not attacking the solidarity of the professional group. Mechanisms would have to be developed which placed the counselor as a loyal member of the group justifiably engaged in opposition.[9]

Counseling organized around advocacy would not resemble the administrative formulation or, as indicated, the therapist conception. Persons engaged in this kind of role would, we imagine, begin to look like lawyers and stress the skills of pleading and analysis; we might even see the emergence of a kind of administrative law system in schools with formal arrangements for dispensing justice and arbitrating issues. Advocate counselors would probably emphasize such values as humanism, individualism, and concern themselves deeply with "the good of the child." One suspects they would leave to others such matters as the integrity of the organization and the logics of cost and efficiency. This kind of specialization, in other words, would in-

---

[9] There are promising opportunities here for research on the current situation. On what occasions do counselors stand ready to "go out on a limb" for a student? Do some counselors occupy a position which permits them to play the advocacy role regularly? If yes, what are the bases on which this position has been built? Are counselors who incline to this formulation different in personality terms; for example, are they more generally rebellious than those who have little interest in advocacy function? These and many other questions need answering before we can assess the force behind this particular formulation of the guidance role.

clude moral as well as technical specialization. The drive underlying the role would be the *relevant* treatment of the individual child, and the school would be held accountable for the human implications of its general procedures, rules and policies. Nor is the stance that of the therapist who, in helping the student work through his problems, locates the problem as something within the student. To the advocate counselor, reality *is* a problem and students have the right to skilled intervention and support in getting the treatment most appropriate for them. The curriculum or the schedule—even an individual teacher—can be wrong.

We can speculate that were counseling to move in this direction, different skills and values would emerge to dominate the profession. Forensic abilities, the preparation of a "brief," skill in discriminating between neurotic and realistic complaints—these would probably emerge as valued abilities among such counselors. One would also expect counselors to develop an ideology consistent with their function—a set of beliefs stressing, in this instance, the importance of offsetting bureaucratic and standardizing forces in our schools. Research might center on such issues as how situational factors inhibit or encourage learning and personal growth, and on how individual variations affect response to different educational structures. The core ethic of this type of counselor would be one which placed clear priority on the responsibility of the counselor for the individual child.

Answers would have to be found for many complicated questions were counselors to move toward this conceptualization of their mission. What norms, for example, should govern the relationship between the counselor and the student he decides to assist? What powers, if any, should counselors be given to right wrongs they uncover? Should counselors intervene in family matters? If so, in what ways do their responsibilities differ from school social workers'? To simply list these questions dramatizes the complexity involved in moving to this definition of the counselor's role. Yet one can question very seriously whether American schools can make good on their affirmations of individualism in the years ahead unless specific arrangements are made to defend the individual student against powerful bureaucratizing forces. Will counselors be the ones to seize this responsibility as their core task?

IV

Those expert in the art and science of psychotherapy agree on the importance of the therapist-client relationship in influencing the outcome of the therapeutic transaction. Such authorities maintain that the client must be able to extend full and unquestioning trust in the integrity and ultimate sympathy of the counselor, and that the establishment of this trust is a primary task confronting the therapist. Yet few authors raise questions about the sociological context necessary for achieving this kind of relationship, for most discussions focus on the counselor's obligations to win trust without serious analysis of the constraints which can act on him from his broader role commitments. Imagine, however, the likelihood that a student called by the counselor for disciplining will perceive the complete absence of "explicit or implicit disapproval" stressed by van Kaam.[10] What chance does the counselor have to convey the "warm and acceptant" feelings emphasized by Rogers where he is tightly bound by pre-existing policies which he must implement?[11] We know intuitively the impossibility of these juxtapositions; yet we often ignore the situational and role prerequisites to effective psychotherapy.

It is clear that the trust relationship rests upon the client's feeling that his interests will come first, and that he is free, as client, to explore a variety of alternative actions, emotions, etc. without excessive moral constraint emanating from the therapist. (Some moral constraints will, of course, always exist.) Specifically, the client must never feel that the solutions he considers and assesses in association with the therapist will be screened in terms of unique organizational requirements. The therapist must be able to convince the client, legitimately, that he is assisting him and placing his interests before that of an employer or school official or court.[12]

The therapist must also be free to follow the client's total interests and be in a position to explore many facets of his total life situation. Schools, for example, generally treat youngsters in their charge in terms of a specific status—that of "student." The existence of the latter status, paired as it is with several counter-statuses, limits the nature, extent and expression of interest school personnel show the

10 See pp. 66–81.

11 See pp. 49–65.

12 When the counselor "counsels" a student he may be doing, as I see it, one of three things. He may be giving him information about the school and its operations—this is essentially an instructional function and does not differentiate the counselor from the teacher. He may, as discussed in our review of the administrative function, be directing the student in ways congruent with the organizational plan—this is clearly administrative. Therapy would presumably include all situations where the counselor seeks to improve the student's capacity to deal with problems which occur in his life space—the end goal is, in this instance, increased psychological capacity on the part of the student.

individual youngster. But no troubled young person is ever, in his eyes, solely a student in School X—he possesses other statuses, crucial affiliations and concerns which transcend one particular organization. The person who would, through therapy, seek to help him explore and understand his world must be willing to accompany him down many paths which lead away from his school experience. An externally imposed definition of psychological problems into "educational" or "noneducational" is hardly likely to coincide with the actuality of the youngster's inner experience—the therapist, in sum, must interact with the student as a total person.

This double imperative of therapy—the necessity to give priority to client interests and the need to relate to him in a total way—makes it extremely difficult to incorporate the therapeutic relationship into a preexisting hierarchy of authority and formal status. Inasmuch as the therapist must enforce even limited aspects of the organization's special expectations, he cannot be certain to place the interests of the client first. Inasmuch as the therapist must limit his relationship to predesignated spheres of life, be they work, study or citizenship, he cannot engage himself with the object of his help as a whole person; yet to show interest in all relevant spheres of the client's life is to create suspicion that the organization is overreaching its boundaries. Almost all therapeutic relationships outside of mental institutions are *separated* from other critical facets of the person's round. Individual psychotherapy is, as well, frequently mediated by a fee-for-service arrangement which dramatizes the professional-client relationship, but even where the service is provided in a publicly supported clinic, the actual therapy is conducted in a physically isolated setting and with no regular communication channels to other persons who figure prominently in the client's life. These structural arrangements are, it seems, not accidental—they relate closely to the double imperative we have examined.

What would be involved in establishing counseling in schools as essentially psychotherapeutic in nature? The counselor would have to be relieved of all administrative and semiadministrative responsibilities, and special mechanisms would be necessary to clarify his lack of organizational authority; he could not, as we noted earlier, expect full trust and revelatory behavior from students who perceived him as a person with influence over their daily school life. The counselor would have to show an interest in many sides of the student's life which are not currently part of the school's mandate. Nor would student expectations which are consistent with the therapist's stance accord with those sought by the advocate counselor. One wonders, in fact, just how he could be placed in the school's regular social structure since the usual ties and obligations of a school professional have disruptive potential for his therapeutic work. The problematic nature of his role would place him under a particular strain to justify his location in the school—he would be asked what he does in school that he could not do as well outside it.

To institutionalize therapy as the core function of the school counselor would require differentiation of his role from that of others engaged in psychotherapeutic activities. Organizationally, one would expect school boards and top administrators to resist the therapeutic emphasis if it involved what they perceived as a major change in the overall function of the school. Creating a new profession of school counseling based on therapy would also be difficult if close examination revealed that school counselors feature the same skills, knowledge and social relationships needed in already established psychotherapeutic fields. Can school counselors develop a new and special conception of therapy which is clearly suited to the school situation and requires the location of the therapist on site?

Our era is one marked by a new realization of the significance of mental health among children as well as among adults. It is ironic that of the three functions we have examined, the psychotherapeutic formulation of the counselor's role would require the most extensive redefinition of that role and, indeed, of the mandate and organization of our public schools.

V

Selection of any one of the three functions we have reviewed as the core activity of school counselors would result in a different profession. Entry arrangements, professional training and career system would differ for administrative, advocate and therapist types of counseling. Guidance based on the administrative function, for example, would probably feature relatively late entry (our tests for leadership potential are not yet good enough to stand in for demonstrated capacity), a curriculum largely similar to that used in preparing school administrators and a career line which could logically terminate in the superintendency.

The preparation of advocates and therapists, however, would call for different persons to start with and different curricula in their training. Recruiting advocates would be challenging, as it would require persons with unusual intellectual abilities, commitment to individualistic values and the personality which would lead to effective work under conflict situations. Furthermore, a new career line would have to be developed to reward the core values of this new profession. But the recruitment, training and career routing of therapists, unless a new and profound differentiation of school therapy emerges, would be based on patterns already worked out in clinical psychology, psychiatry and social work. Three different central functions would require three different sets of answers to questions facing all new professions.

If one major value of the writer underlies this discussion, that value is the belief that counselors should select the function, or functions, they wish to serve and build a structure appropriate to it or to them. There is a genuine risk that if they fail to do so, structural decisions (e.g., admission requirements, educational programs, job organization, etc.) will coerce functional outcomes. Counselors might, for example, recruit new members primarily from those established as teachers only to find that prior socialization makes it impossible to move toward an advocate or therapeutic definition of the role. On the other hand, university curricula might produce graduates imbued with an advocacy mission but no school in which to express it. In social affairs, function *can* follow structure.

The decisions facing counselors are difficult, manifold and time-consuming. As leaders toward a more refined and rich division of labor in schools, it is my hope that they will persist in efforts to find the set of duties which makes the maximum contribution of which they are capable. This will, I believe, require extended study and analysis not only of counseling but of other functions and groups within schools; counselors are not the only persons in schools who, concerned with their status, are considering important changes. We need thoughtful estimates of what services will be critical in the future and close analysis of the interlocking relationships of counselors and teachers and social workers and assistant principals. We will need much careful work, protracted discussion and, I suspect, considerable good will on the part of all if a more effective organization of our schools is to emerge.

Counselors must ask themselves what services they can best perform over the years ahead. Thorough and sensitive research, coupled with frank, widespread discussion, is the only strategy that I can visualize which will lead to a reasonably harmonious and rational division of labor in our public schools. If school counselors wish to play a vital part in that emerging order, they had best heed Robert Park's advice to another occupation and find their craft before they build their profession.

Guidance in the University Setting

GUIDANCE PERSONNEL IN HIGHER EDUCATION need to be especially perceptive about the environment in which they are working as well as about the special problems faced by individuals in this environment. Theory, however, has not emphasized the relationship between the intra-personal stages of development, and the distinctive institutional qualities of the environment in which an individual is located during a particular period in his life. In this article, I would like to focus on two important problems that arise from this relationship. One is the effect on student development of having a certain status in the social system of the university-college; in this instance, the status of academic averageness. The other is the basis of decision making, which here involves the choice of a major field. In this discussion the major ideas will be documented with quotations taken from interviews with graduates of Harvard College.

In every institution, there are values that provide general standards against which the student rebels or to which he tries to conform. Individual freedom and intellectual excellence are values basic to educational environments such as Harvard's. This college proclaims to its students: "Think as you will, but think. Hold to your own opinion; just be sure you have reasons for it." Such words exert an undeniable charm, and not only on the seventeen or eighteen year old. Harvard is successful in bringing its student population to an acceptance of the validity of its ethic because its demands are such that few men could resist them—be independent, be an individual, be free, think for yourself. Such an ethic has a basic appeal that only the rare adolescent would want to reject. These are values that in essence are most championed by young people, and would most enlist the sympathies of young men at the brink of adulthood, embarking on lives of their own, and ready to reduce their dependence upon the emotional and physical sustenance of their families.

We know that students bring varying degrees of readiness for meeting and resolving successfully what can often seem to be the brutal demands of an independence which has been thrust upon them. If a man were asked whether or not he would *accept* such responsibilities, can we doubt his reply? The student with any pride and personal integrity would feel forced to choose independence over dependence, freedom over restriction. As abstract standards, such values appeal to youth more than do most others.

As I describe the effects of an academically average status, I think it will become clear that the prevailing values at Harvard are accepted by the undergraduate population. Students who did not accept a value system encompassing excellence and achievement, would not feel so acutely the pressures of the environment and would not express as pointedly as they do the impact of an average position. This is an important point, for the more academically able student populations become, the greater will be the students' desire to conform to such expectations, and in round-robin fashion the more able the student body, the more the institution will stress freedom and independence.

Yet it can be very difficult for the freshman in the modern university-college to abstract personal resourcefulness from such an ethic. This the ethic is supposed to create, by forcing the man to realize his own possibilities, and what one graduate called "realization that one may do with oneself what one will." Such resourcefulness is often difficult during the period when isolation and independence are most threatening and most difficult to control. Coupling with this what I found to be the most serious deterrent to the student's satisfactory acclimatization into the college community—the academic ranking he achieved in an environment stressing excellence of scholarly achievement—we begin to recognize the dilemmas created for all but the ablest of students. Further, the academic press of educational climates is not going to ease off in the decade ahead. It is, rather, increasing rapidly in this era of selectivity in college admissions and of serious and concerted emphasis on academic programs.

This past summer I spent a good deal of time mulling over the problem of selectivity with admissions officers from as diverse a set of colleges as exist in the spectrum of higher education. These men and women, attending the Harvard Summer Institute on College Admissions which I was directing, seemed, when speaking of the problem of selectivity, consistently to be referring to their college's attempts to up-grade the bottom half of the student population to the ability level of the top half. In other words, colleges would like to be selective in the sense of excluding those students who now fill the bottom half of their classes. When we think of selectivity we seem universally to focus on only one criterion, the criterion of academic ability. This, of course, reflects the emphasis in American higher education at this point in our history.

As colleges and universities emphasize academic excellence they become obliged to recognize the special psycho-social problems of an academically oriented student population and especially, as I am stressing here, the concomitants of academic averageness. Such problems arise out of student attitudes, affecting their interaction with the college environment. We know that with the increased academic ability and orientation of our students, there is more of a student attempt actually to meet and master the kinds of course material with which they are presented.

Because a student population is more able does not mean that the faculty markedly increases the number of high grades. Thus, competition becomes stiffer, and pressures increase on students who accept more seriously the goals of academic success and take mediocrity and failure more to heart. An extreme example of this was found in a study done at MIT.[1] In this institution, where the main value of the environment is academic excellence and where this is about the only area for achievement and outstanding performance, students below the top decile in grade ranking feel they are failures. Adding to the increased competitiveness of such environments as Harvard's and MIT's, is the fact that far more students now feel they have to maintain high grade averages in view of the later competition they will meet in seeking admission to graduate schools.

Just what kind of reaction to their academic status do we find in men who were finding themselves "average," often for the first time in their school careers? To what degree was this something of concern to the student himself? In an environment as competitive intellectually as Harvard, averageness can consign the student to his own sense of mediocrity, and sometimes to a status where he can justify his anonym-

[1] *MIT Observer*, VIII, 1 (October, 1961), 1–4.

ity by looking at the other hundreds like him who are just "numbers on an examination paper." To quote directly from the interview material:

> I'm afraid I didn't encourage contact (with the tutors). I did not try to seek out people to talk with very much, perhaps scared away because they were usually surrounded with some people who appeared to me to be better than I and I didn't want to appear . . . second rate to (the House Master) or some other (tutors) in the House.

> I think I was a little afraid of (faculty) and a little unsure of my own ability. I think I had the feeling during a good part of my education . . . that I was intellectually inadequate as compared with many of the students among my fellow classmates. . . .

My interview samples came from two Harvard classes. It is interesting that the class which had been away from the college environment for five years showed less vehemence in their remarks about the average status than did the more recent class. Their increasingly higher secondary school ranking, as a group, when they entered Harvard, caused our more recent graduates to find this transition to average ranking even more jolting than did classes of several years ago. They were appalled to discover half the class more able than they.

> I think that one of the shocking things is having to realize . . . there are at least 500 people better than I am. . . . I knew they were pretty good, but I didn't know that they were that good. . . . I took the coward's way out. I decided I can't get A's, there is no disgrace in getting B's. Do the best I can and not worry about what the other guy is doing. . . . During my sophomore and junior years, I went into sort of a depression, not feeling myself adequate for the university . . . it wasn't until about the middle of my junior year . . . that I realized well, gee, I'm not such a clod after all.

The shock of averageness was brought up spontaneously by graduates in the interview covering the college years, for it was their reaction to a high-powered environment. The impact of averageness (and its ramifications) emerged as the most significant deterrent to greater participation of this group in the intellectual life of a college. It accounted in large part for their feeling of inability either to overcome the perceived impersonality of a large university-college environment or to achieve recognition as individuals.

Any student confronting a college setting such as Harvard's is indeed being dunked into the "cold bath" of intellectual reality and

forced to "sink or swim." We can talk all we like about the reinforcement to personal effort that a college environment, as a fairly controlled and discrete society, affords the student. But when the very
values esteemed by that society are freedom, independence, and excellence, the society itself provides rewards and bulwarks at a rather
abstract level, not at the functioning day-to-day level where comfort
is needed, but not usually found.

Here are the words of an academically average man from a recent
graduating class. Just before his graduation he expressed his feelings
about his college experience: in them we have a particularly good
résumé of a student's impressions of the passage through college; here
is a man who pinpoints for us a whole constellation of thoughts,
feelings, and attitudes.

> Looking back on the freshman year, it seems like a nightmare. It
> was really very difficult. . . . Another thing that I found particularly
> difficult at that time, the fact that I couldn't find any adequate
> advice. . . . When I got in here, I was rather hostile. . . . Just coming
> out of high school [it] is strictly your family life which I feel per-
> vades your particular outlook. Someone would possibly advise you
> from now till doomsday, unless you learn these things on your own,
> you would not take his advice . . . possibly you could have the stu-
> dent accept the advice if it were explained to him and also some
> understanding of himself as an individual . . . of course, it is a
> function of your education to get a better understanding of yourself.
> But after two years have gone by, it is a shame to waste those first
> two years. . . . I realize that it does sound rather difficult even as I
> speak about it—understanding in an individual, especially in his
> freshman year. But I feel something should be started then, and that
> it is at that point that a person needs his strongest advice. . . . You
> bring the students that we have here at the college and stick them
> together. There is such a vast difference that you begin to feel your
> way and find where you belong and this can really throw you about
> in here. You see that your way of life isn't the only one . . . when you
> come here you find different ways of doing (things) and it can
> really bat you about for a while and as you pick up an understanding
> of it, you can see. But if you never pick up this understanding and
> you never realize that there are other things and how they came
> about, then it can completely destroy you.

For some students such as this man, the difficulty, the traumatic
aspects of the freshman year, are fully as frightful as a "nightmare."
Attributes of the large university-college environment are defined as

coldness, independence, being thrown on individual resources. Then he goes on to reveal to us that he has learned, in the four-year interim, to accept the independence and self-reliance that Harvard College expects of him: "Someone could advise you from now to doomsday, unless you learn these things on your own you would not take his advice." Unless—and here the student is voicing the kind of hopes he has assimilated as a liberally educated man—unless someone tried to explain a personal position from an intellectual, rational angle. But again he goes back to the fact that education should lead to understanding of oneself, and therefore, that the ultimate responsibility for self-realization can rest only on the individual.

This man beautifully expresses the process of education that is unquestionably dependent upon (but also, unquestionably more important than) specific course content, field of concentration, and the situations by which the college expressly attempts to educate. What he defines is the larger effect of education that will pervade the life style of the individual.

When we consider the impact of a university-college environment of freedom that must be tempered by personal discipline, we should keep in mind the extreme impressionability of the college student. In trying to understand what happens to the man in the college environment, this should never be far from our thoughts. It helps to explain just about every kind of reaction we encounter; and especially this reaction against the impersonality of an environment.

> . . . flashes of insight . . . new revelations . . . maybe this was what I was looking for. . . .

This could well be the universal cry of the adolescent on the brink of adulthood. Much has been written on the search for role, for identity, and for meaning in life by the college age group. One cannot search without some kind of open attitude, without a degree of vulnerability, without accompanying confusion. This search is not accountable to the formal situational learning process, but ultimately influences it and must be brought to some kind of culmination in goal-direction and in assimilation into the college culture. If not, the student will suffer so acutely from alienation and anomie that he will never be able to become sufficiently involved in his academic work to find valid meaning there.

I did find that contact with professor, tutor, and House Master was an important factor to these academically average men in developing a sense of personal direction. Yet the very status of "averageness" kept many of them, as students, from entering situations where such contact would be possible, and thus, kept them from finding the kind of guidance they were seeking.

In addition, the degree of impersonality they encounter in the environment can become an excuse in explaining to themselves why they are not "successes" in the terms most accepted by the college society—academic achievement. Since they are not receiving the rewards of the academic successes, they can say that it is this lack of direction and lack of personal understanding from authority figures that are in large part responsible for their position.

Certain programs and goals do assist in focusing undergraduate energy, however. Many of these men, for example, found that their senior year thesis—which is independent work supervised by a tutor, and which culminates in an honors degree—was the most challenging and rewarding experience of their college years.

In other words, the first step a college must make is to recognize that special problems exist for such students, and then to try to cope with these problems by tailoring programs to individuals, by stressing seminars, by setting up tutorials and by trying to bring the honors program to more and more of the undergraduates. These are ways Harvard has tried to make each student feel the college is concerned with the course of his education and with his status as an individual.

There is a real problem of personal identity for the "average" man. His is the struggle to emerge as an individual from the mass of students: he needs to become, in his own eyes, more than "a number on an examination paper." The struggle is the more pronounced because he is being subjected to the anxieties created by an education emphasizing a pluralistic view of the world.

Perhaps this also helps to explain why "average" students emphasize personal qualities. For one thing, the student in today's university learns that the world of intellectual endeavor is grounded in constantly shifting sands. Wholeness and permanence of idea are not the attributes of the modern world: to be able to withstand these assaults on stability, the student seeks integrity of personality.

If a student accepts the fact that he will seldom, if ever, arrive at an answer that cannot be modified he must then be able to trust in man's human nature. This is a major reason why the academically average student, forced to settle for a mediocre position in academic standing at a time in university history when there has never been a stronger emphasis on academic and intellectual excellence and achievement, looks so intently for faculty leadership in areas of personal quality and concern.[2]

Much of the theory and study in the clinical area adds to the insight we can gain from college students themselves. For example, Robert W. White has discussed the concept of competence in a manner that illuminates the psychological effects of the academically average status.

In discussing the limitations of the Freudian models of psychosexual stages of development and his concept of competence, he has stated:

> Since the adolescent is reaching adult size, strength, and mental development, the behavior in question lies in the realm of serious accomplishment—serious in the terms either of the youth culture or of adult society. I am referring to the adolescent equivalent of what Erikson calls a *sense of industry* in the latency period, and I see this problem as continuing rather more strongly after puberty than seems to be implied in Erikson's account. No doubt I bring to this judgment an occupational bias different from that of a therapist. My professional life is spent among late adolescents whose sexual problems and social relations have for the most part not overwhelmed them. We talk together about their plans for study, their abilities and limitations, their struggles with materials to be learned and skills to be attained, their occupational leanings, career plans, and concerns about modern society as the scene of their future endeavors. We talk, in other words, mostly about their competence, and I do not believe that understanding is fostered by interpreting these concerns too much as displacements of instinctual drives, defense mechanisms, or interpersonal relations. They are real.[3]

Few students come to Harvard without a sense of their own competence to perform well in an academic setting, but for a large portion of the population, this feeling of competence soon becomes qualified in the sense that the student cannot excel. Thus the sequence of development toward adult competence is retarded or, perhaps more accurately, blocked. If a student does not develop a sense of compe-

---

[2] The role of the faculty as seen by the average student was the subject of my article, "Encounters with Learning," *Harvard Educational Review*, XXX, 4 (Fall, 1960), 331–49.

[3] Robert W. White, "Competence and the Psychosexual Stages of Development," *Nebraska Symposium on Motivation*, 1960, p. 142.

tence in meeting the expectations of the institution, he obviously has added to his problems of resolving the search for identity in the adult, work-oriented world.

In much the same manner, choice of a college major, when not made from strength (as reflected in competence), emphasizes all the difficulties of the academically average position, since this is one of the crucial decisions the student must make.

The great hope in this area of concentration choice has long been differential prediction: through statistical analysis of aptitude and interest test scores, information would be provided to students and guidance personnel that would result in the most realistic and satisfying choice of major. Yet differential prediction has not really lived up to its billing. Is this perhaps because the real bases for making satisfying decisions are as dependent upon the personal experiences and encounters in the college setting that affect the psycho-social development of the student, as they are upon the predictions resulting from more objective measures of aptitude and interest?[4]

Hopefully, the college student develops not only interest in many fields of knowledge but also the ability to use his capacities in depth. This latter capability is put to the test in the mastering of a particular discipline. At many colleges, the program is set up so that late in the freshman year students elect a major field of study. They then go on to take a prescribed number of courses in this and, sometimes, related fields, completing their programs by satisfying distribution requirements or personal interest. It sounds straightforward and relatively uncomplicated on the surface, a rather clear progression from general studies to specialization. The student finds a field that attracts him and settles down to mastering it as best he can in three years of study.

Yet like all the decisions the "average" student must make in the large university-college, this is typically influenced by traces of

---

[4] Lee Cronbach in discussing differential aptitude tests pinpoints one of the major problems inherent in differential prediction when he states that "no ability save verbal or numerical affects many courses" (Lee J. Cronbach, *Essentials of Psychological Testing* [New York: Harper & Row, 1960], p. 279). So much of the ability necessary to be successful in an academic area is common to all academic work that success, consequently, can be as effectively predicted by the G(eneral) factor measures, such as verbal and quantitative, as by differential aptitude measures. For example, the correlations between grades in a field of study and aptitude test scores on corresponding tests, seldom exceed those between these grades and general measures of verbal and mathematical aptitude. While interest tests to date have offered more differential predictive effectiveness than aptitude tests, even these are more effective in predicting satisfaction with vocational choice than with college major.

disturbing or satisfying encounters, and by the necessity of reconciling what one can best do with what one most wishes to do.

> Well, I didn't intend to choose history. As I said, I started here . . . with the idea that I'd like to go into medicine, and that was fortunately taken out of my mind. . . . And so I don't know if that chemistry upset was my fault entirely or the Chemistry Department's fault, I have the feeling it's both. . . . I wanted to go into something that was, great admission, reasonably comfortable and not too hard and not too specialized so that you'd have to narrow yourself down into a field, where you would concentrate. . . . And history puts you in contact with all sorts of philosophies and fields and when you go into business or something . . . you don't say, I am majoring in geological engineering and you are obviously a geological engineer. You can keep as diverse as possible.

A majority of the men I interviewed chose a particular concentration for one of two reasons—as vocational preparation, or as a relatively safe anchoring place for the college years (courses in other fields having proven disastrous experiences). Where vocational goals were not an influencing factor, specific decisions often seemed the result of such random factors as having friends in the concentration, the chance encounter with a particular course, the influence of a professor who made a subject mean enough to merit further effort. Because the average student is not a star performer who earns high professional respect from the faculty, he is especially apt to stress the personal qualities of professors as the determiners of choice.

> I began as a history and science major. . . . In the middle of sophomore year I had Professor ——— in the Chemistry Department who I thought was a very fine scientist, but also a real humanitarian person, humanitarian type person. He was very kind. . . . I switched to chemistry then. I thought, well, the department has these kinds of men, well, I'll be very happy to stay in it.

Choice of concentration—one of the decisions that gives focus to college study—may be made by chance, or because it is a relatively safe or easy choice, or because the personality of the teacher is charismatic. In such cases where the impetus toward that discipline is essentially external rather than a commitment to the field as a body of knowledge, it is more natural (and helps us to understand) that the student continues to look for a stimulant extraneous to the material.

> I didn't start out with any concepts of what I wanted to do except to . . . possibly get my pre-med credits but then that fell by the way-

side in my second year. I just didn't have enough drive to do it. I
didn't give that much of a damn. I only entered into it because of
my old man. But then I floundered for, ah, from the latter half of my
second year . . . but by the third year I started to generate quite a
bit of interest in European history. . . . I don't know how I got into
it. . . . Maybe through Professor ———, maybe listening to him throw
the baloney around about it . . . and he livened it up for me.

We all, of course, have known what it is to be pricked by a number
of goads. Natural curiosity and desire to find solutions and answers to
problems are among our least selfish motives. The promise of personal
recognition or rewards offer more extraneous, and yet more self-
centered, motivations. By educating, we are ideally reducing the pre-
dominance of external motive in a student's desire to master his work,
and promoting an involvement in learning that no longer depends
upon external goads. This is among the most difficult of the aims of
education.

What does it mean to a man to be forced to choose concentration as
much from weakness as from strength? Reinforcing the effects of the
competitive climate, the averageness, and the sense of anonymity in
the academic community, would be failure to handle successfully the
courses in one's concentration. The necessity to admit a defeat here,
would be visible evidence of the student's lack of ability to maneuver
his own way through this perilous field of learning. The most frequent reason given for changing concentration was the impact of the
college, "the cold bath of intellectual reality." I know not only from
academic records but from the remarks of men themselves, that people
in this average group tend to move out of a field because they cannot
perform to their satisfaction there.

In the freshman and sophomore years, there seems to be a good
deal of confusion and anxiety about concentration that is never satis-
factorily resolved. Several men stressed the difficulties of finding what
they called "adequate advice." This seems to be the eternal complaint
of undergraduates and must be taken for what it is worth. What they
seem to be revealing is that since they themselves often have vague
ideas about what they want to or should do, they are looking around
for suggestions. These should not be merely general but should
provide them with specific clues to the content and approaches of the
different fields. The departments at Harvard do provide special opportunities for students to learn about courses and content, and students
are also urged to audit classes to become familiar with work in various
departments. The average student, however, often lacks a certain

assertiveness in personal contacts. To get him to take advantage of the many opportunities *offered* is the problem. The student often looks to his adviser for information and some guidance, but because of the size of the university-college, very often an adviser has little knowledge of offerings other than in his own area or field.

> I wanted to go into science. I have always been inclined to the sciences. Perhaps [a] constructive criticism that I could offer the university as far as their freshman adviser program goes . . . when it came time to choose a major, my adviser was totally unfamiliar at least as far as I could determine, with the sciences period. . . . I still had the idea of attending medical school afterwards and whether it would be a good idea to, say, be a non-science concentrator which would be better for me because I realize that my major is not pre-graduate training. . . . I was originally a [Social Relations] major when I first signed up and I changed to biochemical sciences at the very beginning of sophomore year. In other words, I essentially never did get into the social relations field because I realized that much of my decision was not my decision but just the strong impression that my adviser had made. . . . [He] sort of looked down his nose at the sciences, and discouraged me from going into them, as being a narrowing process.

Since few of our average men were thinking of an academic profession, academic subject matter could hold only as much interest as the essentially "amateur" scholar—the student—could bring to it. He could not, by definition, feel the same deep commitment to a field as the scholar or teacher whose life work it is. He has a limited investment, and this necessarily affects his openness toward areas of concentration that are not directly pre-professional (as, for example, are bio-chemical sciences in preparation for medical school).

On the other hand, Richard Hughes' statement in *The Fox in the Attic* cannot be ignored when we think about the meaning of student life.

> After all, it is only grown men who ever think of school as a microcosm, a preparation for adult life: to most boys at any time school *is* life, is itself the cosmos: a rope in the air you will climb, higher and higher, and—then, quite vanish into somewhere incomprehensible anyhow.[5]

College is a world to the student, *even* if he sees that world leading to some future role. For this reason he must be, truly, a student, or the

[5] Richard Hughes, *The Fox in the Attic* (New York: Harper & Row, 1961), p. 110.

college as an institution of learning falls short of its function in serving him. Extracurricular, athletic, social service activities—none of these can compensate for academic apathy, and lack of involvement. These extracurricular pursuits can be fine and important activities, but they are, by the nature of a university, peripheral. They cannot be justified as foci of student concern. It is important that the student make a choice of concentration from a real interest in the subject matter, from a willingness to become immersed in the scholarship and discipline of the field. Without this interest, the natural approach is that of the dilettante. The college curriculum is not a game, and the values of the university-college make gamesmanship morally indefensible.

It is when the student makes a concentration choice out of enthusiasm and "need to know," out of a desire to learn and to follow his field as deeply as his four-year program will allow, that he is usually happiest with his education. Of course, the student who is thus involved and fascinated with his area in turn arouses the interest and admiration of his professors, and in turn becomes eligible for their attention and the individual concern he craves. He also becomes eligible, at Harvard, for the college programs that provide occasions for the type of education that seems to work best for him—the individual attention of a tutor, the satisfaction of producing one's own large piece of creative work in the thesis. It is extremely important to a man's development at the college that he find a field that is right for him.

While choosing an area of concentration did seem to pose special problems for many of our academically average students, these problems in most cases sprang from the college climate itself and that strongly supported attribute of individual freedom which is a main component of Harvard and of similar college environments. But the freedom to choose also involves the burden of choosing. Adults can forget that it is more often their point of view than the students' that this freedom is easy and friendly and encouraging. Although the student might never admit to not knowing quite what to do with this freedom, he does resort in fact to tying his bewilderment into the institutional chain, and sharing the responsibility for making decisions.

> I resent advisers because they [are] always too ambitious, because they always want you to take these terrifically difficult courses, just because they are interesting. Well, you go in there and have a horrible time and get completely disillusioned and I think I was too

ambitious as a freshman. . . . I have found that generally advisers want you to be ambitious. Well, they expect everyone to be brilliant and, of course, some people are. . . . Of course, [departmental advisers] want you to take everything in the department.

Yet the student would not, in the true sense, be a student if he attained professional focus and interest. These graduates made clear that as undergraduates they wanted to arrive at the point where they would feel a pull from the future—a lure toward a direction that had taken on an intrinsic value and vivacity. Some fields of concentration achieved this intrinsic value simply by merit of their ultimate purpose —preparation for a vocation that had already sparked the young man's imagination.

I think if medicine holds an interest for a person throughout his life, there is no boundary in medicine. It seems fascinating, and I, of course, have respect for all the doctors I meet. I haven't had the opportunity to meet a bad doctor yet or, in my eyes, a bad doctor.

In this sense, vocational goals can serve a purpose that liberal educators sometimes refuse to recognize as important: such goals help the student to make a choice from a sense of direction. I interviewed men who gave me the feeling that without these goals, college would have been a dazed encounter—with the student unable to grasp meanings in the work required, and with the academic environment essentially futile for him.

Summarizing, I would suggest that many problems of guidance in the modern university require an understanding of two points of view: the student's subjective interpretation of his experiences, and the institutional values and expectations that create the unique environment of a school. I have tried to illustrate by examples that where the climate is intellectually high-powered and where academic achievement is greatly valued, such a status as average ranking can affect a student's attitude toward learning. He feels unknown to faculty, yet because feelings of mediocrity plague him, he turns away from opportunities for contact because he might "run into something" he "might not be able to cope with." His choice of field is often influenced by these same timidities. It is clear that guidance of students such as these who are academically average hinges upon our helping them strengthen their sense of confidence and vigor. We find wise perspective on our modern profession in the words of Ralph Waldo Emerson, who wrote in *The Conduct of Life:*

Although this garrulity of advising is born with us, I confess that life is rather a subject of wonder, than of didactics. . . . We accompany the youth with sympathy, and manifold old sayings of the wise, to the gate of the arena, but 'tis certain that not by strength of ours, or of the old sayings, but only on strength of his own, unknown to us or to any, he must stand or fall. That by which a man conquers in any passage, is a profound secret to every other being in the world, and it is only as he turns his back on us and on all men, and draws on this most private wisdom, that any good can come to him.[6]

This, after all, is the goal of our attempts to understand and guide the young toward adulthood, the worthy goal of helping each person to come into his own strength, into the "profound secret" of his unique resources.

[6] *The Works of Ralph Waldo Emerson, Four Volumes in One* (New York: Tudor Publishing Co.), pp. 161–62.

WILLIAM W. COOLEY

A Computer-Measurement System for Guidance[1]

THE PRECEDING ARTICLES leave the reader with the impression that the individual counseling of students is the only legitimate activity of today's guidance programs. Testing and the interpretation of test scores are not considered in any of the articles, and one could also be left with the idea that testing is no longer an aspect of guidance. The opposite is found when schools are visited. There, the testing program is the dominating and expanding aspect of guidance. This apparent trend has been documented by recent *Project Talent* data (Flanagan, et al., 1962) which show the increasing use of tests in most high schools, the trend being much more pronounced than that for the addition of counselors, for example.

The differences between what some apparently feel is desirable and the actual situation is partly the result of the problem of numbers. In the United States there are about nine million students in grades 9 to 12 attending about nineteen thousand senior high schools (taking public schools alone). Over one-half of the public high schools in this country have no full-time counselors. Since most of these are very small high schools affecting few students, the overall picture is not quite as gloomy—the best estimate in terms of student-counselor ratios

[1] This paper was prepared while the author was Research Associate at the Center for Research in Careers, Harvard University. It was read at the Institute for Administrators of Pupil Personnel Services, Harvard Summer Guidance Institute, July 30, 1964.

is about 740 students per counselor (Flanagan, et al., 1962). Recommendations of the professionals and the self-appointed critics of the American school suggest 250 to 300 students per counselor, and those ratios seem too large when one recalls that there are only about 180 days per school year. Thus, even if the number of counselors now active in the schools were doubled, it would still be an inadequate number for the students in school today, and more than inadequate for the projected school enrollments by the time the additional counselors were recruited, trained, and practicing in schools.

Although it is expected that counseling will continue to be an important and integral aspect of guidance, many of the time-consuming details can now be automated, freeing time for busy people to do a good job of counseling in those cases where it is most necessary. As they become more aware of these changes, school systems are turning more and more to testing programs as a means of assisting counselors.

Recently many books and articles have appeared which seem to be a reaction against too much testing, and undoubtedly, there has been much wasted and misguided effort in school testing. I should like to consider here some of the ways by which we might improve our ability to deal with test scores and thus reconsider the school testing program. The computer, methods of examining many test scores simultaneously (multi-variate analysis), and results of longitudinal studies make it possible to take a new look at potential improvements.

Perhaps it would be useful to consider briefly the current situation regarding measurement in guidance and the use of computers in the schools. School testing programs today are primarily concerned with achievement testing. Generally, a battery of four or five tests is used to sample a student's knowledge in the major curriculum areas. Also, a general test of scholastic aptitude is administered about every other year. As a result the student is assigned some sort of number or set of numbers, generally a percentile, a score which tells the percentage of students who received lower scores than he did. Often neither the students nor the parents are told anything regarding the outcome of the tests. A major reason for the testing program seems to be that of sectioning students on the basis of previous achievement as measured by these tests. One thing we can be fairly sure of is that a student's test scores are recorded in indelible ink in his cumulative record so that in case some teacher or counselor wants to know how this student "is doing," the record is pulled and the scores are there.

The computer is now being used in many school systems, and more are joining this bandwagon every day. In every installation I know about, the computer applications have been almost exclusively a simple automation of clerical tasks previously done by hand, such as report cards, school attendance, scheduling, test scoring, etc. Those schools which have transferred the student cumulative record to the computer have done so in a very routine fashion. In fact, in many cases one wonders why the computer is involved at all. Information is read into the computer, the computer then prepares a gummed label containing the student's grades or test scores, and this is placed onto the student record card. However, if there is no attempt to ask questions which would assist in interpreting the data, the need for the computer is dubious.

There are many difficulties with current computer-measurement applications. A major one can be illustrated by the use of an analogy. Early automobiles had an oil pressure gauge mounted on the dash board which would continuously record the oil pressure in the motor. This little device was rather useless unless the operator knew the optimum pressure for maximum motor efficiency. Today, the human engineers have convinced car manufacturers that it is more reasonable simply to have a red light come on when the oil pressure is not what it should be, than to try to educate all American drivers to know the desired oil pressure for this particular motor. The analogy is clear. School testing programs need to shift from a system of recording sets of numbers on student cumulative records to a procedure of "flashing red lights" which indicates when certain students seem to be in particular types of danger.

I should like, in the remainder of this paper, to consider in some detail the area of guidance with which I am most familiar, namely educational and vocational planning.

CAREER GUIDANCE

For some time psychologists have been convincing guidance workers that one test score alone is not sufficient evidence to conclude much of anything about a student. Their recommendation was to consider several test scores as a profile of the student. This resulted in the familiar "parallel stalks" model, each stalk standing for a test, with a line passing from stalk to stalk representing a particular student's score combination. Although this gives the impression that all the test score information available on a student is being considered simultaneously, anyone who has worked with this approach knows that it is only a slight graphical improvement over this same set of scores recorded in a cumulative record. *What has been needed is a summary of this test score evidence with respect to particular questions, questions with educational and career relevance for each student.*

I certainly do not visualize a system where the student's test scores are the input and prescribed curriculum and career are the output. Rather, the input consists of test scores, grades, biographical (including family) information, *and* the student's school and career plans. Output from the system would include for example, certain information regarding students who appear to have high-risk plans. The actual form of this computer output could include explanatory paragraphs, if that seemed desirable. The task of the guidance program then, given this information, would be to plan experiences for such students which would give them more information about their plans, and about themselves in relation to those plans.

One key component of the output would be the probable success and satisfaction associated with a particular student plan. Most students seem quite willing and able to make plans and to discuss their plans in terms of probabilities. Interviews with the 700 boys of the *Scientific Careers Study*, a five-year study of career development, consistently found them talking in terms of their chances of doing this or that (Cooley, 1963). "Although I would rather be a doctor, I think I have a better chance of getting into a dental school." "With my grades, what are my chances of making it as a physicist?" "Do boys like me tend to go into law?" The students seemed to be continually searching for the type of data which a computer-measurement system could provide them.

Perhaps a specific example would help to clarify the points being made here. A case was drawn from the *Scientific Careers Study*, and it illustrates a frequent guidance problem. Selection of the case was quite simple. A brief inspection of computer output quickly identified several students with the characteristics needed. The files of that five-year study contained folders on each of 700 boys, and each folder contained about 100 scale scores, 4 questionnaires and 2 interviews. Only with the aid of the computer can students with particular combinations of characteristics be identified quickly and easily from a file of data this extensive.

The Case of Robert S. (Case #SCS 2214)

Bob S. was first contacted in the 8th grade. Our file contains his achievement data prior to 8th grade, as well as the data which were collected from grades 8 to 12 as part of the study.

Bob lives with his natural mother and stepfather. He has two younger brothers and no sisters. His father is a typewriter repairman and his mother does not work.

Ability and achievement information available on Bob when he was in 8th grade gave every indication that he had the potential for further schooling beyond 12th grade. A multivariate statistical summary of his ability and achievement profile indicated that about 83 per cent of the boys with his particular combination of scores do enter some type of college.

Interest and temperament data available indicate that Bob "looks" very much like other boys who have entered careers in some field of science and technology. Of the boys with his pattern of interests, 73 per cent enter some science-technical field. About one-half of the boys who responded to the Temperament Survey as he did, were pursuing careers in science-technology.

A summary of socio-economic data showed that 87 per cent of the boys with Bob's family background do not go to college. These data include such variables as parents' education, father's occupational level, and the parents' expectations with respect to further schooling for the boy.

Notice that the numbers reported above tell something about Bob with respect to such questions as whether he is likely to go to college and/or become an engineer. Those percentages can be thought of as the probabilities associated with a particular type of prediction based upon a certain set of data. The data upon which these predictions are based were available when Bob was in eighth grade. Previously used techniques tend to report test results in terms like, "Bob did better on the mathematics test than did 50 per cent of his classmates," or perhaps simply, "Bob received a score of 500 on the SCRAP mathematics test." It is difficult to decide what to think about such test scores. They are static. No implications are discernible.

Bob's career plans when first contacted in eighth grade were to enter the Coast Guard. He had an uncle and a cousin in the Coast Guard and felt "they had a good life." Otherwise, he might become an airline pilot. At grade 9, he was still talking about the Coast Guard but was also considering becoming a mechanic or engineer. He thought it might be a good idea to be a mechanic in the service because it is "more organized and less chance of business collapsing." In 10th grade he talked about "becoming a mechanical engineer because he liked to work on cars." This goal continued through 11th grade, but when he was last contacted in grade 12 he was planning to enter the service after high school graduation and become an airplane mechanic.

The point of this particular case is to illustrate a high risk in the sense that if Bob developed realistic college goals later during high school (as he did during grades 10 and 11), he would discover that his 8th and 9th grade behavior (e.g. course selection) was not consistent with those goals.

PROGRAMMED EXPERIENCES

By a systematic examination of several different types of data, a variety of potential problem cases can easily be uncovered today among a very large group of students. A computer-measurement system could allow the early identification of potential problems, soon enough to do something about it. The problem then is what to do once a trouble spot has been observed. The recommendation here is to develop a system of *programmed experiences*.

In Bob's case, for example, general mechanical-technical orientation was quite clear. What was not clear was the level at which he might operate. A sequence of experiences could be designed to show the broad range of jobs open to boys like Bob, including the training required. For common problems, such as this one, films could be an excellent method. Included in these experiences would be some indication of the types of financial aid available to boys like Bob, so that college is not unrealistically discounted too early for financial reasons.

Included in his program of experiences would be a talk with a counselor. In fact, this might be the first experience in the sequence, to make sure that the established measurement-computer system did not miss something important, and to examine the prescribed sequence to see if it made sense. It is beyond the scope of this paper to consider other facets of the counseling interview. The plea here is that we do not rely so exclusively on such talks for either diagnosis or "treatment."

The concept of programming experiences perhaps needs further clarification, especially its difference from programmed instruction. Programmed instruction appears to be a very useful technique for teaching students many routine skills, such as arithmetic. Although some workers have attempted to adapt this stimulus-response technique to guidance, it might be more useful to adopt the concept of program, but broaden the units to be programmed. Instead of the sequences of separate one-sentence stimuli needed to take a student through the intricacies of arithmetic, programmed experiences would lead him through the types of experiences needed in order to develop a realistic concept of what a mechanical engineer does, what training he needs to have, what special abilities he has, the current and projected employment situation, etc. Such experiences might include work experience, meeting role models, visiting plants and laboratories, etc.

Several workers (see, for example, Bushnell, 1963) have been developing the concept of computer controlled and monitored instruction. In such systems the computer seems to be viewed as a giant teaching machine, providing the entire instructional sequence. This type of micro-programming of student behavior seems to be a long way off.

Rather than have the computer decide which foreign word a particular student should learn next, a macro-programming concept would program much larger units of student experiences. The macro-program could help the educator-guider decide upon an appropriate sequence of books, films, "courses," lectures, discussions, etc., for each student. Such a concept is not nearly so far from being operational as is micro-programming.

Of course, it is not novel to seek effective and more efficient guidance procedures. Various forms of group guidance have been developed, and most recently, Holland's (1964) paper calls for the restructuring of school experiences as a more reasonable alternative to "traditional vocational counseling." His argument that the new job of student personnel workers should be "to design, manipulate, and coordinate student experience" is very similar to the concept here of programmed experiences. What I am adding is the suggestion that computer-measurement techniques are now developed to the point where they can be used to help the guidance programmer decide which students seem to need what types of experiences.

Additional Applications

At this point, it might be useful to survey other types of problems which a computer-measurement system could easily uncover.

The college placement function is a big consumer of counselor time. College finding services, for example, have demonstrated that much of this problem can be automated. Also, the computer-measurement system could identify trouble-spots which, if acted upon immediately, the counselor could easily help remedy. If not identified early, the problem could grow until the student's situation required extensive remedial action.

One case occasionally observed is the student who is planning to apply to only two colleges and the chances of his being accepted at either one is something like one chance in one thousand. It would not be difficult to develop experiences which could point out to the student the desirability of *also* applying to a college for which he has a much higher probability of being admitted. Counselors are already using a type of intuitive estimate of such probabilities, so they should welcome assistance in this area.

The case just mentioned illustrates the problem of "over-aspiring," whereas Bob's problem, cited earlier, was a type of "under-aspiring." Both are frequent problems in educational and vocational planning, and if identified early, they might be remedied with suitable student experiences. The student may decide not to change his plans, but at least he will know he is pursuing a high-risk path. He may even decide to do something about some of the predictors (e.g., grades), thus changing his probability in that way. The main thing is that he have a rational basis for whatever plan he develops. As Kogan and Wallach (1964) have recently shown, the amount of risk a person is willing to take is a function of his personality, and this aspect could also be built into the computer-measurement system.

Another area in which an active computer-measurement system could accomplish much is in the analysis of student achievement. It is now possible for schools to develop a type of dynamic norm, which would make it possible to detect, for example, a student whose achievement-growth curve has suddenly slacked off. If this is done on a continuous basis, problems can be anticipated before they become serious, such as leading to another drop-out. The need for dynamic norms is considered in the next section.

A computer-measurement system could perform other very important diagnostic functions. Testing programs of the past have tended to assess "how much" the student knows, instead of asking what missing skills or concepts are interfering with his school progress. Perhaps a few weeks' review of fractions would help fill a gap which is currently giving some students trouble in shop work, for example.

The existence of such computer-measurement systems would also allow a systems analysis of school practice, such as that proposed by Kershaw and McKean (1959). Although such analyses would not be directly related to the guidance of individual students, it is not unreasonable to have guidance personnel examine and "guide" institutional practice as it effects student behavior. A continuous, systematic examination of student growth as a function of institutional practice is certainly long over-due.

THE NEED FOR DYNAMIC NORMS

Although there have been several factors which have limited the effective use of measurement in guidance, the problem of obtaining sufficient normative data has been one of the more serious problems. For one thing, norms have been allowed to get out of date. Funds are only now becoming available in the amounts needed to provide their continued updating. Another problem is that norms have been insufficiently developed, limiting the questions which can be asked. Norms are needed which are based upon multiple observations of the same students over time, and these need to be developed on a continuous basis. Also, counselors have not had the information needed for understanding the validity of test scores or the predictive implications of particular test score combinations.

Project Talent (Flanagan, et al., 1962) has shown that it is now possible to develop truly representative norms. These norms are also dynamic in the sense that they are based upon follow-up data which make it possible to ask questions about the subsequent educational or vocational implications of current behavioral and environmental observations, including the current plans of the student.

At regular intervals (say every three years), a five per cent sample of schools could be selected for participation in a national "norming" study. The students would take a battery of tests which broadly sampled student behavior and determined their plans.

Periodic follow-up studies could then determine the pattern of events which followed the testing. The first follow-up might be conducted five years later, when most of the original group will have graduated from high school. This is more or less the current plan of *Project Talent,* and so the feasibility of such an operation is now being demonstrated.

The computer-measurement system being proposed here is completely dependent upon obtaining such adequate normative data. The *Scientific Careers Study* (Cooley, 1963) has shown the potential utility and validity of the probability predictions for individual students based upon multivariate information, but only the *techniques* used there have generalizability. The actual prediction equations from that study are appropriate for a very restricted population (boys of above average ability in Eastern Massachusetts). Undertakings such as *Project Talent* can now provide the type of normative data which has been lacking.

Not all applications of a computer-measurement system require national norms. In fact, "norming" can and should be frequently done on a regional basis. However, follow-up data must be made an aspect of this norming procedure if we expect to be able to utilize the test results in the manner described here.

This proposed, periodic, mass testing program may sound expensive. It certainly is when viewed in terms of the amount of money which has previously been spent on establishing norms and other validating information for tests. Yet it would cost only about $500,000 annually,[2] which is about what it would cost to add only 50 more counselors to the entire United States, a number which would not even make a dent in the current student-counselor ratio. If we really want to learn more about students from the millions of dollars annually spent on school testing programs, if we want to provide the type of information which students seem to want and need, then such undertakings seem necessary and feasible.

The skeptic may also claim that, although computers and multivariate methods are available today, they are out of the financial reach of most school systems. There are ways to solve this financial problem, however. Through establishment of regional data processing centers such as the New England Education Data Systems (NEEDS) project, a central computer facility is able to service many school systems, including the analysis of test scores for guidance purposes. In a few years each school could be directly connected to a central computer by a remote typewriter-type terminal which would enable school personnel to ask questions of their school data stored at the central computer center.

THEORETICAL BASIS

The discussion thus far has been more or less exclusively about rather vague operations. By now the reader is probably concerned about the theoretical basis for this type of wild talk. Actually there

---

[2] Estimate based on approximate *Project Talent* budget.

are several bases, depending upon the area of application for the computer-measurement system. Perhaps it would be useful to examine the view of man which is behind the recommendations for applications in the area of student educational and vocational planning.

The basic proposition is that different plans are appropriate for different people. This proposition requires a taxonomy for plans and people, and a method for dealing with relationships between types of plans and kinds of people.

Factor theory provides a more operational basis for talking about people differences and their relationship to plans. In the factorial conceptualization of human behavior, personality has its locus in an m-dimensional space. An individual's personality is his unique location in this space, the location determined by the total pattern of the m behavioral measures which are available for that individual. In this context, personality encompasses all behavior, including intellectual functioning. People who have similar patterns of scores will occupy similar regions of this m-dimensional space. That is, people who behave similarly have similar personalities. Career planning and decision making is one aspect of behavior. People with similar personalities *tend* to make similar types of career decisions. Once the regions of the personality space occupied by people who have made particular types of career decisions are defined, the probability that another person will make a certain decision can be estimated.

Before this theoretical position can be further developed, it is necessary to explain the test space concept, and the probability classification procedures which are the analytical techniques employed in the factor approach advocated here.

Say, for example, the task is to distinguish future scientists from non-scientists, Figure 1 represents a one-dimensional test space. An individual's location along axis X depends upon his score on test X.

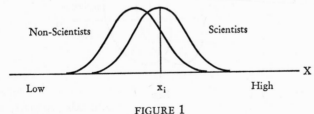

FIGURE 1

A One-dimensional Test Space

The height of the curve for the scientist group at some point, for example at x_i, is the frequency with which scientists receive that particular score on X. Knowing only the test score, you would predict that the person was a non-scientist if the score was low, and a scientist if the score was high. Knowing the heights of the two curves at score x_i, it is possible to compute the proportion of people receiving that score who are scientists, and the proportion who are non-scientists. With new test scores, from a person for whom the scientist: non-scientist designation is unknown, the proportions became probabilities of group membership for that person.

For example, if one-third of the people having a score of x_i are non-scientists, and two-thirds are scientists, then the probability that a person with score x_i is a scientist is .67, and .33 is the probability of non-scientist. This assumes that the two categories exhaust the possibilities for the population under consideration. If the areas under the two curves are equal, this also assumes that the two groups exist in equal numbers within that population. These two conditions (that there are only two categories of people in the mixed population and that they are of equal frequency), are peculiar to this example and are not limitations of the technique.

Of course, a single test score yields inadequate information, so a method is needed for handling more than one test score. Consider the next most simple case, that of two tests. This results in a two-dimensional space similar to Figure 2. In this space, each individual can be

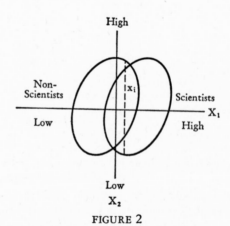

FIGURE 2

A Two-dimensional Test Space

represented as a point with a unique location depending upon his combination of scores on X_1 and X_2. This time questions can be asked about people receiving a *particular combination* of test scores: what proportion are scientists, and what proportion are non-scientists. These proportions are computed from the relative densities of "scientist points" and "non-scientist points" for a given score combination.

The importance of score combinations can be seen in this example. A score of x_i on test X_1 could have different implications depending upon the score X_2. High scores on X_2 with x_i on X_1 indicate the student is more like a non-scientist. Low scores on X_2 with a score of x_i on X_1 indicate greater similarity to the scientist group. If a score on X_2 is viewed alone, nothing can be concluded about the student's resemblance to these two groups. Multivariate procedures make use of this combinational aspect of scores.

Consider another example. If a decision between two alternatives has been made by individuals located in the behavioral space, such

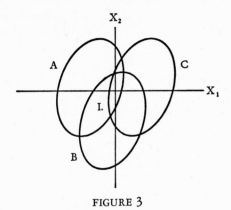

FIGURE 3

Three Group Dispersions in a
Two-dimensional Space

as A) college preparatory curriculum in high school and B) non-college preparatory, the behavioral space will contain regions in which many individuals chose A over B, other regions in which choice B was preferred to A. There may be at least some A choosers in all regions of the personality space, but the A density varies from region to region. Comparison of the density of A choosers to B choosers at a particular point in the space determines the probability that choice A will be made by persons at or near that point. This scheme of analysis is generalizable to decision-making situations involving more than two alternatives and/or two variables. Each new variable adds a new axis to the system. The bivariate normal distributions for three groups on tests X_1 and X_2 are outlined in Figure 3. Once the means and dispersions of these three groups have been estimated, the probability that individual i is a member of group A, B, or C can also be estimated. The computations become rather extensive as the number of variables increases, but this is where the computer comes in.

Mathematically the analytic task is handled by employing the algebra of matrices and vectors. A vector is a row or column of numbers. In a column vector of scores, each number represents a test score for someone. A row vector, if it contains m-scores, locates an individual in an m-dimensional space. If there are N such vectors, representing N people sampled from a population, the region of the test space occupied by that population can be estimated from the sample by assuming that the distribution of points in the population is multivariate normal. The center of the swarm of points is represented by the vector of sample means (called the centroid), and the dispersion of the points about the centroid is described by the variance-covariance matrix. This is the essence of multivariate analysis.

It is certainly not necessary for counselors to become familiar with the details of this type of multivariate analysis. The nature of these techniques was hinted at here for purposes of illustrating the type of thinking and analysis behind the computer output that would monitor student plans. To actually see how such techniques are applied in analysis of data, the reader might consult Cooley and Lohnes (1963) for computational details and Cooley (1964) for career research applications.

SUMMARY

As recently as 1960, participants at a conference on measurement and research (Traxler, ed., 1961) have pleaded that counselors and teachers be taught how to interpret test scores in relation to all other data available on the same student. Although this is a noble goal, it is unrealistic. Even if they had the follow-up data which would make predictive interpretations possible, people are just not able to process that much information reliably.

It is possible to achieve this goal of sounder interpretation by use of the computer, methods of multivariate analysis, and results of continuous, normative, longitudinal studies. I do not mean to imply that such a system is ready to be installed tomorrow in any school that wants a computer-measurement system. The point is that, for the first time, the parts are all clearly discernible and feasible.

This paper and these arguments seem necessary because of the emphasis today on the counseling process. There seem to be too few people in guidance today who are concerned with the role of measurement in guidance and the ways in which new techniques might assist counselors in the task of helping our millions of students through school and into careers. The hope is that this type of article might stimulate renewed action along these lines.

REFERENCES

Bushnell, D. D. "The Role of the Computer in Further Instructional Systems," *Audio Visual Communication Review*, Vol. 11, No. 2, Monograph No. 2 of the Technological Development Project, March-April, 1963.

Cooley, W. W. *Career Development of Scientists*. Cambridge, Mass.: Harvard Graduate School of Education, 1963.

Cooley, W. W., and Lohnes, P. R. *Multivariate Procedures for the Behavioral Sciences*. New York: J. Wiley & Sons, 1962.

Findley, W. G. (ed.). *The Impact and Improvement of School Testing Programs*. 62nd Yearbook, Part II, NSSE, Chicago: Univ. of Chicago Press, 1963.

Flanagan, J. C., Dailey, J. T., Shaycoft, M. F., Orr, D. B., and Goldberg, I. *Studies of the American High School*. Pittsburgh, Pa.: Univ. of Pittsburgh, 1962.

Holland, J. L. "Some New Directions for Vocational Counseling." Paper read at AERA meeting, February, 1964.

Kershaw, J. A., and McKean, R. N. *Systems Analysis and Education*. Santa Monica, Calif.: The Rand Corporation, 1959.

Kogan, N., and Wallach, M. A. *Risk Taking—A Study in Cognition and Personality*. New York: Holt, Rinehart, and Winston, 1964.

Traxler, A. E. (ed.). *Measurement and Research in Today's Schools*. Washington, D.C.: American Council on Education, 1961.

The School and Self-Understanding

THE GUIDANCE PROCESS inevitably aims at self-understanding by the client, by definition a key aspect of mental health. This is a precondition for making mature choices, for the assumption of responsibility for self. This kind of learning, perhaps the most important in the world, must start before the individual attempts to relate himself to the working world. Its logical place is in the elementary school. This paper[1] addresses itself to the problem but does so pleading a special case: the greater use of cognitive techniques.

What is the school's situation in fostering this self-understanding? It is confronted with a most difficult job. On the one hand the school is expected to prepare its inhabitants for the good life. Youth must become competent, of course, in the ordinary sense of the term but also should achieve a level of self-understanding, accept self and others, live with others in cooperation and trust rather than in suspicion, be concerned and helpful rather than competitive and cynical. On the other hand, there is the way to make a quick dollar. In this context Hutson (12) notes that the educative principle and the competitive principle so characteristic of our culture and economy cannot be reconciled.

It is wonderful to have the world's goods in the supermarket, but there is a price to be paid for it and we are paying it, quite hand-

[1] I am indebted to Eli M. Bower of the National Institute of Mental Health and John R. Lawson of the University of Maryland for the opportunity to discuss the ideas in this paper with them. This does not mean that Dr. Bower or Dr. Lawson necessarily endorse these ideas.

somely. There is no surcease offered here. The point is that in the schools alone we are not going to remake our culture.

Not that we have not tried, but the number of such attempts is dishearteningly limited. A few years ago the *Personnel and Guidance Journal* sought to pull together noteworthy programs in mental health in the schools (2). Out of this reasonably thorough search it was possible to present only six reports: the programs at the Institute for Child Study at the University of Maryland, Ojemann's work at the State University of Iowa, Hall's description of his efforts at the Nebraska Human Resources Research Foundation, Moustakas' human relations seminar at the Merrill-Palmer School, John R. Seeley's "human relations classes" at Forest Hill Village, and the ambitious program of teacher education at the Bank Street College of Education.

These and similar programs referred to by Withall (34), for instance, are generally moving and exciting programs. Yet the reason for what seems to be limited progress must reside in factors beyond budget. Of course there must be a phenomenal difference between teacher attention to the individuals in a class of thirty-two and, as has been found necessary in special education, in a class of ten or twelve. However, the idea of doubling or tripling the educational budget seems quite unrealistic. More important, there can be no assurance that teachers with such small classes automatically become desirable models. It may well be that money will buy more than the skeptic will allow, but even so there are the limiting factors of the humanity with which teachers are endowed, their personal security, tolerance of differences among others, and their ability to inspire trust in others. Nor will a fancy establishment or a democratically run school counter the many hostile facets of our culture. Even a partial list of what goes on all around us is unnerving: cutthroat competition; not only absence of ethical behavior but absence also of indignation at the lack of ethical behavior; cynical disregard of the rights of others; gerrymandering; bribery and blackmail of public officials; separation of men and women from society under barbarous conditions when crimes are committed; and an immense death and accident toll on the highways, largely preventable. In 1961, in the Fourth John Dewey Address, Gardner Murphy (19) properly asked whether a teacher can teach rationality in such massive unreason as flourishes in our time.

This is proper ground for despair and a possible proposal that the Lord start over again. However, there are some opposite signs. There is the response to the Peace Corps, for instance; the insistent civil rights program; and the constant, if painful, democratic process of correcting our own inequities. It is possible to take heart from these and to work in productive directions in the hope that to an extent we can redress the balance.

One emphasis in some school mental health programs is on broadening the teacher's understanding and increasing her personal security. Following another, children are taught to consider multiple motivation and behavior dynamics. In the process, there is a certain amount of practice in self-search. These are the goals also of those school counselors who tend to identify with the major movements in mental health. This is desirable and necessary and should be continued and expanded. However, such programs are not widespread, nor is their number growing at a great rate.

In this circumstance the imagination turns to additional possibilities. This is the burden of this paper. In a number of ways the school mental health program mirrors the formal therapeutic situation. In such a program the relationship between student and teacher is characterized by trust. There is understanding and acceptance of the student by the teacher. It does not seem too much to say that transference is manifested, and, perhaps less obviously, also counter-transference. The major concern of the mental health worker in the schools is with the feeling life; and, as self-understanding is fostered, the great discoveries and inventions of classic psychoanalysis come into play.

In following the therapeutic model, in focusing on the feeling life, in seeking really to restructure personality, the program follows the classic psychoanalytic formulation of basic motivation. This is a view which amply supports the existence of profound unconscious elements in personality and the pre-eminence of drive, need, personality defense, and sublimation in the organization and maintenance of behavior. The minimal influence of cognition, if indeed it is influence at all, is clear in Freud's teaching. In his view, the ego is the agent of the id, the blind and primitive pleasure-seeking drive, and is designed to further the aims of the id. The ego's energy and power are derived from the id's great demanding impulses and has no viability of its own.

This is the classic view and prevails in many settings. For instance, even the neo-Freudians subordinate cognitive ego functions to the need for the emotional experience. Fromm-Reichmann's statement (6) is characteristic:

Working through should be continued until the time is reached when the intellectual understanding of the problem, of its previously dissociated causes, and of its various interlocking mental and emotional ramifications is gradually transformed into real creative emotional insights.

Granting what theory and experience indicate, and taking into account that this may be only a cry of pain, a defense against the more arduous enterprise, something else may be possible. However, a new line of thinking has emerged in the analytic field and in more orthodox psychology. It is doubtful that these developments are taken into account sufficiently in mental health work in the schools.

A New Emphasis: Cognition

It is now almost two decades since Hartmann, Kris, and Lowenstein (9) offered a revolutionary reappraisal of Freudian personality typology. The idea that the ego is not an agent of primitive pleasure-seeking drives, but has energy and vitality of its own made it possible to emerge with new conceptions, led to change in emphasis and technique in the therapeutic relationship, and initiated the alert and self-conscious movement in ego psychology.

The theorists who have emphasized cognition include Schachtel (30), who urges the influence of man's search for meaning in life, Heider (10) and Hartmann (8), who call attention to the influence of intention, as does Allport (1). Also cited by Allport are Wallas, who includes an "instinct of thought" in man's motives, and Bartlett and Cantrill as regarding man's search for meaning as perhaps the ultimate motive in life.

Starting with Schachtel's ideas, Neisser's (22) examination of childhood amnesia led him to question the concept of repression and to look for an answer in the discontinuities in cognitive functioning which accompany growth into adulthood. Thus conceived, childhood amnesia is amenable to quite a different kind of treatment than is now available.

McGuire (17) starts his syllogistic analysis of cognitive relationships by pointing out that the idea of the "rational man, long out of style, is now undergoing a remarkable revival." He refers to an impressive list of theoretical and experimental approaches referring variously to "tendency toward balance" (Heider), "balanced structure" (Cartwright and Harary), "balanced matrices" (Abelson and Rosenberg), "stress toward symmetry" (Newcomb), and most recently, "cognitive dissonance" (Festinger).

Although it must be searched for, there is clinical literature which illustrates a therapeutic approach utilizing strong cognitive elements. This is the technique that Dollard and Miller (3) follow in their discussion of "discrimination." Similarly Monroe (18) presents the case of Mrs. S., who, for example, is asked productively by the therapist whether she has heard of a particular psychological theory. In Thorne's (33) eclectic volume, the last 124 pages are devoted to the problem of maximizing intellectual orientation.

Lakin Phillips (26) denies the need for a concept of unconscious motivation and works with his clients in terms of their conscious awareness and understanding. On the face of it, his method is therapy using cognition as the major vehicle. The reiterated work of Albert Ellis (4) probably is well known. Less well known is a paper by Betty Ganzhorn (7) and one by the present writer (28) on using the client's available resources, including cognition, much more greatly than we now do. As can be seen there is no tidal wave of cognitive approaches. Nevertheless there is a clear direction, reiterated by observers, researchers and clinicians, toward the use of intellectual understanding.

The theoretical proposals and the clinical instances are intended to buttress the point that increasing attention is being paid to cognitive approaches and techniques in fostering personality growth. Can the schools travel this road? What can the schools do?

THE SCHOOL, COGNITION, AND SELF-UNDERSTANDING

It seems strange to say that the school should look to rationality and cognition in fulfilling its purposes. This is, almost by definition, the school's stock in trade. However, our prevalent counseling philosophies, i.e., Rogerian and watered down elements of psychoanalysis, run counter to use of rationality and cognition.

What can the schools do? They can continue and extend present forward-looking practices. As teachers learn to use the six-area framework of the University of Maryland Institute for Child Study, their view of children will become more objective and understanding. The teacher-in-training exposed to Moustakas' seminars stands a very good chance of coming out a more secure person with greater maturity than before, and, therefore, should be a better teacher. The twelve-year-old in Ojemann's University School should come out of his exposures inoculated against black and white judgments and aware of some of the underlying motives for behavior.

The goal of these and similar programs is "the examined life," a phrase that Socrates 2,500 years ago fortunately did not copyright. The examination of one's own motives or the motives of others is one aspect of Socrates' great teaching. There are ways in which this can become a most important enterprise—what, in man's condition, is more important?—but not before the school becomes committed to such examination as in itself desirable and necessary. It is pointless to take the schools to task; it is too easy and popular an exercise anyway. Yet with respect to guidance people, it is to be noted that Shoben[2] feels that the nonfacilitation of an active search for values among students, an aspect of his view of the examined life, constitutes a failure of guidance and the school.

So many have written so movingly about the experience of coming out of the dark that it seems pointless to repeat what by now is in modern folklore. Although the climb is endless, the view is increasingly breathtaking. In more mundane fashion, therapists say that there are deeper and deeper levels of understanding. This climb is the goal. Its end is always beyond our reach. What are some of the techniques possible within the school which would enable the student to see this goal in a cognitive framework?

Teaching the Dynamics of Behavior

There is nothing at all new in such an idea. Ojemann (23) has done it handsomely for a decade and a half and bolstered it with the backbreaking task of rewriting the texts used in the Iowa University School so that they mirror, for instance, multi-values and many-faceted motivations. Increasingly, first-year college courses in psychology are seeping into the high schools. The stream should become wider, deeper, and more powerful. If two conditions are met, it does not really matter what philosophy is advocated by teacher or discussion leader. The chief consideration is whether the rationale provided (e.g., learning theory of one or another persuasion, ego psychology, neo-behaviorism, analytic psychology of the Freudian or Adlerian variety, or any other) offers clarifying concepts. The point is that, whatever the rationale, it should help the student to observe and

2 See pp. 117–18.

follow his own behavior and, as he feels it necessary and possible, attempt to intercept and change it.

The conditions to be met are: first, that this kind of investigation by teacher and students be moved out of the thirty-two-pupil class into the ten- to twelve-member discussion group. The reason is no doubt too obvious to belabor but basically flows out of the second condition: that development of these ideas start with, or as quickly as possible be made pertinent to, the individual in the group. This is essential here since what is to be learned must arise from and be integrated in one's own living. The term "cognitive" is capable of carrying such sterile connotations as to negate what is here intended. While this is not group therapy, it is not barren intellectualizing either. Just as the central nervous system cannot operate independently of the autonomic nervous system, so intelligence and cognition, to have validity, must take into account the rich life of feeling.

However, if pupils' private feelings are to be discussed, there will be charges of intrusion of privacy. The school will be charged with meddling in the family, and all the old sanctities will be raised. This will receive attention at a further point.

Of course such a program is easier to talk about than to carry out, but the saying does provide a map. At least the direction is clear if one wants to go that way. Even so, the proposal to teach behavior dynamics is so general that a specific example will be useful.

If I were to lead such a group, I would use Sullivanian concepts as a framework for the reason that they have been clarifying and exceedingly useful in my need to understand my own sometimes unhappy behavior, and to make progress in intercepting it. Also, in my own teaching, which is, to be sure, at the university level, these ideas have been exciting to communicate and also quite clearly useful to students. I refer specifically to the central concept of anxiety and the self-system, which as it happens comes complete with directions for recognition of clues.

The Control of Behavior

The Freudian revolution presented us with the containment of impulse, id-based, as a central and necessary direction for behavior of man in society. Perhaps as part of the foundation for the emergence of ego psychology, perhaps in reaction to the extreme view of man as moved by blind and primitive libidinal needs and wishes, a number of observers, among them Maslow (16), make a case for impulse gratification as against control. The very strong probability is that the two are synergetic. Gardner Murphy (20) says it movingly and beautifully.

> . . . the nurture of rationality may perhaps lie in other efforts than the sheer encouragement of rational thought; indeed, . . . the rational may best continue to grow in the instinctive soil in which it was engendered, and . . . too clear and sterile a surgical separation of thought from its ancestral and parental roots in love and impulse may threaten its viability. And if this should by any chance be true, it would mean that the learner must not be deprived of the riches of his impulse-life, and that the teacher must be a quickener of that impulse-life through which thought can grow, indeed a shaper and molder of the impulse into the rationality which comes from a healthy craving for contact with reality.

Perhaps we can abandon both extremes, the control of impulse and so to speak its gratification, in a mode of living that utilizes various degrees of control, depending upon the situation and its meaning. However, in evaluating when feelings are to be subordinated, there is a need for some reference point. While I can provide no ready and precise arithmetic and while I know that what is offered is capable of distortion, I suggest simply that feelings are to be *controlled* when, if expressed, others would suffer unwarrantably.

An example out of our current difficulties in living with each other may make the intention clear. A man says that no matter how much he is urged in church and elsewhere, he cannot bring himself to like Negroes, much less love them. This is not the issue at the moment, which is that he *behave* decently. The issue is as simple as that. The example is intended to highlight a class of instances in which native feelings are to be subordinated, suppressed, held in check. They are *not* to be an excuse for inability to behave decently to others. Proper behavior should become a set of expectations and part of the role of being human. These expectations should be as taken for granted and in a way beyond question as are the ordinary roles of being male or female. The difficulty, of course, is determining what *is* desirable and under what conditions.

This approach in no way supplants the more basic responsibility of looking into ourselves and coming to terms in positive ways with the disaster and hate in us that results in our inimical behavior to others. What is urged perhaps is second best, but, if so, it is second best to an ideal. In its own terms, it is important to note that as behavior is adopted and practiced, the associations and rewards associated with it should reinforce it and in time affect feelings.

THE EXPLICIT SUPPORT OF VALUES

Subordination of feelings and control of behavior can be seen as a value. If, as I hope, this is not immediately abhorrent, the idea can be carried further to the point of identifying a number of values which guidance personnel in the schools should support in working with their school clients.

The issue of support of given values by the school is not really for discussion. It is clear that as a social institution, the school's values are not only implicit in the function it performs, but explicit in the communications made to students, parents, and the general public. By virtue of its being, the school says education is important; one should be educated. One should be responsible, studious, clean, neat, courteous, outgoing, cooperative. Present rewards should be forgone for future goals. Counselors in the schools may be ready to grant this since it is well-nigh indisputable, but may point out that in their professional role they cannot and may not deliberately or subtly push the particulars of any values.

There is no space to develop this great problem. From prior consideration of at least some of its facets, a number of statements can be made. Three of these are safe and can be documented, but the fourth is arguable.

1. There is no task, including research in the hard sciences, that is not value inflected.

2. Values are communicated in ways other than in formal language. Very specifically and despite professions to the contrary, counseling has a value system built into it.

3. Since values, with or without counselor awareness, will be communicated to the counseling client, the counselor should become aware of them.

4. Since by virtue of the counseling task, the particular relationship, and the presumable goals to be achieved, there will be stress on some values and at least implicit derogation of others, agreement might be reached on at least specified values to be supported.

The problem may seem less sacrilegious if it is stipulated at the outset that no large charter will be drawn. No attempt will be made to rewrite the ten commandments. Instead, perhaps agreement can be reached on a minimum number of values to be supported, and we can agree also about such values that they will be regarded as capable of having exceptions to their general applicability.

What can be accepted? Surely we can agree that there is virtue to the examined life. To an extent this is capable of influencing thought and action. Since the organism is unitary, it seems not unlikely that one accepted value will lead to another. The need for thoughtful self-examination, not self-review, seems to lead to a need to review what has become a fetish with us, the jealousy of privacy. It seems hazardous to argue against privacy. However, the point is that we have too much rather than too little privacy. This does not mean that the bathroom door should not be locked but that we must construct, in Schachtel's and Dorothy Lee's terms, *the open self* as against *the closed self*. The cult of privatism has need for the fences to be up and in good repair, for the self to be well guarded. The opposite is urged. What are all the dreadful secrets anyway except evidence of our humanity? Openness can be hewed to as a value to work toward, to say how one feels, to be spontaneous, and to identify what one is uneasy about. Of course, there are limits that ordinary sensitivity will supply.

This beginning list is not intended to start an inventory of values. Probably I am sufficiently foolish to offer such a list, but the emphasis here is on values that can be taught in reasonably cognitive ways. It is readily possible to list the presumably desirable values, for instance, those that Jahoda (14) reports as meeting substantial agreement in the form of attributes of positive mental health. It is difficult to see, however, how maturity, self-acceptance, cooperativeness, responsibility, and others can in effect be taught. Rather they seem subject to learning from models, from proper experiences with others, from experiencing physical and psychological safety rather than from expectations set before one. It may be, of course, that ingenious teachers, perhaps building on a psychology of implicit expectations, can devise means of fostering agreed-upon values in these areas. For the present, it is proposed that specified values be supported affirmatively and without apology. These are the examined life, openness, and the control of feelings when their expression leads to inimical behavior. That it may make very good sense to hew to absolutes is indicated by Farnsworth (5) in discussing the problem of premarital sexual intercourse among college students.

A short time ago a president of a women's college asked me, just for the purpose of focussing our ideas, "Is premarital sexual intercourse always wrong?" and I said "Yes." This surprised her somewhat, because psychiatrists are not supposed to employ terms that carry value judgments. We argued it back and forth a good deal, and she backed me into a corner several times, but my final defense was, "If you exhibit uncertainty or ambivalence on this question, then you are faced with the task of making decisions as to when it is right and when it is wrong." I said I prefer to take the viewpoint that if college students are found to be having intercourse, that's understandable. It's been going on for as long as there have been colleges. We do not condemn them, but we do not confuse them by saying that what they did was right. Rather, the college maintains the ideal standard of society in general, even though it is not adhered to by large segments of society. The idea exists, and it is the job of those of us who work with students not to pass judgment, not to moralize, but to help them live up to the idea.

If this can be done, values, as John E. Smith (31) indicates, can be made to stand as the referent points for decisions and action. This should be quite clear from the example given concerning feelings and behavior with respect to Negroes. It is not impossible that a whole set of unhappy and inimical behaviors can be intercepted and changed through reference to given guidelines.

In the loosening of religious precepts and in the inevitable changes in the times we have lost a set of guidelines for behavior and living. This is as it should be. But, in fact, in these complex times, a vacuum has been created—probably just when we could least afford it. Something must take its place, and no doubt something will. Hopefully, whatever it is, it will move us away rather than toward "Walden Two." The cry for guiding principles, evolved by ourselves, although by no means popular, is yet not a cry in the wilderness.

Although the setting is in higher education, it is not inappropriate to hear George Stern, whose work on differential college cultures is well known, on the problem of student needs (32).

> The excitement of ideas and discussion which I once found at Chicago as an undergraduate, I have re-discovered in some of my own classes today. But the challenge of abstractions, principles, and values in these current instances has been aroused not by intellectualism but by inter-personalism. Students today seem interested in inter-personal behavior, the analysis of motivation, and the problems of dealing effectively and with decency in human relations. Any material placed in this context arouses a depth and intensity of response which belies the apathy and privation encountered elsewhere.
>
> But there is another aspect to this problem. For many of the students in today's college classrooms, the ability to participate even

under the circumstances just described seems severely limited by a deeply ingrained fear of introspection, self-expression, and departure from stereotyped views. Above all, they fear the consequences of personal freedom and seek security in dependence and conformity.

ON THE EXAMINED LIFE[3]

The examined life has been cited as a value but requires more detailed attention. As a goal, as a commitment, its hold on man is ages old and has been attested to by great souls in all times. In countless generations past this task had to be done intuitively, or only in the autumn of life; in our time there is a methodology for progress toward it.

How can the school reinforce or help to bring it about?

In addition to specific procedures, and in the same way that it emphasizes good citizenship in many school settings, it can maintain search and awareness of self as a general educational goal. Since available subject-matter texts do not generally have this type of orientation, teachers will provide their own adaptations if only they are convinced of the validity of the problem and its potential contribution. Of course, to do this they must know what they are about.

This should be one of the school's leitmotivs. In this area there are quite specific teachings that the school can provide and learnings that it can foster.

MAINTAINING SELF-RECORDS

The initial work in the maintenance of behavior logs, of others, but not self, is reported by Prescott (27) and by Peck and Prescott (25). This is part of an ambitious program in teacher-training at the University of Maryland Institute for Child Study which, however, is addressed to adults. Briefly, the observer learns to view and record

---

[3] It is taken for granted that by definition counselors are in the business of helping students in examination of their motives, assessing the energy and weight behind each, and seeing them as a pattern. The counselor's job is to assist the student, to use the pat phrase, to achieve degrees of self-understanding. This is the purpose of psychological testing, and the way in which occupational information should be utilized. Counseling interviews should serve precisely the same purpose. It is on the basis of self-understanding that choices should be made, as a result of weighing of alternatives. For each available choice, information is considered in terms of probable outcome and importance to the individual according to his own needs and his own development.

behavior objectively and in specific detail. As nearly as it is possible
to do so, he becomes a camera eye and recording ear. He becomes
aware of the distorting effect of interjecting his own values and pre-
dispositions in noting behavior. This is the critically important first
stage. After a sufficient number of such samples of behavior are
gathered, characteristic behavior is identified and interpreted.[4]

Two departures are proposed for consideration in adapting this
type of methodology for the schools. First, the records to be maintained are self-records, not observation records of others. In some respects this makes the task easier; in others difficulties arise. It is less
threatening to observe others since the self is not immediately involved. The walls do not go up automatically, the fences are not
immediately charged with electricity. Corrections in method by the
observer are capable of being accepted without considerable ego
involvement. This is even more pertinent when data are to be pulled
together for interpretation. On the other hand, the individual, as his
own subject, is always available. This is a greater advantage than
might be granted at first thought. Although they may be hidden and
distorted, the all-important areas of feelings, fears, embarrassments,
guilts, gratifications, unhappinesses, satisfactions, at best inferred from
observation of others, are here at hand.

Little work has been done in the maintenance of self-records,
although in a way all self-study proposals require keeping notes of
some kind. Horney's system (11) requires keeping track of free associations and involves developing a shorthand system for quick nota-
tions. In the context of the need for training in self-study, Dollard
and Miller (3) note that this may seem a laborious amount of training
to inflict upon a child and go on to make a useful point:

> We think, however, that this kind of training would not have to be
> invoked very long before the child would begin to get the hang of
> it. For all we know, it might be as easy to learn as the multiplication
> table. We have no doubt that however strange such training may
> seem at the present time it will sometime be part of the repertory of
> human culture.
> The mind of the child could be trained to deal with such prob-

---

[4] Data on the usefulness and contribution of the program is presented in reference
13. No doubt there are related approaches elsewhere. For instance, Richard Jones'
(15) report of his own work but on a preparatory school level is noteworthy. The
Institute for Child Study program should stand as an example only of what is
possible.

lems if the home and the school were able to train it. Much that has later to be done by exhausting treatment of adults might be taught mass-wise at elementary levels. Both parent and elementary-school teacher must eventually learn to train children to use their minds in solving emotional problems. As adults, such children would then naturally have recourse to self-study when they were faced with bothersome problems.

Elsewhere, the present writer (29) has called attention to other literature in this area including Peck's study, which showed that with minimum help the untrained individual can make notable progress toward greater insight into his own behavior. In a six-month self-record aimed at identifying anxiety and the related security operations, his subjects, under Peck's guidance, presented courageous personal material. They began to see their characteristic patterns of behavior and made appropriate inferences concerning their living. To a limited extent, the present writer has used Peck's method with occasional students in mental hygiene classes. A brief excerpt from Peck's research (24) may illustrate the self-observation record:

> There are one or two people in my section who previously annoyed me because of overbearing attitudes which resulted in any number of people being embarrassed by these two individuals at different times (this annoyed me even when it was not directed at me, because in my being witness to such). This particular young lady seemed to be completely satisfied once she had made some sarcastic retort. (I believe it was my subconscious awareness of my duplication of such actions in my own relation to my sister—that I was getting too much of a "kick" out of being sarcastic—that I had become aware of its implications.) Her actions no longer annoy me and I found myself injecting a few remarks into her conversation with another recently, which went something like this: "Millie, I hope you don't think like you talk as far as real feelings are concerned. I believe it is from your mouth out and I conclude your bark is worse than the bite." She laughed as she walked toward my desk and said "You sound like the only person around here who understands me."

The second departure is that these records will be maintained by school pupils. Although at present lower age limits can only be guessed at, the method probably ought not to be tried with children below junior high school age. If the basic idea is tenable, these limits can be established in standard experimental fashion.

The specter of privatism might just as well be faced since it is, in

any case, abroad. The fearful must defend their fears and we shall
have to do the best we can, which now and again may not be very
much. Ideally, a program of self-records or any program in this area
might have its origin in discussion at teacher and PTA meetings.
School personnel and parents should grow together in understanding
and acceptance of this type of program. The strong threats that drawing the shades has, in terms of what one's fancy fears might be exposed, must be taken into account.

THE INTERPRETATION OF DREAMS

The very use of these words may raise hackles. The beads of sweat
may rise at the idea of so personal, difficult, and disconcerting a task.
The idea may be too difficult, require too much skill on the part of
those who attempt to impart it, and require too much to be learned
by those who attempt to learn. The idea may be a very poor one;
friends with whom it has been discussed shake their heads very doubt-
fully, but it ought to be considered. It does not necessarily mean that
dreams will be produced and interpreted in the group situation. It
could mean that the mode of understanding one's dreams might be
taught. After all, it *is* a skill in understanding; many have been taught
the skill and have demonstrated that they can become quite good at it
and that understandings gained have been very useful to them, sometimes phenomenally so. Other than to indicate that there are a number
of major contributions in this area of experience, e.g., Bonime's *The
Clinical Use of Dreams*, and Diamond's popular book *The Science of
Dreams*, it does not seem fruitful to enter into discussion of this fertile
area for man's understanding of himself. If this area is explored in a
school setting it will require competence of a type that needs no list of
titles of books for assistance.

It is not proposed that the curriculum be made to include a course
with the title of this brief subsection. Such material properly belongs
in a framework which includes various aspects of self. Since dreams,
like examination of anxiety-loaded behavior, can be a road to self-
understanding, this section might properly have been included in the
notes on teaching the dynamics of behavior. It has been separated
in order to highlight it. Nevertheless, the vehicle for self-exploration
is at hand in quite a few schools in the formal psychology courses and
less formal group discussions of human behavior, personality, or
understanding.

ON MONEY AND SKILLS

Friends who have seen this material have asked, even granting the pertinence of some points, who is going to provide the instruction and who will pay the bills? The answers are not comfortable, but they are simple enough. Such a program will cost money. But money is easier to come by than comfort. It is not really a problem. If we want this kind of program badly enough, we will provide the money. What we need to start with is the interest and conviction; ways to finance it will be found.

The problem of finding skilled instructors is in part related to budget. However, such a program should be very attractive to concerned workers who see little profit in ameliorative and curative procedures. The school can follow the example of other concerned groups in a time of competition for scarce skills and train selected faculty for the new roles they are to play. It can also call on mental health personnel, even though they are in a very short supply, because this is precisely how scarce personnel should be used, where greatest influence can be exercised.

REFERENCES

1. Allport, G. W. *Pattern and Growth in Personality.* New York: Holt, Rinehart & Winston, 1961, p. 223.
2. *Basic Approaches to Mental Health in the Schools.* Reprint Series from the *Personnel and Guidance Journal.* Washington, D. C.: American Personnel and Guidance Association, 1959.
3. Dollard, J., and Miller, N. E. *Personality and Psychotherapy.* New York: McGraw-Hill, 1950.
4. Ellis, Albert. Rational Psychotherapy. *J. Gen. Psychol.,* 1959, 35–49.
5. Farnsworth, Dana. The Need for a Comprehensive Mental Health Program: Accent on Prevention, in *Higher Education and Mental Health, Proceedings of a Conference,* Gainesville, Fla.: The University of Florida, Sept. 25–26, 1963, p. 71.
6. Fromm-Reichmann, Frieda. *Principles of Intensive Psychotherapy.* Chicago: The University of Chicago Press, 1950, p. 95.
7. Ganzhorn, Betty. A Cognitive Point of View in Counseling College Students. *J. of College Student Personnel,* March, 1962, 126–29.
8. Hartmann, Heinz. *Essays in Ego Psychology.* New York: International Universities Press, 1964, p. 173.
9. Hartmann, H., Kris, E., and Lowenstein, R. M. Comments on the Formation of the Psychic Structure, in *The Psychoanalytic Study of*

the Child, Vol. II. New York: International Universities Press, 1946, p. 19.

10. Heider, Fritz. *The Psychology of Interpersonal Relations.* New York: John Wiley & Sons, 1958, p. 111.

11. Horney, Karen. *Self-Analysis.* New York: W. W. Norton, 1942.

12. Hutson, P. W. *The Guidance Function in Education.* New York: Appleton-Century-Crofts, 1958.

13. Institute for Child Study, The University of Maryland. *A Report to the Grant Foundation.* April, 1958 (mimeographed).

14. Jahoda, Marie. *Current Concepts of Positive Mental Health.* Monograph Series No. 1, Joint Commission on Mental Health. New York: Basic Books, 1958.

15. Jones, R. M. The Role of Self-Knowledge in the Educative Process. *Harvard Educational Review,* 1962, *32,* 200–09.

16. Maslow, A. H. *Motivation and Personality.* New York: Harper & Row, 1954.

17. McGuire, W. J. A Syllogistic Analysis of Cognitive Relationships, in *Attitude Organization and Change, Yale Studies in Attitude and Communication,* Vol. III, Hoveland, C. I., and Rosenberg, M. J. (eds.). New Haven: Yale University Press, 1960, p. 65.

18. Monroe, R. L. Intellectualizing Techniques in Psychotherapy, in *Case Studies in Counseling and Psychotherapy,* Burton, Arthur (ed.). Englewood Cliffs, N. J.: Prentice Hall, 1959.

19. Murphy, Gardner. *Freeing Intelligence Through Teaching.* New York: Harper & Row, 1961.

20. Murphy, Gardner. *Freeing Intelligence Through Teaching.* New York: Harper & Row, 1961, p. 22.

21. Murray, H. A., and Kluckhohn, C. Outline of a Conception of Personality, in *Personality in Nature, Society, and Culture,* Kluckhohn, C., Murray, H. A., and Schneider, D. M. (eds.), 2nd ed., New York: Alfred A. Knopf, 1953, p. 40.

22. Neisser, Ulric. Cultural and Cognitive Discontinuity, in *Anthropology and Human Behavior,* Gladwin, T., and Sturtevant, W. C. (eds.). Washington, D.C.: The Anthropological Society of Washington, 1962.

23. Ojemann, R. J., Levitt, E. E., Lyle, W. H., and Whiteside, M. F. The Effect of a "Causal" Teacher-Training Program and Certain Curricular Changes on Grade School Children. *J. Exp. Educ.* 1955, *2,* 95–114.

24. Peck, Bernard. Effect of Self-Observation upon Self-Awareness: An Exploratory Study. Unpublished Doctoral Thesis, University of Maryland, 1957.

25. Peck, B., and Prescott, D. A. The Program at the Institute for Child

Study, the University of Maryland. *Personnel Guidance J.*, 1958, 2, 114–22.

26. Phillips, E. L. *Psychotherapy: A Modern Theory and Practice.* Englewood Cliffs, N. J.: Prentice-Hall, 1957.

27. Prescott, D. *The Child in the Educative Process.* New York: McGraw-Hill, 1957.

28. Samler, Joseph. An Examination of Client Strength and Counselor Responsibility. *J. Counsel. Psychol.*, 1962, 9, 5–11.

29. ————. Basic Approaches to Mental Health: An Attempt at Synthesis. *Personnel Guid. J.* 1959, 37, 639–43.

30. Schachtel, Ernest C. *Metamorphosis.* New York: Basic Books, 1959.

31. Smith, John E. *Value Convictions and Higher Education.* New Haven: The Edward W. Hagen Foundation, 1958.

32. Stern, George. Student Values and Their Relationship to the College Environment, in *Research on College Students,* The Western Interstate Commission for Higher Education, Boulder, and the Center for Higher Education, Berkeley. December, 1960, p. 103.

33. Thorne, F. C. *Principles of Personality Counseling.* Brandon, Vt.: *J. Clinical Psychol.*, 1950.

34. Withall, John. Mental Health in the Classroom, *J. Teacher Education,* 1964, 2, 193–99.

DAVID V. TIEDEMAN
FRANK L. FIELD

Guidance: The Science of Purposeful Action Applied Through Education

FROM CONDITIONING TO LIBERATION THROUGH GUIDANCE-IN-EDUCATION

IT IS OUR BELIEF that, in general, people would like education to be liberating rather than conditioning. We believe that this expectation is held for education in all of its forms: in schools, in colleges and universities, and in industries. Admittedly this is a generalization; throughout history there are frequent instances in which education has been used consciously to condition students, to make them capable of achieving ends chosen for them in advance. However, despite hot and cold wars and the very real requirements they impose upon us, our present culture has advanced to a state where *overt* conditioning is incompatible with our expressed goals. Science has convinced us that conditioning, to be most effective, must be so overt, so obviously undertaken, that our particular American goals become travesties when pursued in such fashion.

Does this mean, then, that education in our schools, colleges, and industrial training programs is already designed solely to liberate, to make the student more capable of choosing and achieving his own ends? If not, what has all this to do with guidance?

Our answer to these questions is that current educational policies do not reflect an objective consideration of the liberating-conditioning issue, and that guidance has begun to focus educators' attention upon this great lack of objective consideration. Furthermore, Guidance[1]—as we define it, at least—can contribute to the identification of this problem, and perhaps to its better solution as well. Consequently, we choose to base our argument for a more operationally defined and more powerful Guidance function upon a clearer understanding both of the setting in which such a function must take place, and of the specific educational goals derived from such understanding.

Hopefully, it will become clear that our procedure for achieving this goal, *i.e.*, developing a new model *of* Guidance-in-education, parallels the functional approach we propose for the fuller achievement of specific individual goals *through* Guidance-in-education. In brief, we will assess what guidance is now, develop a concept of what we now would like it to be, and design a guide for choosing actions to attain our current goal.

THE CURRENT STATUS OF GUIDANCE: TECHNOLOGY, NOT PROFESSION

Schools and colleges were organized and institutionalized long before the first "counselor" was formally employed as such. It therefore seems clear to us that the current practice of guidance stems from the traditional desires of educational authorities and practitioners to make teach*ing* more powerful without limiting the authority of teach*ers*. This role of *aiding* teachers is necessarily based upon the assumption that the teacher is in a position superior to that of the counselor. Such a relationship further implies that the counselor is necessarily a technician; his theory that of a technology. Thus the guidance counselor's technology stems from studies to improve teaching and learning as defined by educational authorities, *primarily teachers or those concerned solely with teaching*. In this framework, it is easy to comprehend the efforts of early guidance practitioners to evaluate, to select, and to place pupils in order to achieve the goals of the school and of the community. As technicians they were neither expected nor invited to play a professional role in deciding what these goals might be.

However, as these practitioners functioned under authority stemming from principals, deans, or teachers (and perhaps because they

---

[1] The term "Guidance" (capitalized) will denote the professional use of a science of purposeful action within a specific structure of education. Other relevant, but not identical, connotations of guidance will be denoted, whenever grammatically possible, without capitalization of the word.

were trained partially by psychologists) they came into far more revealing contact with students than had teachers and administrators. They saw more than the "traditional" teaching-learning process, and their ideas began to have an impact upon educators. Education itself began to appear more complex, both in practice and in theory. As a result of this, and of progress in the behavioral sciences in general, we now possess sufficient knowledge of human behavior to make significant contributions to the process by which individuals assume responsibility for their own particular goals.

However incomplete this knowledge, we hope to apply it more fully and more effectively to the process of education in this country. Unfortunately the current nature of guidance practice—taking place *beside* rather than *in* education—blocks such a full and effective application. There are two major reasons for this situation:

1. It is impossible either to marshal or develop the resources—scholarship, basic research, rigorous training, and occupational opportunity—necessary to outgrow our status as technicians and/or trainers of technicians. Because we lack a valid professional identity, we are still neither expected nor invited *creatively* to develop the science of education. Rather, we are hired to *apply borrowed principles* from current behavioral sciences in order to assist teachers in pursuing their own "established" educational goals. In essence, we believe that our ancillary role has derived from the position of the teacher as the central figure, rather than a partner, in American Education.

2. Those of us who do manage to achieve professional status (but usually as psychologists or sociologists, scientists or professors rather than as guidance personnel) are nevertheless employed to enhance the practice of teachers, to operate under the management of persons representing *different* occupations, *i.e.*, teachers or psychotherapists, principals or deans, superintendents or presidents.

As long as this situation continues we will be the first to admit that there is no Guidance profession in and of itself, and furthermore, that *there should be none.* Perhaps a brief digression will clarify our admission, and our hopes as well.

WHAT IS A PROFESSION?

From our point of view, professional activity requires, first of all, the *creative* application of current knowledge to solve a particular type of problem. Secondly, because these problems involve the well-being of many people, society requires that professional practice be responsible as well as creative. In essence, then, the ingredients making up a profession are:

1. an ever-developing body of knowledge;
2. a desire to achieve certain general conditions in and through specific instances;
3. individuals capable of creatively achieving the desired general condition in particular instances; and finally,
4. a social "mandate" to use, within certain limits, the considerable power inherent in the possession of such expertise. When we use the term "professional practice" our referent includes all these ingredients. Consequently, we feel that at present the term "guidance" does not refer to any such definable practice.

We observe, first, that there are several bodies of knowledge making up the behavioral sciences, each dealing with one or more artificially separated aspect(s) of human behavior. Diversities of interest, technique, and goal have prevented an integrated science (the science of applying behavioral sciences) from developing. We observe, secondly, that the resulting disciplinary specialization impedes the development of *general* goals for guidance—or even for education. There is, in other words, little consensus regarding a future condition which would be more generally desirable. We observe, thirdly, that the resulting diffusion of ends prevents the development of criteria for determining the relevance of available knowledge. It is difficult, if not impossible, to choose the best means to an end when the end is not reasonably well defined. Finally, the various applied disciplines have been granted separate mandates, which vary considerably with regard to limits. Compare, for example, the mandate given the medical practitioner with that given the educator or the psychologist—let alone the guidance practitioner. But compare, also, their training and supervision—their gradual assumption of responsibility. What would *you* say to the potential suicide teetering on a ledge?

RECENT EFFORTS TO MAKE GUIDANCE A PROFESSION

The issue of professionalization in guidance became central during the 1950's. Statements have developed from concern on the part of two major occupational associations, Federal and local government, various foundations, and individual scholars and/or practitioners. For example:

A. The Associational View

1. The American Psychological Association has attempted to establish and maintain certain distinctions between the professions of psychiatry and psychology. Within the Association itself, professional psychologists have examined and discussed distinctions among clinical, counseling, industrial, and school psychologies (5, 6).

2. The American Personnel and Guidance Association has recently made it more possible to distinguish members according to training/experience, since membership is often held in two or more Divisions of the Association. Several members are now engaged in ascertaining the meaning, consequences, and possibilities of professionalization (7). The officers of the Association and its divisions are also trying to improve the education of counselors (2, 11, 18).

B. The Influence of Money and of Law

1. The National Defense Education Act of 1958 reflected considerable governmental concern with the nature and purpose of guidance. However, the most immediate result of the Act was really a threat to then-emerging attempts to make guidance a profession; underlying generally desirable but undefined goals such as "individual freedom," the *operational* goal of the legislation was to develop and support a technology designed to implement governmental interests. Fortunately, the increased level of support made possible by the Act has still served to improve practice. Indirectly through conferences, wider consultation, and subsidized training programs and institutes, guidance practice has been provided with a firmer basis with regard to training—and *re*training.

2. Departments of Education in several states also seem to be discussing new modifications in the certification of counselors. Foundations and government agencies have supported several conferences (1, 14). Generally, however, foundations also tar guidance with the brush of "technology" and seem to make little effort to support the development of a profession. Fellowships and other such support for training programs are not readily available. Guidance still has to clarify its own goals if it is to escape public and foundation distrust of "pupil adjustment," "mental health," and the like.

C. The View of Our Theorists

Since 1950 many individuals have written of professionalization in guidance. We shall point specifically to only Professors Robert H. Mathewson, Donald E. Super, and C. Gilbert Wrenn, however.

1. Mathewson was one of the first to struggle with matters of theory *and* practice in an introductory text (8). He has also chaired several committees and informal discussion groups which examined various theories from the behavioral sciences in a search for ideas relevant to guidance practice. He is one, at least, who has shown a desire to grow in response to the need, to keep his theory alive.

2. Super has simultaneously been developing theory in vocational development (13), and a goal for counseling psychology (12). He has used several associational offices and professional appointments to advance the cause of a profession of counseling psychology. He has been instrumental in gaining support for a conference on vocational development theory (14), for a monograph on theories in career development, and he is now seeking support for a conference on training for counseling psychology.

3. Wrenn is one of the very few who has struggled with *philosophical* issues in the practice of guidance (17). He is also one of several now concerned with clarification of a long-standing problem in the practice of counseling, *i.e.*, the danger of imposing the counselors' values upon the student. Furthermore, he has gone beyond the "mere" identification of this issue—and of several others as well. He was singled out by the American Personnel and Guidance Association to conduct the American Guidance Inquiry (18). This report recommends training for guidance practice which would represent great improvement, but even this training would not make possible the assumption of responsibility necessary to achieve the goal we propose.

These men have been singled out with reluctance because there are many deserving of mention. The statements heretofore noted do attest to the concern for the present "vitality" of guidance, however. Those interested in a history of the many controversies can readily catch their spirit in the pages of *The American Psychologist, Counselor Education and Supervision* (particularly the issue for Spring, 1962), *Journal of Counseling Psychology,* and the *Personnel and Guidance Journal.*

DEFICIENCIES IN CURRENT VIEWS OF GUIDANCE

As we reflect upon these and other efforts to define the problems involved in creating a profession to meet a recognized need, it is clear that each has fallen short—far short—of its mark. Even though the need *is* for a broad design, we observe that the broader the proposed theories of guidance, the farther short of the mark they fall; current theories expand upon some singular point of view (usually technical), and therefore cannot become comprehensive as well as broad. The particular orientation of each writer has constricted his proposal; personal, occupational, or theoretical—nearly all statements about guidance reflect firm (though rarely overt) commitment to maintain a *status quo.*

We must confess to a degree of puzzlement on this score, because most introductions and prefaces within the guidance literature contain frequent reference to "crises," "turning points," and the need for "drastic revisions." We cannot understand why conditions conjuring up such fearful images should at the same time command such strong vested interest, or be approached with such profound conservatism. Consider, for example, the following premises for definition, all common in the literature:

1. "Guidance is what I (am required to) do, because I was hired as a guidance counselor."
2. "Guidance is what I (am able to) do, because I was trained in a guidance program."
3. Guidance involves the practice of non-directive (or analytic, ego, eclectic) counseling because . . ."
4. "Guidance is psychotherapy (or preventive mental health, or counseling psychology, or etc.)."

Although the problems underlying many of these issues have been evident, they have not been clearly presented to those now engaged in the practice of guidance. There is a relative lack of literature in guidance which *simultaneously* considers the matters of setting, of purpose, of developing theory, and of perfecting technique. The few broad studies available do not reflect consideration to a depth sufficient for identifying issues in professionalization, or to offer a basis for preference which can be examined, criticized, and gradually refined. Such an opinion has been offered by Barry and Wolf (3, 4), Scanlan (10) and Tiedeman (16).

It is our primary thesis that *simultaneous* examination of setting, purpose, theory, and technique in guidance will clarify issues not present in the debates we have cited. Furthermore, we believe that such simultaneous examination will substantiate our two other contentions:

1. that Guidance as a professional practice must exist within the total framework of education; and,

2. that the authority of educational administrators for Guidance must be modified.

We therefore turn next to our consideration of setting, purpose, theory, and technique.

A Proposed Setting for Guidance Practice

Guidance, as we define it, can exist only within a process of *liberating* education. This means a process in which the student is free from overt conditioning or indoctrination, and, as much as possible, from ignorance or bias of which the teacher is unaware. Guidance is an integral part of, and also dependent upon, such education. Education, in other words, is not synonymous with either teaching or learning. Nor is education only the interaction of teacher and learner. Rather it involves the full transaction resulting from a mutual pursuit of something desired by students and teachers alike. Teaching, learning, guidance—all are *necessary* to such education, but none is *sufficient* by itself or in partial combination.

Toward the Establishment of Purpose Through Guidance

We believe that to establish purpose in Guidance, ends must come into existence before, or simultaneously with, means. This premise does not involve the issue of teleology, as might be argued. A goal, if defined as "a desired *future* state," certainly cannot exist prior to the means for its achievement. But a *concept* of this desired future state can exist in the present. Thus it is quite possible to compare the present state of X with the concept of a future state of X, to note the difference, and to choose, develop, modify and perform a series of actions designed to reduce this difference.

This process is what we mean by the term "purposeful action." It describes:

1. the behavior we hope to encourage on the part of individual students;

2. the behavior we hope to make more practicable for individual Guidance professionals in education; and,

3. the behavior we hope to make more operational in training such professionals through the mutual development of professional theory.

Thus "purposeful" means "not random," *i.e.,* "more likely to achieve the currently desired by acting contingently upon the currently observed." It is our current observation that contemporary activity in education is undesirably random in general and undesirably constricted in particular instances.

THE ORIGINS OF OUR GOAL

That which we desire to make generally possible can already be observed in many particular cases. There are numerous individuals who manage, on their own, to pass successfully through the processes we are about to describe. Their success, if not perfect or complete, is certainly substantial enough to elicit our desire to make it more operational. Let us now develop our notion of *discontinuity*, and follow one youth through a period of such discontinuity imposed upon him by society.

We observe that people constantly change. They grow older, larger, stronger, more capable—and eventually they begin to grow weaker again. They learn, ignore, forget and/or apply the results of their own and others' experience. All these processes have their "inside" effects, not all of which enter the individual's awareness.

We also observe that peoples' environments change. The environment can be described as a series of states or conditions, a series of situations. As such, it can be seen to change when the individual moves from one situation to another, and also, because each situation is dynamic, while the individual is present "within" it. Just as the individual is not fully aware of his "inside" changes, so is he partially unaware of those taking place "outside."

The individual who provides our example is a youth in junior high school—for him, a situation. During a period of several years our youth grows older, stronger, larger. He encounters considerable information, he retains somewhat less, and he uses still less with purpose —his purpose. (Recall our definition.) Our youth changes, nevertheless, far more than he can realize at any one time.

During this same period the school gradually changes, too. Such changes may include structure, organization, actual personnel, and the competence of personnel. In other words, the youth's younger brother will encounter quite a different situation as he "passes through" several years later. By this time, however, *our* youth will have passed on to high school. In so doing, he will have experienced one *major discontinuity* in his environment.

Our observation of this *imposed* discontinuity is the key to our whole argument. It provides a basis for structuring:

1. some of what we know to be relevant from the behavioral sciences;

2. an anaylsis of our youth's current situation (in this case, that of a high school student);

3. our concept of an "ideal"—more desirable—state for him; and,

4. our theory for a "science of the purposeful, integrated application of various basic and applied behavioral sciences," *i.e.*, for structuring our theory for Guidance.

Let us very briefly consider these tasks in order.

A. What do we know from behavioral science?

We know that our youth is changing physically, in obvious, readily observable fashion and also in a more subtle, pervasive fashion. Our youth has adolescent problems to handle, together with increased and quite different academic and social demands, plus increased amounts of acquired information to integrate with his personal functioning. These are observed facts requiring no further comment.

B. What is his present state?

We know that our high school youth has experienced a major external discontinuity, as well as the internal changes resulting from his physical-emotional development. He has, in other words, become a functioning new member of a sustantively different system. He will find it necessary to learn new ways of experiencing new things; a point of view once appropriate for junior high school is suddenly obsolete. He will also find that he is no longer the same person who held these obsolete points of view. In brief, then, our observation of his current stage suggests that he *definitely* needs:

1. information about his new situation;

2. revised criteria for evaluating this new information in order to use it for his own developing purposes; and,

3. knowledge regarding available sources of assistance.

In addition to this "introduction" to his new state, our youth *may* need:

1. help in establishing or modifying purposes of his own;

2. help in increasing his awareness of the internal and/or external changes that have taken and are taking place;

3. help in acquiring "academic content"; and/or
4. extensive psychotherapy.

Note that one or more of these last four needs may or may not exist; the problems are certainly real for most students, but not everyone requires *individualized* help with them.

There is yet another aspect of our high school youth's current state, one that is less noticeable in the transition from junior to senior high school, but one which would immediately attract our attention if the transition were to college, work, or military service. This is the less introductory, more *evaluative* consideration regarding whether or not, for our youth, the new situation:

1. Is an appropriate step beyond the previous state; *e.g., should* our youth be a new member (yet or ever)—is he able or prepared to pass through it?
2. Is it an appropriate step toward our youth's goal, or toward what we hope will remain possible for him; *e.g.,* does our youth *need* to pass through this state?
3. Is this a state containing a "choice point" or a "point of no return," regarding which we feel constrained closely to watch, if not to intervene, in his youthful decisions?

In general, then, an analysis of the current state of our high school freshman, structured as above, results in the conclusion that the best teaching in the world will not, by itself, lead to what we desire for him. Nor will the most refined teaching or subject matter. Consequently, we can profit from the formation of a concept regarding an "ideal"[2]—*i.e.,* more desirable—state for our youth to experience; in short, a goal for education.

C. What would constitute an "ideal" new state for our youth to enter? And how would the ideal differ from the current state we have just analyzed?

As long as we are being idealistic, we can say that an ideal state would be one in which the awareness of discontinuity in individual

---

[2] The "ideal" is a desired state, of course. However, not all desired states are "ideal" either to the person seeking passage into the desired state or to another person reflecting upon the first person's attainment of the desired state. Furthermore, person and observer may differ in the construction of the desired state and of the bases for seeking it. We use the term to emphasize the "yet to be achieved" nature of the goals.

experience would *contribute* to independent individual development. "Onward and upward" would describe the process perfectly. However, in addition to being idealistic we aspire to be scientific; our concept must be operationally defined, emphasizing the difference between what we want to create and what currently exists.

At this point it might be well to justify (and limit) our idealism to some extent. Thus there are some individuals who experience what we describe as discontinuity, and who nevertheless manage to seek out, recognize, and use the information necessary for their development. As we stated earlier, if their development isn't perfect, it is certainly good enough to make us wish we could guarantee it to everyone. So we don't expect miracles or perfection; we hope instead to enable *more* people to realize as much of their potential as *some* do already.

Analyzing the current state of our high school youth leads to a conclusion that discontinuity in experience is a partial (and wholly natural) result of individual development "inside" and individual progress "outside"—actually transition from one "outside" to another. In other words, the individual's experience changes, and so does that which is available for him to experience.

Discontinuity is also a partial result of the frequently step-by-step nature of the experiencing process. Thus the oft-cited "aha experience" results in a jump from one point of view to another, a partial resolution of discontinuity. From this point it is possible to begin forming a concept of the desired future state: it is one containing elements which increase the individual's chances to achieve his own moments of sudden new awareness, and conversely, one that does not contain elements to inhibit such achievement. The task of guidance, then, is to control these elements. A structured description of how this task might be achieved becomes—lo and behold—a theory for Guidance.

D.   What theoretical structure would suggest an integrated, scientific application of knowledge from various behavioral sciences to adaptive individual resolutions of discontinuity?

In essence, we see the answer in a structure requiring the presence of a person equipped to represent to students the particular system of which they have just become parts. In one sense such a person would serve to *introduce* the new environment to the student, to provide information about it, to help the student become aware of the important differences in his new surroundings. Freshman orientation—in some colleges—is an example of this function. It goes beyond the provision of simple facts, as implied by the term "orientation"; "reorientation" might be more descriptive of the purpose underlying such programs.

As suggested previously, in discussing the present state of our particular youth, there are other problems facing new members of any educational system. The previously proposed representative must *evaluate* or *assess* as well as introduce. The evaluation should include, for example:

1. Should the student be a member yet?
2. Does he need to "pass through" this system at all?
3. How can the process contribute to his movement toward an appropriate subsequent system?
4. Does the student require any specialized assistance?

Each of the behavioral sciences, whether basic or applied, consists of many individuals' reports concerning their experiences with behavior. These reports contain, or can be used to establish, bases for predicting and controlling aspects of human behavior. Some such sciences produce these bases, others produce practitioners. But despite current opinions or claims, none produces practitioners of guidance per se. Each can produce information, rules, or individuals that can contribute to the achievement of our goal for Guidance, but none embodies that goal—as is right and proper. Guidance, as we define it, does not exist in the various outgrowths of this or that science, practice, or art. If it does come to exist, it will consist of a flexible but *purposeful* integration of various skilled, individual functions.

Let us hasten to add that we do not envisage either a "Renaissance Man" or a "Jack of all Trades" who would necessarily be "Master of None." Rather, we envision a master of *creatively administering the application* of many "trades" to the familiar problems encountered in passing through an equally familiar system. Our ideal Guidance practitioner would serve to bring together student and information, pupil and teacher, client and counselor, patient and therapist. He would hold a general conceptual model of the "ideal student making ideal progress through or within an ideal system." He would possess the ability to see where an individual fell short of this ideal concept. And finally, he would possess the knowledge necessary to marshal the special skills and/or information most relevant to an individual's idiosyncratic problems.

It becomes obvious that such a practitioner would also be practicing a profession, even in terms of our rather stringent definition. It becomes equally obvious that our ideal practitioner does not have very many currently existing counterparts.

SOME QUALIFICATIONS

We have implied that the basic interest to be served by Guidance is that of the individual. On this we stand. We offer the following qualifying statements in the hope that they will prevent unnecessary objections based upon preconceptions, specifically hasty conclusions that we represent certain "whipping boys" of the past. Thus:

1. We are not preaching any known form of "life adjustment"; the term suggests many desirable ends, but fails to define any specific, operational means. Good *is* better than evil, but this knowledge hardly specifies the next step.

2. We are not proposing any form of coddling, spoon-feeding, or so-called progressive measures. In fact, rather than helping students avoid the frequently unpleasant realities encountered during their development, we hope to provide a structure, and suggest a function, that would make such avoidance difficult (at least for those individuals who do not display marked pathology).

3. In a similar vein, we do not mean to suggest any form of social engineering, or brainwashing, aimed at providing a "good set of middle-class values" for our youth. We envision no homogeneous goal for the socialization process, no need to destroy sub-cultures. High aspiration, religion—even patriotism—are, in reality, matters for individual choice. It is irrational to pretend that an *educational* system can alter this fundamental fact.

A REEXAMINATION OF THE DIFFERENCES BETWEEN TEACHING AND GUIDANCE

We have argued:

1. that education should serve the interests of students;
2. that Guidance is a function within the process of education; and,
3. that Guidance should be granted a mandate distinct from that of the teacher.

It now becomes possible to establish a basis for differentiating the two complementary functions. In terms of our argument, teaching involves a communication of *others'* experiences—data and conclusions. Guidance, on the other hand, involves primarily an examination of the individual student's experiences—data and the *process of forming* conclusions about them. Teaching continually creates useful discontinuity by saying, "Here are things you do not know, or know how to do." Guidance, on the other hand, deals with the individualized reduction of discontinuity:

1. by pointing out where discontinuity has (or has not yet!) come to exist;

2. by making it *not* seem undesirable or overwhelming, but useful; and,

3. by making it more possible for the individual to choose actions designed to reduce (or establish and *then* reduce) such discontinuity.

It becomes clear that Guidance involves behavioral change, a change quite different from that necessarily induced by teaching. Consequently, quite different aspects of behavioral science become relevant to the practice of Guidance. As suggested previously, the basic difference involves a consideration of purpose, *i.e.,* of action patterns chosen and established to create desired states from observed states. Unfortunately there is no ready-made body of relevant basic theory. Although much of the necessary data may well exist, it has not been integrated by scholars and scientists concerned with *both* behavioral change *and* independence on the part of the individual who is changing. This is why teaching in and of itself is not education. This is why both teaching and Guidance are necessary for the kind of education we claim as our goal. This is why current guidance must be developed into a profession.

We have proposed the beginnings of a goal for Guidance, a goal based upon current observation, current aspiration, and the difference between the two. However, we have not yet suggested what immediate actions might begin to establish our purpose.

The Future in Guidance: Profession, not Technology?

We have implied the existence of basic obstacles to further progress toward professionalization, obstacles which can now be clearly specified. First, the current organization of education places *both* teaching and administration in positions superior to that of guidance, even though the very nature of professional practice requires autonomy. Consequently this situation must be altered *in the schools* before the professional practice of Guidance can become possible.

Second, there is as yet no "science of applying the behavioral sciences" on which the profession of Guidance can be based. *Such a science must come from a scholarly orientation that does not yet exist as a basis for training*; it requires the employment of multidisciplinary means for metadisciplinary ends. In other words, there is no existing facility for training even the scholars needed to develop the profession of Guidance, not "even" at Harvard. Or is there?

It is difficult to justify our conclusion that we have no facility for training the personnel needed to develop Guidance as a profession. At this time we can do no more than show that this is true within Harvard, the situation we know best.

As we engage in proving our point for Harvard, however, we urge you to consider our example in a larger frame. We have done two things as we have written: (1) used a model, (2) to specify a model. We are using a theoretical model to suggest a parallel among several types of purposeful action—by the individual, by the professional, by the profession itself, and by the science underlying the profession—action designed to reduce the discrepancy between the currently experienced and the currently desired. Such an analysis would be incomplete without considering, operationally, *how* the transition can be accomplished. We have already noted many needed modifications in school organization and in the practice of guidance. We must now turn to the university, the second link requiring modification if the now desired goal is to be reached. The facilities necessary for training will continue to be subjects for *debate* (cf. "Recent Efforts to Make Guidance a Profession") until a university *acts*. In all likelihood the debate will continue thereafter, too, but at least it will be based upon some empirical roots. It is for this reason that we turn now to our report on the educational experiment undertaken at Harvard.

An Experiment in Training for Guidance

What of the "currently observed" at Harvard? The program in guidance at Harvard has a capacity it did not have a short decade ago. Some of the hopes Tiedeman outlined in 1957 (15) have now materialized. The Faculty in guidance enjoys support from members of several other Faculties within the University as well as from the Faculty of the Graduate School of Education. The entry of the Graduate School of Education into the School-University Program for Research and Development (SUPRAD) has created for us an unprecedented opportunity for supervised laboratory experience, in both teaching and guidance, in the school systems of Concord, Lexington, and Newton, Massachusetts (9). Members of the Faculty in guidance have research underway in career development, counseling, and psychodiagnosis. Support has been forthcoming for a Center for Research in Careers. Several members of staffs in the training facilities are involved in guidance research and development activities, the School having made several joint appointments with other organizations—schools, colleges and clinics.

The scope of these diverse opportunities provides the guidance student with much of the *background* necessary for the practice of Guidance; our next task is to provide an integrating theoretical framework. Thus the student is exposed to concepts advanced (1) through teaching at the University, and (2) through specialized professional practice in a natural setting—a great improvement over the situation where professors teach what they have never attempted to practice, or where busy practitioners pass on their experience to only a few internes or disciples. However the emerging educator-practitioner is still not a representative of Guidance—as we have defined it. Therefore, we next consider the "currently desired." We do so in terms of two of its operational aspects, function and organization.

A. Function

In terms of function, our present goals are as follows:

1. We need to establish a basis for determining what aspects of any existing science or practice are relevant to future practice by *our students*. For example, the teacher-clinical psychologist is not appointed here to train clinical psychologists, to teach clinical psychology as such, or even to "teach about" clinical psychology. But it remains difficult to establish just what such diverse individual specialists *are* to teach. It seems clear to us that the needed science, and hence the needed teaching, must deal with both the continual modification of a current state *and* of a currently desired goal. In our consideration, the two aspects of this problem must be kept wedded as they are studied, because they are co-functional; we must recognize that we are dealing

with a process of investigation, of practice, *and of revision*. We obviously lack much of the needed science. Unfortunately, we even lack general understanding of the need for such a science. This is why we consider this first, essentially scholarly, task, so important for our goal.

2. We need to establish a basis for guaranteeing the responsibility of our students, for determining their professional adequacy, and for communicating to them a *valid* sense of professional identity. In other words we need standards, and this, too, requires criteria derived from a common purpose. Consider once more the experiences of the medical interne, and compare them with those of guidance internes!

3. We need to develop for our Faculty not only *teacher*-practitioners who understand and accept our more comprehensive goals, but professional *supervisors* as well. Such individuals must oversee student practice in a constantly changing profession, and they must do so without sacrificing standards, falling back upon their own *original* (and diverse) professional identities, or losing sight of our basic goal for Guidance.

4. We need to formulate and to gain acceptance of a charter for the practice of a common profession of Guidance in school and college, and in the educational endeavors organized within governmental agencies and industries. We must assume responsibility for providing professional opportunity—not merely employment—for our graduates. It therefore appears that the primary need in this area will be:

   a. to specify the authority needed for practice in a particular sphere; and

   b. to specify means for resolving truly professional differences between teacher and counselor on issues not clearly within the sphere of one professional or the other.

It seems intuitively clear that the differences noted in (b), above, must be resolved by the superior officer of the two professionals, namely the principal or the superintendent (and to do so, he, too, must be a creative professional).

B. Organization

These four general needs will require revision of the present organizational pattern in our Guidance program. The needed pattern requires augmentation of resources and, undoubtedly, an operational reassessment of responsibility and authority. Since such reorganization depends upon the augmentation of resources, little can be said of the latter until the former become specific. We shall trouble to portray a guideline or two, however, because those guides may further clarify our "research proposal" and the progress of our "pilot study."

Our resources need augmentation in several ways. First, with regard to our faculty, we need greater depth and a wider range. The advantages of the latter are obvious; the advantage of depth, on the other hand, is derived largely from the need for a continual revision of ends and means. Such progress requires both creative and careful change, which in turn requires educator-experimenters of established responsibility and appropriate academic/professional stature. Here depth is essential.

Second, we need to be able to guarantee and to specify the initial jobs of our graduates for a limited time, say two years. This desired expansion in our relations with schools and colleges is needed for recruitment, for training, and for placement. For several years we have attracted very capable students who have had no teaching experience.[3] Greater certainty of initial placement in Guidance is needed for these graduates, or else our sources for students of such quality will quickly become depleted. More importantly, however, *we need these places in order to complete the training of our graduates.* In the year or so that students in guidance are with us we can offer them only an apprenticeship as a counselor. Before assuming responsibilities as master counselor, however, students should serve a two-year[4] stint as journeymen. This stint should be designed so that it will enhance the graduate's knowledge, increase his confidence, provide him with a comfortable sense of professional identity, and complete his qualifications for later independence. We feel that *personal* independence must precede professional independence, *i.e.*, that the practitioner must *feel qualified* as well as be certified.

What, now, of academic responsibility and authority? Must our goals be largely achieved before a school of education dares consider such issues, or are such issues the real bases underlying our proposal? The purpose we seek to establish is that leading to a center for training in the professional application of a science of behavioral change,

---

[3] The absence of prerequisite teaching experience is in keeping with our belief regarding the need for autonomous authority for the counselor in his own sphere. *The counselor need not necessarily be a former teacher. He is not to teach any more.*

[4] Those who stay for the doctorate with us may not need to serve so long as a journeyman; however, even the student qualified for the doctorate in Guidance can benefit from effective supervision.

a science which does not, as yet, exist. And as we stated earlier, it cannot be built *solely* from bits and pieces of other scholarly, scientific, and professional areas. While it is true that the profession we envisage has scholarly and scientific roots in universities as a whole (a fact which has economic as well as scientific advantages), the roots are more deeply imbedded in professional schools of education.

Universities are institutionalized to provide both education and research. However the nature of each process and the degree to which they are kept functionally related varies among universities; and, within universities, between professional faculties and faculties of arts and sciences.

Some research is based upon curiosity and conducted according to the "rules of simon-pure science and scholarship." Another kind of research is based upon curiosity *about* something. When this "something" is man's development, research involves purpose and responsibility as well as creativity and discovery.

Rather than trying to keep the experimenter "out of" the experiment (which is never possible anyway), the new science must *include* the experimenter together with all his hopes and dreams. The vested interest is not in rigorous objectivity as *opposed* to subjectivity, but in the unique class of data containing *both* objectivity and subjectivity— *i.e.*, in man. This is science for man, not man for science.

Returning to the issues of academic responsibility and authority, we find that they do in fact underlie our proposal. We have really called for a new *type* of science, not merely a new science forged from traditional elements available in the arts and sciences. The basic departure lies in the *overt* introduction of desire into the pursuit of scientific results. Like the medical researcher, we would know what we want for man, not just what we want to *find out about* him. To train personnel for this type of investigation, without sacrificing either subjectivity or the equally necessary rigor and objectivity, requires a training facility such as that we have described. This is our belief, and it provides the basis for both our proposal and "our" experiment.

The Essence of Guidance-in-Education

We began with a brief overview of current guidance practice which emphasized a need for change; guidance and education are not now achieving our purposes. However, the survey revealed still another fact, *i.e.*, that current guidance is not by itself an adequate base upon which to build a profession of Guidance. We therefore proposed that the basis must lie in the total process of education, offering the following principal arguments:

1. Liberating education requires an addition to the process of teaching and learning, an addition in the form of a professional practice complementary, not supplementary, to those of administration and teaching.

2. The bases for such a profession lie in an entirely new science, that of applying existing behavioral sciences to achieve a chosen goal.

3. The basis for this science—the goal—must be established by scholarship, by basic research in the area of behavioral change.

4. A new type of training is required to produce the needed scholars, experimenters, educator-professionals, and practitioners—a type suggested by the preliminary results of the "Harvard experiment," but a type, also, which the Harvard Graduate School of Education is not yet truly prepared to train.

We conclude on an optimistic note, however, because we feel that the application of purpose will complete our preparation, and make it practicable to begin training for the profession of Guidance.

References

1. American Association for the Advancement of Science. *Identification and Guidance of Able Students.* Washington, D. C.: The Association, May, 1958.
2. American Personnel and Guidance Association. "The Policy Statement on Counselor Education," *Personnel and Guidance Journal,* XL (December, 1961), 401–07.
3. Barry, Ruth E., and Wolf, Beverly. *Modern Issues in Guidance—Personnel Work.* New York: Teachers College, Columbia University, Bureau of Publications, 1957.
4. ———. *Epitaph for Vocational Guidance.* New York: Teachers College, Columbia University, Bureau of Publications, 1962.
5. Division of Counseling Psychology, APA. "The Current Status of Counseling Psychology," New York: Division 17, The Psychological Corp., 1961.
6. ———. "The Scope and Standards of Preparation in Psychology for School Counselors," *American Psychologist,* XVII (March, 1962), 149–52.
7. McCully, C. Harold. "The School Counselor: Strategy for Profes-

sionalization," *Personnel and Guidance Journal,* XL (April, 1962), 681–89.

8. Matthewson, Robert H. *Guidance Policy and Practice.* (Revised Edition). New York: Harper & Row, 1955.

9. Perry, Paul A. "A Matter of Quality," *Harvard Graduate School of Education Alumni Bulletin,* VII (Summer, 1962), 2–24.

10. Scanlan, Edward C. "A Theory of Guidance." Cambridge, Mass.: Harvard Graduate School of Education, June, 1961. (Unpublished doctoral dissertation.)

11. Stripling, Robert O., and Dugan, Willis E. "The Cooperative Study of Counselor Education Standards," *Counselor Education and Supervision* (Spring, 1961), 34–35.

12. Super, Donald E. "Personality Integration Through Vocational Counseling," *Journal of Counseling Psychology,* II (1955), 217–26.

13. ———. *The Psychology of Careers.* New York: Harper & Row, 1957.

14. Super, Donald E., and Bachrach, Paul B. *Scientific Careers: Vocational Development Theory.* New York: Teachers College, Columbia University, Bureau of Publications, 1957.

15. Tiedeman, David V. "Guidance for Tomorrow," *Harvard Graduate School of Education Alumni Bulletin,* March, 1957, pp. 3–7.

16. ———. "The Status of Professional Theory," Cambridge, Mass.: The author, 1961 (mimeographed).

17. Wrenn, C. Gilbert. "Philosophical and Psychological Bases of Personnel Services in Education," in Henry, E. B. (ed.), *Personnel Services in Education,* 58th Yearbook of the National Society for the Study of Education, Part II. Chicago, Illinois: University of Chicago Press, 1959.

18. ———. *The Counselor in a Changing World* (Report of The Commission on Guidance in American Schools, to the American Personnel and Guidance Association). Washington, D. C.: The Association, 1962.

C. GILBERT WRENN

The Culturally Encapsulated
Counselor

THE REPORT of the Commission on Guidance in American
Schools[1] presents a statement of anticipated developments in
school counseling against a backdrop of projected changes in our
culture. Since what we speak of as the guidance function in American
schools[2] has grown out of certain values in our culture, changes in
that culture presumably will affect the role of counselors in the school.
Such changes will also affect the nature of their education for the task.

ANTICIPATED CHANGES

Change has always been the one thing of which we could be sure.
What then is different about the changes of the next decade? Two
things only, but these are awesome enough—the rapidity and the
extensiveness of the changes anticipated. It is easy to repeat the
familiar and overgeneralized statement that it took 1,750 years for the
number of known facts existing at the time of Christ to double in
amount, but that the number doubled again by 1900, again by 1950,
and again by 1960. Whether or not there is numerical accuracy in
these figures, they dramatize the acceleration of change. The difficulty

[1] C. Gilbert Wrenn, *The Counselor in a Changing World* (Washington, D.C.:
The American Personnel and Guidance Association, 1962).
[2] Specifically "guidance" is a psychological and philosophical point of view which
influences curriculum and teacher attitudes, as well as resulting in the employment
of school counselors and other pupil personnel workers, such as school psychologists,
school social workers, and others.

is that these abnormally decreasing intervals simply do not have meaning. They are too threatening for us to be able to accept readily. From 1,750 years to 150 to 50 to 10—is the interval already down to 5 years? Is the fraction of knowledge that we can absorb in a lifetime already so small that man is at the mercy of knowledge? Must an individual's "existence" be thus circumscribed?

The Commission Report attempted to deal with changes in the American culture against a backdrop of world changes. Perhaps the analysis should have been made against a larger backdrop—against changes in our understanding of the universe, not merely the world. It seems quite likely that man is not alone in the universe, that life exists in solar systems other than our own, and proof of this will be a sharp challenge to our present "provincial" view of man. The astronomer Harlow Shapley estimated that there may be as many as 100 million stars whose planets are favorably constituted and located for the support of life. Many of these solar systems are billions of years older than our own and may be assumed to have developed some form of intelligence and culture far more complex than our own. We are now actively seeking to receive radio signals from other solar systems, but some of those systems may have been seeking such signals for millions of years.

We can make two statements with reasonable certainty. Life—of any complexity at all—will be found outside of our own small solar system. And the probabilities are very remote that such life will be in a form similar to our own, either anatomically or chemically.

Up until 300 years or so ago the earth was thought to be the center of the universe; then the sun was held to be the center of all. Then our sun, once so important, became a star of minor significance at the edge of a galaxy of 100 billion stars. Now we know that our galaxy is merely one of 100 million galaxies! How will man face the knowledge of life on other worlds, life of a form different from his own, perhaps enormously more mature as a species than man? The evidence that we are ready for such realization is not convincing. Yet of all the changes to be anticipated this may prove to be the most crucial, a need for a change in the "inner space" of man that will enable him to develop his relations with outer space. Will the number of "cultural barbarians" in the world—those who believe that anyone different from themselves is inferior to them—be adequately balanced by those who can deal rationally with contacts with other worlds?

Our own small world is becoming smaller by the moment—and

more densely populated. Earth is facing a paradoxical development of, on the one hand, closer contact between peoples through improved communication and transportation, and on the other, a rapid rise in the numbers of people to be thus related to each other. There is urgent need to develop skills in human relations that are equal to the tensions that arise because of great unevenness in wealth, particularly in food production. In 1957 it was predicted that if a rate of only one per cent annual increase in world population was maintained, a population of 7,000,000,000 can be projected by the year 2050.[3] This suggested average annual population increase of one per cent a year over the next 85 years looks modest indeed in the face of a world increase of 2.1 per cent reported for 1960–1962, slightly up from the 2.0 per cent reported for 1958–1962.[4]

In this development food will be a more crucial issue than nuclear weapons. Currently some sections of the world have a higher birthrate and a lower per capita food production than they had 20 years ago. In the six nations of Central America, for example, the birthrates for 1963 range from 40.8 to 49.9 per 1,000 population, almost double the 1963 birthrate in the United States of 21.6 per 1,000, yet we are producing more food per capita than those nations.[5]

We can grow food enough for this projected world population of seven billion only under certain stringent conditions that have been well specified as involving a far greater change in attitude than can be contemplated simply in expectation of further developments in agricultural technology.[6] The fact that America is an island no longer has any significance. Our economy of abundance must rub elbows with many economies of scarcity—with peoples who have only a fraction of what we have and yet who are well aware of what the United States has and is.

Changes are taking place within our own nation which are far reaching and difficult to accept. The increasing affluence of our country carries its own hazards. How will the 1970 projected increase in Gross National Product of 60 per cent over 1960 affect the way we live?[7] Affluence must be shared and must result in an increase in the

[3] Harrison Brown, James Bonner, and John Weir. *The Next Hundred Years: Man's Natural and Technological Resources* (New York: Viking Press, 1957).

[4] *Demographic Yearbook, 1963* (New York: United Nations, 1964), p. 142.

[5] *Ibid.*

[6] Brown, Bonner and Weir, *op. cit.*

[7] In June, 1964, GNP was at an adjusted annual rate of $608 billion and is now projected to be $825 billion in 1961 prices in 1970 (*Education for a Changing*

general level of ideas and appreciations or it becomes a hazard—a continuing increase in goods and leisure could be debilitating. Affluence can also become a threat to that sector of the population that does not share in it. In 1964 some 35 million out of our 192 million population (June, 1964) lived in families with less than $3,000 annual income. Yet the disposable personal income (after taxes) in the United States in 1963 was $402 billion, an average of $2,125 for each man, woman, and child. Affluence and poverty are uncomfortably close neighbors in our country.

A second national development of great significance is the increasing concern of the federal government with the quality of education and of social health at state and local levels. Contrary to popular opinion this is not a recent development but one having its origin with Alexander Hamilton in the beginning decades of our existence as a nation. The concern is acute now because national survival depends on a uniformly effective use of educated manpower as well as on a quality of urban health that is an asset and not a liability to the nation. At the same time this federal concern may unduly relieve the state, community, and individual of responsibility for concerns that should be their own—may decrease the independence and autonomy of the local groups. If we are to maintain our position among the family of nations, it seems inevitable that federal concern over local conditions will increase, but how will we handle this concern? Will we gerry-build it, allow it to overcome us, or control it wisely as we accept its inevitability?

People increasingly cluster in cities. America has become a constellation of urban galaxies. Metropolitan area boundaries which cut across county and state lines may become more significant economic and social boundaries than are state and county lines.

The pattern of family living prevalent in the early part of this century is gone, to appear no more. New patterns of family life are realities to be accepted and dealt with. Youthful marriages are in the ascendency. In 1960 the average marriage age of men was 22.6 years, of women 20.4. Youthful marriages are not believed to be a temporary phenomenon or one that is stopped by "tush-tushing" on the part of elders. The situation can be dealt with intelligently only after it is understood, and understanding comes after *acceptance* as a reality.

Perhaps the greatest influence in the changing pattern of family

---

World of Work, Washington: Government Printing Office, 1963). By way of comparison our GNP was $450 billion in 1958.

living is the increasing proportion of married women who enter the labor market. In 1950 single-pay-check families outnumbered double-pay-check families by 6 million. By 1964 the relationship was reversed with one million more families having two pay checks than one pay check. The Department of Labor estimates that by 1970 well over one third of the total labor force will be women, most of them married. In 1920 the average woman worker was single and 28 years old. In 1963 she was married and 41 years old. "About half of today's young women are married by age 20 and have their last child by age 26; by the time the youngest is in school, the mother may have 40 more years of her life ahead of her."[8] The role of women in society generally is changing markedly—each generation sees more who have high school and college education, more who want to make some work contribution outside the home as well as in the home. Women have one half (or more!) of the brains of the country. They intend to use them in a wide variety of ways.

Occupations will disappear and new ones appear with a speed that has little regard for the information about occupations that is now provided in printed form. Occupations may bear little resemblance to occupations carrying the same label a few years ago. (For example, the term "school counselor" as used two decades ago involved a very different set of functions than is implied by the current usage of the term.) The "automation revolution" will have a more profound effect upon people's lives than did the Industrial Revolution, if for no other reason than that the computer, the tape-operated machine, and the many information retrieval and coding devices replace routine *brain* work, whereas steam and electricity merely replaced muscle. Such a replacement is threatening to one's sense of personal significance.[9] In addition, there is no assurance that automation will create as many jobs as it eliminates. Occupational choice will no longer be an event, but a life-long process. An individual will be in and out of several occupations during his lifetime or will have to engage in some type of formal education repeatedly in order to keep up with the same vocation.

Marked alterations are also appearing in our educational system.

[8] "Fact Sheet on the Changing Pattern of Women's Lives," Women's Bureau, U. S. Department of Labor, October, 1964.

[9] For an analysis of the changing function of work in our society see Henry Borow (ed.), *Man in a World at Work* (Boston: Houghton Mifflin, 1964), especially Harold L. Wilensky, "Varieties of Work Experience" and C. Gilbert Wrenn, "Human Values and Work in American Life."

The kind and amount of education is now a matter of economic survival—it is not a privilege but a necessity. For without the appropriate education a young man or woman simply will not get the job—the essential element is education, not merely youth or strength. Few will be able to "work up from the bottom" without formal education to some point beyond high school. As a consequence post-high school vocational education at a technician level is expanding rapidly, as is the enrollment in junior colleges. There is a trend too for the latter to become community colleges which offer both formal and informal education for members of the community at all adult age levels. "Continuation education" is a term used to describe the tendency for people to return to formal school or college at various times throughout their life. It would appear that one's formal, structured education will never be completed.

PSYCHOLOGICAL DEFENSES AGAINST CHANGE

Like Job of old we protest the inevitable; we argue about it. Even better than Job we protect ourselves from the disturbing reality of change by surrounding ourselves with *a cocoon of pretended reality*—a reality which is based upon the past and the known, upon seeing that which is as though it would always be. This is "cultural encapsulation," an encapsulation within our world, within our culture and sub-culture, within a pretense that the present is enduring. Some of this evasion of reality is defensible, for one can absorb the new at only a limited rate. More than this, we move more freely when we know the limits within which we can safely operate. But the rate of change is another thing. The rate of change in science, in technology, and in the interacting complex of pressures in our society pays little heed to what we see within our cocoon. The walls of our cocoon must be permeable so that pressure does not build up between the "reality" within the cocoon and the reality without.

The Commission Report makes certain recommendations for the counselor's role with students, teachers, and parents, the counselor's place in the total school program, and the professional education of the school counselor. These recommendations are argued from the projected changes in our culture. It is true that the specific recommendations may be in error as inferences from cultural change, or the culture changes themselves may be of a different order, but the *amount* of change to be anticipated in the next decade or two will be the largest in our country's history. What will keep these changes from being applied to the role, education, and life of the counselor— what indeed but the counselor's resistance to change?

It can be assumed that counselors are subject to reality evasion. Perhaps counselors have particular cocoon patterns of their own because of their sensitivity to others and their desire to help. In his enthusiasm for helping, a counselor builds upon his own securities. He communicates concepts and values which have given him security and which are actually appropriate to his past, perhaps even his present. But even if the counselor tries to work from his present to the client's present, a hard enough task, this is not enough. Counselors frequently must work to the client's future as well. To deal with two presents and one future is the counselor's major assignment—and a most difficult one.

Following are some of the cultural encapsulations which the counselor must examine. They may not all be distinctive for the counselor. What happens is that the counselor faces them with a sense of urgency because of the critical nature of his relationship to the growing personality of the student.

Some Cultural Encapsulations

The tendency to be surprised or even unbelieving that what we regard as truth ever changes.

It is comforting to believe that at least some of what we regard as truth is ultimate truth, or is at least true for our lifetimes. This cocoon is a hard one to leave. Of course we recall that at one time it was "true" that the "earth is flat," that "matter is matter and energy is energy," that "man's major motivations arise from instincts." What we forget is that our awareness of truth is so very young because we are so young a race of man. If we assume that man has been on earth for perhaps one million years (it may have been two million), this is a small part indeed of the total time in which man may exist and learn. Whereas earth's future may be a matter of five or six billion years in terms of the anticipated disintegration of our solar system, the expansion of the sun and its increasing radiation will mean that in something like two billion years the seas will be boiling and all life will be extinguished. The striking difference between the one million years we may have existed and *the two thousand million years* we may have yet to go suggests a shocking infancy of man and his knowledge. Who then is to think that what we now consider truth is always to be truth, indeed, any part of truth?

This may hold true for empirically determined truth, but what if we also accept revealed truth? This is where I am safe! But am I? Why must we assume that revelation has ceased and is limited to the sacred literature now in existence? Is our concept of God so limited as to assume that it must remain fixated at the level of Buddha, Christ, and Mohammed—2,500, 2,000, and 1,400 years ago? Would it not be strange indeed if all inspired truth had been revealed to the very young, to the infant who has lived only 1/2000th of his possible lifetime? Why can we not assume that inspired truth is being continually experienced—through artists, poets, and sages, if not through prophets?

Certainly the values that one holds—convictions of the worth of things and of people—are culture-bound. They are also time-bound. The virtue of "work for its own sake," of "being mature before you marry," of "knowing what you want to do and then hewing closely to the line," may be far less significant values for our children than for us. If the youth of tomorrow see work, marriage, and vocational decision in different perspective from that of the youth of yesterday, who is to say that we are nearer the truth than they will be? They are reared for different worlds and for different values associated with these worlds. So if I rest secure in the cocoon that what I know is an ultimate truth or what I believe is an ageless value, that cocoon will betray me. My values are for now and for me—not for all time or for all people.

The cushioning of the school counselor in some academic cocoons which have little reference to our total culture.

Academic folklore holds that grades are the most important thing in a student's life, that having a vocational choice helps each person in his academic life, that students who fit in and express themselves well should be rewarded. We are academic people, and our academic cocoons may be most unrealistic in terms of either the future scope of human behavior or the reality of the world outside the school.

Similarly, what the counselor thinks he knows of the nature of human behavior may be unrealistic. At least it is tentative. Whatever we "firmly" know now may be firm as a principle but not as a law. Perhaps we have no laws of behavior as yet. Because man changes as his knowledge of man increases, we may never have laws. We must proceed upon the principles we now have, but since we operate within such large areas of uncertainty we should be humble indeed. Above all, let us avoid dogmatism and encapsulation where the evidence is conflicting. For example, we do not now know how to resolve the antithesis of Skinner and Rogers. We are certain both cannot be right, at least not right to the extent that each thinks himself now to be. Operant conditioning, with its sure movement of the person in the direction of only that behavior which is reinforced, cannot be a complete explanation of behavior if Rogers' concept of the subjective self and some degree of personal autonomy is also true. Who is to say that we now have any more than a small glimmer of light on the resolution of this crucial problem? Encapsulation at this stage of our knowledge of behavior will mean professional stagnation of a critical order.

The assumption that the counselor may safely draw upon his own educational and vocational experience in counseling the student.

There is a danger that the counselor may draw upon his past experiences to help the student solve his present and future problems. The world in which the counselor went to school and had his early job experiences is no longer in existence. The more rapid the rate of change, the greater the gap between yesterday and tomorrow. It is most human indeed to "draw upon our experience" in helping another, but of this the counselor must beware. Most of our experience was valuable for our yesterday, but not for the student's tomorrow.

SOME MEASURES AGAINST ENCAPSULATION

For the counselor to become more accessible to today and to tomorrow:

He should persist in a regimen of "unlearning" something each day.

Each day he should take some fact which is no longer a fact and replace it with a relevant item of information which is currently valid. Each day he should examine some situation which seems very familiar to him but which is no longer present in our society. Each day he should question some social relationship which was not present when he was a child but is very present now, for instance, the emergence of the new African nations, the proximity of our Communist adversaries, or the new patterns of marriage and family living.

Each day he should question something that he believes but that other people of integrity may reject. This is to remind him that there is a difference between his culture and the culture of the parent, the culture of the teacher, and the culture of the child. The thing that he believes in deeply may be something that someone else has every right not to believe in.

He should accept as an obligation the encouragement of students whose thinking is different from his own.

Students who think differently are never popular, but they may be the hope of the world. Who, if not the counselor, is to recognize these differences and encourage them? If the counselor disagrees with a person, his task is still to help that person become *his own man* rather than someone made in the image of the counselor. Peter Viereck has suggested that the "hero of the day" is the man who is adjusted to the ages but unadjusted to this age.[10] How can the counselor help a student to respect his own differences rather than to deprecate them? How indeed unless the counselor respects them first? The counselor has an obligation to help a student develop his own integrity even though it may vary from that of the counselor.

Finally, the counselor must batter down any tendency to be self-righteous.

What is "right" for the counselor may not be right for another person. A counselor may believe in some things that are beyond fact, but can he believe in something bigger than himself without feeling superior to those poor mortals who do not have such faiths and such beliefs? It is important that he believes if he can do so without feeling superior about it. There can be a snobbishness about faith as there is about fancy.

Everyone has a need for security, but the counselor must be reminded that what he seeks must be security in *presently operating principles*, not facts; security in *faith*; and security in the *process* of becoming. In seeking purpose in life he may find purpose in a way of relating himself to others, in a way of behaving because of believing. Allport's two principles of tentativeness and commitment[11] seem basic enough to be convincing to behaviorists as well as to existentialists. To believe that truth is forever emerging and never fully found is followed most necessarily by the principle that one must give one's life for what one *now* knows and believes. Commitment to what one knows not to be final is required of man in order to *be* a man.

10 Peter R. E. Viereck, "The Unadjusted Man—Last Refuge of Civilization's Secret Fires," *The Saturday Review*, November, 1958 (or) *The Unadjusted Man: A New Hero for Americans* (Boston: Beacon Press), 1956.

11 See p. 19 of this book.

And so the counselor must face change without trepidation and fight encapsulation with vigor. He will need to have humility in the face of ignorance, compassion for those who want to be loved, courage as he struggles for the assurance that he may always seek but never find. Two men, many hundreds of years apart, have said it well: "For whoso seeks the truth will find in nowise peace of heart" (Boethius); "You may seek either truth or repose. You must choose, for you cannot have both" (Emerson).

It will not be easy to be a counselor. Only the strong need apply.